4-5-22

Alan Cowell

SIMON & SCHUSTER

New York London Toronto

Sydney Tokyo Singapore

KILLING the WIZARDS

---

*Wars of
Power and Freedom
from Zaire
to South Africa*

SIMON & SCHUSTER
Simon & Schuster Building
Rockefeller Center
1230 Avenue of the Americas
New York, New York 10020

SIMON & SCHUSTER and colophon are registered trademarks
of Simon & Schuster Inc.

Designed by Carla Weise/Levavi & Levavi
Manufactured in the United States of America

1   3   5   7   9   10   8   6   4   2

Library of Congress Cataloging-in-Publication Data

Cowell, Alan.
Killing the wizards : wars of power and freedom from Zaire to
South Africa / Alan Cowell.
p.   cm.
Includes index.
1. Africa, Southern—History, Military.   2. South Africa—
History, Military—1961–   I. Title.
DT1165.C68   1992
968—dc20   91–43523
CIP

ISBN: 0-671-69629-7

ACKNOWLEDGMENTS

There is no easy way of listing all the people who, over more than a decade in Africa, helped me along the route that led to this book. But it would not have been possible without the help and support of those at Reuters News Agency and *The New York Times* who assigned me to the places that became the theater of so many adventures and experiences. Ian MacDowall, of Reuters, was the man who sent me to Africa in the first place. At *The New York Times*, Michael Kaufman recommended me and Robert Semple hired me to continue the African tenure. Over the years, Craig Whitney, Warren Hoge, John Darnton, and A. M. Rosenthal variously assigned me to, supported me in, and managed to postpone for nine months my expulsion from South Africa. Joseph Lelyveld offered me another life in Africa's broad, continental sweep by appointing me Cairo Bureau Chief. And Bernard Gwertzman did me two great favors, firstly by permitting me to write the book while assigned to the Middle East, and secondly by sending me back to South Africa for a spell in mid-1990 when conditions there changed.

I had never envisaged writing a book from the perspective of Africa's leaders, rather from the perspective of those they led. So, many of those who helped me the most were just the nice, kind, unassuming people who invited me into their homes to talk, from the shanties of Kinshasa, Zaire, to the equally cramped quarters of Kwazakele and other townships in South Africa. I hope I have relayed what they told me with fairness and accuracy. They are the people I cherish the most from those years.

Others, of course, had greater prominence in their own lands—in Lusaka, Milimo Punabantu, at State House, and Naphy Nyalugwe, at the *Times* of Zambia; in Zimbabwe, vice presidents Simon Mzenda and Joshua Nkomo, and, during the guerrilla war, military com-

5

manders Josiah Tongogara and Dumiso Dabengwa gave generously of their time. In Mozambique, I recall with particular fondness, I was fortunate enough to spend time with Fernando Honwana before his death in a plane crash in 1986 that also killed President Samora Machel. The list from South Africa is a long one and could not possibly include all the people who shared their experiences with me. But, among my journalistic colleagues, I think of Zwelakhe Sisulu, Mono Badela, Deon du Plessis, Kulu Sibiya, Allister Sparks, and Harald Parkendorf. And, among many others, I owe thanks to Gavin and Molly Blackburn and Mkuseli Jack in Port Elizabeth, Archbishop Desmond Tutu and Helen Suzman in Cape Town, Popo Molefe, Cyril Ramaphosa, and Bobby Godsell in Johannesburg. In their exile, two figures from the ANC were especially kind, Stanley Mabizela and Peter Tsikare. And, among many South African officials who explained their side of the story, I recall particularly Tienie Fourie, David Steward, and Barend du Plessis.

For the genesis of the book I am most grateful to my agent, Michael Carlisle in New York, and for its evolution to my editors at Simon and Schuster, Alice Mayhew and Ari Hoogenboom. And for help and advice during its writing, I turned often to Michael Holman of the *Financial Times* in London.

Much of my time in Africa was spent on the road with fellow foreign correspondents whose company turned grueling travel into fun, among them—particularly—David Cowell, Michael Holman, Ray Wilkinson, John Edlin, John Borrell, Allen Pizzey, Bernd Debusman, and Charles Powers. And while I traveled, I was sustained by the thought of those who would welcome me home again, especially my children.

Rome, 1991

FOR STANLEY AND DOROTHY,
MY PARENTS

CONTENTS

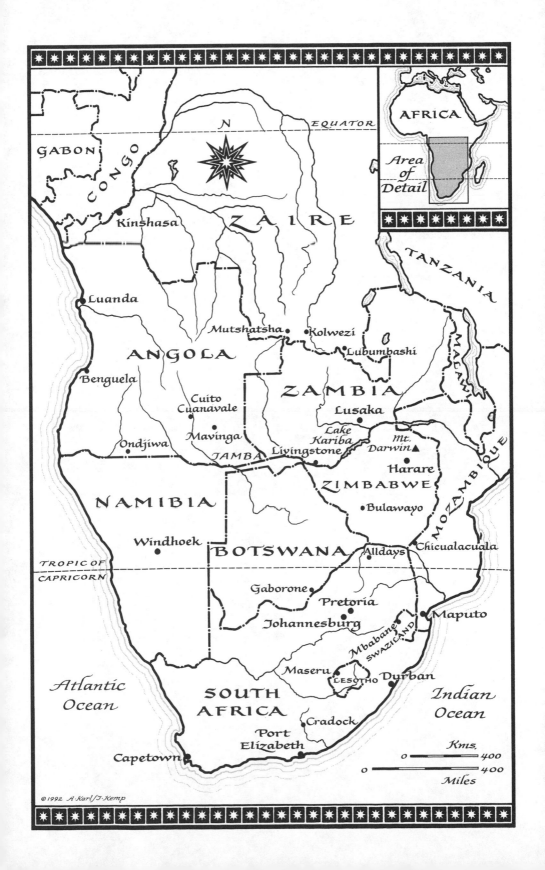

GABON

CONGO

ZAIRE

EQUATOR

N

Kinshasa

Luanda

ANGOLA

Benguela

Mutshatsha • • Kolwezi
• Lubumbashi

ZAMBIA

Cuito
Cuanavale

Mavinga

Ondjiwa

JAMBA

Lusaka

Lake
Kariba
Livingstone

Mt.
Darwin ▲

TANZANIA

MALAWI

MOZAMBIQUE

Harare

ZIMBABWE

• Bulawayo

NAMIBIA

Windhoek

BOTSWANA

Alldays

Chicualacuala

TROPIC OF
CAPRICORN

Gaborone

Pretoria

Johannesburg

Mbabane
SWAZILAND

Maputo

Atlantic
Ocean

Maseru

LESOTHO

Durban

SOUTH
AFRICA

Cradock

Indian
Ocean

Port
Elizabeth

Capetown

AFRICA

Area
of
Detail

Kms.
0   400
0   400
Miles

©1992 A.Karl/J.Kemp

"When the dance was at its height, Dingane suddenly leaped to his feet and screamed, *'Bambani abaThakathi!'* (Kill the Wizards!)"
—Donald R. Morris, in *The Washing of the Spears*, recounting
the events of 1838, when Zulus massacred Boer trekkers in
South Africa's Transvaal

"They come at night with the white men. They smash everything and they shout: Kill the Wizard."
—Resident of Kagiso township, west of Johannesburg,
recounting the events of 1990, when eight hundred people died
in factional clashes in South Africa's Transvaal Province

Prologue:

Frontline State

"En Afrique, il n'y a jamais de grandes batailles" (In Africa, there are never big battles).

FRENCH MILITARY ATTACHE in Kinshasa, Zaire, to the author, May 1977

An editor said: go to Africa. So I went.

I flew in a hurry by way of Cairo and Nairobi, stopping briefly to see friends, see the Nile, see the Pyramids. I saw the Nile by moonlight, and the Pyramids of Giza from the rear seat of a friend's motorcycle at 85 miles per hour. By the pool of the Norfolk Hotel in Nairobi, I turned a very English pink in a very African sun. It was July 1976.

My destination was Zambia. Everyone I met said I'd regret it. Nothing happens in Zambia, they said. The journey was a voyage to the unknown: when the editor had called to offer the job, I'd taken down an atlas to peruse the block of Central African land that was to be my new home. The atlas was so old it still showed the place painted pink, the cartographer's chromatic choice for the British Empire, and called it "Northern Rhodesia." The names of some towns and places seemed throwbacks to a lost era—Livingstone, the Victoria Falls. The Zambezi River was shown snaking along the southern border, the Congo lowering to the north—mysterious names that evoked other intrusions into Africa, people like David Livingstone and Henry Morton Stanley.

Going to Africa was a return to the history that had drawn my forebears to a continent of which they were as ignorant as I. But it was also a venture into a modern era stained with the conflicts that had been their bequest.

In South Africa, Soweto's first explosion of riot and protest had just

15

started. To the west, between Zambia and the distant Atlantic, Angola was at the beginning of what seemed a terminal spin, twisted by Cubans, the CIA, South Africans, white mercenaries, Angolans of all ideological shading. To the immediate south, straddling Zambia's trade routes, Rhodesia had yet to become Zimbabwe and its intransigent white leaders meant to postpone the name change, and the black majority rule that came with it, for as long as possible. To the southwest, in Namibia, guerrillas, based in Zambia, were trying to fight a war against a much too powerful adversary—South Africa. And Pretoria, the continent's tortured colossus, was trying to implant its vision of a new kind of empire, of a constellation of pliant, black-ruled states surrounding and protecting its borders like an ideological palisade.

To the east, blocking access to the Indian Ocean along the coastline and uplands of Mozambique, an uprising by black guerrillas armed by white men had just begun to stir. Its aim was to unseat the young, revolutionary regime of Samora Machel, and thus hold back the winds of change that breathed through the continent.

Southern Africa's geography had become a jigsaw of insurgency, a patchwork of wars with many things in common—race, tribe, Marx, power, revolution. Guerrilla armies fed on ideologies that required Africa's newest soldiers to call one another by the imported term "comrade" in the struggle against alien rule. Beyond them all, dimly perceived by a newcomer like me, lay the contests of the Cold War that saw Africa in the way outsiders had always seen it—as a checkerboard of alien ambitions.

Africa had generated plenty of problems of its own. But the greatest traumas to gnaw at its self-respect—the slave trade, the missionaries, colonialism itself—had been imposed from the outside, beginning as long ago as the fifteenth century.

In 1976, it seemed ironic and sad that, in response, it should take up alien slogans and ideologies, too, and live with their flaws in return for sponsorship by one superpower or the other, or even both.

Over the centuries many outsiders had brought their magic to Africa, disguised as technology or Bibles or seeds for cash crops to feed distant markets. But now—rebelling against the oppression that came with all that—southern Africa had turned to killing the wizards of foreign intrusion. The sorcerers were not all outsiders, though: Africa had its own malevolent wizards, who, since the first stirrings of independence in the 1960s, had transmuted the dream of freedom, with few exceptions, into one-party autocracies and worse.

For more than a decade, the editor's orders threw me into wars and conflicts from Zaire, to Zimbabwe, Angola, and Mozambique, and finally to South Africa itself, forcing me to try to understand two things: the reflexes these contests drew on and demanded from their combatants, and the pattern they established of black African power moving south as white African power moved north to challenge it.

This book is an attempt to try to chart some of those conflicts—the flaws and nobilities of "the struggle," as many black Africans called their wars against unsought domination, and the fears and vainglory that drove whites in Africa to resist them. It is one reporter's account of a decade in Africa, a political voyage by a newcomer who stayed longer than he had planned. It is not intended as a scholastic or anthropological study of southern Africa's contortions.

It also seeks to follow the way violence itself percolated through the era, beginning as a statement of revolutionary ideology in response to the inherent violence of foreign rule, ending as the very currency of the political debate between Africans and their rulers and between Africans themselves. And it is, in part, a story of the Cold War that sought its own answer to the central questions: Whose identity would now be stamped on the parcels of land that colonialism molded as Africa's nation-states? How would power be wielded? Was there, really, much difference between its misuses in Zaire or Zimbabwe or Zambia and its distortion in South Africa? Sometimes, the repositories of power—held by small and privileged elites interested only in the maintenance of their dominance—seemed to mirror one another. But only in South Africa did an elite need such a web of hurtful and destructive racial legislation to create for itself the illusion of moral justification.

The Afrikaners of South Africa had sought divine justification for apartheid in the Calvinist faith of the Dutch Reformed Church, itself an institution riven by racial distinction. Their adversaries had found revolutionary justification for violent struggle in the teachings of Frantz Fanon, in the models of Vietnam and Algeria, in the very essence of campaigns supposed to replace tyranny with freedom and democracy. In their ways and by their own lights, both sides claimed just causes, but, I was to discover, the hidden agenda was often the same: the maintenance of power and the survival of the elite.

. . .

In contrast to the turbulence in the lands around it, Lusaka, the capital of Zambia, seemed becalmed when I first arrived there. The country itself was one of the so-called "frontline" states confronting white minority rule in Rhodesia and South Africa by offering sanctuary to a host of guerrilla groups. The city teemed with representatives of acronymic liberation movements—SWAPO, UNITA, ZANU, AND ZAPU—but their wars intruded less than their rhetoric. African presidents came and went, holding summit talks, hidden in Mercedes limousines, with motorcycle outriders who forced the less exalted into the drainage ditches by the roadside. Diplomatic initiatives flitted by, like shadows cast on a silk screen, seeming full of moment but bearing no substance. Western spies swapped notes over tepid canapés and games of squash. Communiqués bubbled to the surface and sank without trace, easily absorbed by the endless bushlands of Central Africa.

The president, Kenneth Kaunda, played golf on his own nine-hole course in the grounds of State House—a latterday Nero with a five-iron replacing the fiddle. (His colonnaded residence with a garden full of peacocks had once been the British colonial governor's home, which went some way to explaining why we attended presidential press conferences in a ballroom with a sprung floor designed, presumably, to enhance those long-gone evenings aglow with chiffon and tuxedos—as much one of colonialism's odd legacies as the golf course.)

The country's wealth—copper—miraculously came out of the ground from deep, wet mines and large open holes, and was sold for low prices on depressed markets, purveyed in great, thick bars, or refined into the dull glow of cobalt. Zambian women, stoic in the heat, lined up for salt and sugar, babies on their backs, within earshot of the Lusaka Club's red clay tennis courts, where the membership was predominantly formed by white expatriates. The Soviet ambassador sat in his fortified embassy plotting the Kremlin's takeover of southern Africa, while, across a strip of scrub and diplomatic no-man's-land, the American ambassador plotted in his how to stop him. On shaded porches and verandahs, white people surveyed the demise of what they once dominated over sundowner drinks and games of tennis and lawn bowls, almost as if the brief candle of white supremacy had not begun to gutter all over Africa. Sometimes, as the seasons followed one another with metronomic regularity—dry winter, hot summer with rain—it was difficult to grasp that these were times of momentous change, and all around, other lands were gripped by events that would remold them irrevocably.

I had arrived in a continent caught between hope and disaster, sliding toward the latter; a continent where hunger and bloodshed and decline shared a stage with the striving for decency and self-respect. And I stayed in Africa until, a little over a decade later, the South African government told me that my work permit would not be renewed and would I therefore make arrangements to leave by January 10, 1987.

The message came through a little before Christmas, in December 1986, as I tarried under the great sweep of Table Mountain in Cape Town. I was due to leave at the end of my tour of duty. The authorities, however, had decided to seize upon my departure as the opportunity for a more radical step, taken in a fit of pique at the way their land was being covered and depicted in the United States. To make their outrage as graphic as possible, they had decided to close down *The New York Times* bureau in South Africa. While I was told to leave, my appointed successor was told he would not be allowed to enter the country. The door slammed shut. The man who bore the tidings, Dr. van Zyl of the Interior Ministry, never did say why I was being expelled. But, speaking on the phone from Pretoria on December 23, he did wish me a Merry Christmas. And he chuckled.

On January 10, 1987, I left South Africa and the swathe of lands that had been my home since July 21, 1976. Those dates are the bookends of a life in sub-Saharan Africa. But that vast continent does not easily relinquish its orphans and stragglers. After a brief spell in Greece, another editor sent me back to Africa and a new base at its northern bulwark, Egypt. And in 1990, inexorably, the great changes afoot in South Africa—the release of Nelson Mandela, the stirrings of unprecedented negotiation between black and white—drew me back again. This time, the authorities were not so harsh: I could visit any time, just send a fax in advance, said Mrs. Smith, the cheerful new voice of the Interior Ministry, songbird of the "new" South Africa.

Back in 1976, I did not really know what awaited me. Africa had been remote, romantic, murkily defined somewhere between Tarzan and Livingstone. Old-time expatriates offered cryptic and often useless advice. "Don't expect lions in the streets, old boy," one said, but on arrival I was still disappointed to find the neat, geometric streets of Lusaka offering nothing more exotic than old bicycles and locally assembled Fiats.

"Of course, you'll really be at the end of the line down there," a Kenyan offered with the degree of infinite superiority that marked a country then viewed as an African success story. That was literally true. We were at the end of a railroad the Chinese built from Dar Es Salaam, which brought none of the small delights that help define First World complacency or the staples that define Third World survival. And President Kaunda, enforcing the United Nations sanctions that were supposed to bring Rhodesia to its senses overnight, had long ago closed the border that straddled the "southern route"—the lifeline to the ports of South Africa.

Rhodesia did not oblige by collapsing. But Zambia's own economy did. There were no apples. So we made ersatz apple pie from papayas that fell when ripe from a tree in the garden and were then marinaded in lemon juice. Liquor was hard to come by. So was candy for the children. Visiting friends received urgent cables: bring chocolate and real whisky or don't come at all. All the while, the railroad, which might have brought salt and sugar—not to mention apples—brought in Soviet tanks and guns as part of the Soviet ambassador's plan, a plan that turned out to be about as flawed as any concocted by the Western imperialism it was supposed to thwart.

But in another way, which I did not really grasp until much later, my experiences in Zambia were the beginning of a line—a line of discovery, one that would force me into a reluctant appraisal of my forebears' achievements and abuses.

Over the next eleven years, there would be many adventures along the way. I sent despatches by carrier pigeon in Zimbabwe and became a regular commuter on the dug-out canoes that plied the Shari River between Cameroon and Chad. Other great African streams—the Zambezi, the Kafue, and the Luangwa—introduced me to crocodile and hippopotami at close quarters. I went to look for pygmies in Zaire, mountain gorillas in Rwanda, endangered rhinoceros in Zambia. There were flights to the rebels of southern Angola in old South African Dakota transport planes, and rambunctious rides by Jeep and truck in the Sudan on tracks that gave way to camel routes and ambush by locusts.

Most of all, however, my stay in Africa coincided with what I came to think of as the "time of the comrades"—a time when violent protest and armed struggle, entwined with the rivalries of the Cold War and overlaid with socialist dogma, became legitimized as the means of changing the fundamental relationship between the nations of the region and the nature of the states that ran them.

When President Kaunda met the press in what had once been the colonial ballroom with its sprung floor, his underlings—and some East European journalists, too—would address him as "Comrade President." The usage was common to the times. Joshua Nkomo, the Zimbabwean patriarch, and Robert Mugabe, who became Zimbabwe's leader, called themselves "Comrade," and so did Nelson Mandela and Oliver Tambo. In Angola and Mozambique, they used the Portuguese word—*camarada*—and the sense was same: it was a statement rejecting colonialism and its associated sense of white, capitalist domination. It provided the thread between the guerrillas who roamed the bushlands of Central Africa in the sixties and seventies and the youthful warriors of South Africa in the 1980s.

Comrade meant a leaning toward socialism, an acknowledgment of the "natural alliance" of the Cold War years that tied Africa insurgencies to Eastern Europe and the Soviet Union with bonds of purported solidarity and supplies of AK-47 rifles, limpet mines, and bazookas. When communism collapsed throughout the Eastern bloc, significantly enough, it was the South African Communist Party that maintained the torch should not be dimmed, arguing into the 1990s that, essentially, everyone else had gotten the application wrong, but there was nothing basically flawed in the ideology.

The easy adoption of the word "comrade" said something too about an emergent continent's quest for a political identity once the colonialists had gone, leaving new rulers in charge of assemblages of divergent tribal loyalties that did not add up to cohesive nation-states. And it showed as clearly as anything else how closely the Cold War was intertwined with Africa's contorted post-colonial history: the Soviets offered the guns and the MiGs—on commercial and not-so-comradely terms; and the West offered the butter and the aid packages—at a price exacted often as not by the International Monetary

Fund with its setpiece deal: financial assistance for wrecked economies and help with the debt rescheduling in return for free market economic reforms that denied both the comradely ethos and the political legitimacy that African leaders sought from it.

Socialism had failed in Africa long before its dominoes fell in 1989 in Eastern Europe, but no one was prepared to admit it, so people kept on calling one another "comrade" and hoped that, somehow, it would all come right in the end.

The idea of "just" struggles had long been endorsed by both the Soviets and the Chinese as they sponsored their surrogates in Africa. That made those same struggles anathema to Western interests. Yet, those embroiled in their small wars in Angola and Mozambique, Namibia or Zimbabwe, all insisted that the West had offered them no choice: when they penetrated the Western chanceries in the early 1960s, seeking help, they were turned away; and when they went next door, to the Soviets or the Chinese, they were welcomed with open arms, swept up by the ideological commitment to world communism that mirrored their own perceptions of Western rejection and exploitation. If South Africa's rulers saw events in their own country as part of Moscow's "Total Onslaught," it was not surprising because many of those ranged against them were armed and ideologized by the Soviet Union, and Soviet policy elsewhere in Africa—from Ethiopia to Angola—had left no doubt that the Kremlin was indeed interested in whatever African windfalls it could coax from the disorder of the times.

It was a time that elicited personal responses beyond impersonal dispatches, among people who demanded a stand—for or against; supportive of Africa's new order, or jealous of a past that had gone beyond recall. There was no neutrality.

It was a time of fallen empires—the Portuguese in Angola and Mozambique, and the last vestiges of British colonial dominion in Rhodesia. And it was a time, too, when South Africa sought to rebuild the imperial barricades through surrogate armies and direct pressure on those lands that had taken socialism as the rallying cry of the battle against foreign rule and apartheid.

Many people have studied the individual turmoils of South Africa and its northern neighbors. Yet it seemed to me from the places I lived in and visited that there was another process at work, an umbilical link that tied the various conflicts together. Like a great magnet, South

Africa drew the struggle southward to its very heart, even as it sought to repel the onslaught.

Maybe—as a French military attaché was to tell me in Kinshasa—it was true: there were no big battles in Africa in a conventional military sense. But the struggles drew on momentous themes of race, identity, and survival.

I had covered wars before, in Lebanon at the start of its turmoil in 1975, in eastern Turkey when the Kurds fled before the armed might of Iraq as the Shah of Iran sold their cause for a slice of a waterway. I had seen Israeli warplanes spiral over Syria in 1973. But, like many of my generation, I still clung to the old-fashioned version of conflict—good guys and bad guys, defenders standing up for God and nation, aggressors seeking dominance over land and resources and people to which they had no rightful claim. My father had fought in World War II with the Royal Air Force in North Africa and Italy and, it seemed, he and the others had achieved a clear and noble victory in the defeat of fascism. That was what wars did—they put the evil adversary to rout and reasserted the virtuous status quo.

It was a naive view, and one that left me unprepared for these small and sometimes dirty wars, wars that escaped simple definitions, bludgeoned the status quo, and forced those who witnessed them to define their feelings about the new ways that would come in their wake. Being in Africa peeled away old assumptions and forced a painful reexamination of all the subliminal messages of an imperial history.

In Lusaka, for instance, I invited for Christmas dinner a grizzled man, a carpenter and friend who hadn't seen his own family for years and so enjoyed adopting mine in the incongruous setting of an African Yuletide—temperatures in the 90s, plum pudding on the table. My friend later became vice president of Zimbabwe—his name was Simon Mzenda. Here was a modern warrior, of sorts, at home with me at Christmas while the guerrillas to whom he played godfather attacked civilian targets a hundred miles to the south. Was he terrorist or freedom fighter? Did our friendship blind me or enlighten me to the realities of his cause? Would the society he helped create in Zimbabwe, when Rhodesia crumbled in 1980, bloom from the soil of nationalist idealism, or grow barren in a continent's greed and decay? Here, finally, at my dinner table, was a leader of those same guerrillas who would undo everything white supremacy had started. Colonialism had caused him great pain and loss. He had not seen his own kin for eleven years, and his daily routine was to house and tend young people who had fled the war across the southern border—or been abducted by the guerrillas to feed their ranks. For him, the British were oppressors who had denied his people's humanity. The perception created no personal bitterness: we could be friends, even if our ancestors set us on opposite sides of a great divide.

For well over a decade, I would find myself in places where people gathered to the rallying cry of self-determination like moths about a flame, knowing, but not fearing, the combustibility. But the central liberal belief of the twentieth century that democracy is universally applicable and indivisible was a notion that sat uneasily on African lands whose leaders corrupted the very notions of freedom that gave them power.

The editors who sent me to Africa, for Reuters News Agency first and then for *The New York Times*, inadvertently offered me a first-hand seat at the unfolding of colonialism's final hours. Virtually every-where I set up my African homes, my forebears had ruled at one time or another. Then they had gone, leaving their successors to deal with the results of their judgments. So where did I stand on those huge themes—race and faith, democracy and self-determination, and the patina of intolerance that spread with the Marxist slogans? Had I the right to criticize the new Africa or defend the past? How would I cope with the paradoxes?

At the height of the Rhodesian war, I was invited to the home of a white Zambian, Guy Scott, who farmed a range of crops from corn to strawberries, to play croquet on his lawn. At each corner of the irrigated expanse of kikuyu grass, he had ordered his staff to build thatched shelters to provide shade. And at strategic moments during the game, his Zambian manservant, Whiteson, would descend from the homestead in a white uniform with a plum-colored sash, bearing a tray of gin, tonics, ice, and bitters. As we refreshed ourselves between games, other Zambians—soldiers with AK-47 assault rifles—would slouch by the croquet lawn on their way to man the anti-aircraft missile batteries the authorities had installed on a hill on Guy's farm, part of the defenses required by a war to the south in Rhodesia against the same privileges as we were enjoying. Across the Zambezi, a life such as mine and Guy's would be a target; indeed, one of Guy's own brothers

was down there, fighting the war. With gin and croquet, Guy was
doing quite well in Africa. (Indeed, he later became agriculture minister, when President Kaunda was finally voted from office in 1991.)
With guns and resistance, Guy's brother was not. But for both of them,
the same question recurred: Did outsiders have the right to use these
great uplands of Central Africa as the theater of their competing notions
and experiments?

Political independence had come to many new states, but economic
independence lagged, still held by outsiders who controlled both the
technology that generated wealth and the pricing systems that dictated
the value of commodities from copper to wheat. Outsiders could live
with complacencies because, when it was all over, there was a home
to go to someplace else and there was money to sustain them. But
those among whom they lived were caught up in the immediacies of
raw survival. On the northern bank of Lake Kariba, on the border
between Zambia and Zimbabwe, I met a young man who told me his
name was Simon Peter. He was armed with a length of nylon line
and homemade slingshot; his mission that day, he said, was to catch
small fish or kill small birds, both for the pot. If he failed, neither he
nor his family would eat. Not even the poorest I knew back home
lived with such complete uncertainty, but this was part of Simon Peter's
life, and Africa was home to an awful lot of people like him.

The contrasts persisted as I moved from home to home in Lusaka,
Harare, Nairobi, Johannesburg, Athens, and Cairo, and spent time
in most of Africa's states—always the outsider looking in, trying to
combine an understanding of ways to which I had not been born with
the need to build the props of a familiar existence.

In July 1976, as the Kenya Airways 707 dipped over Lusaka and Africa
edged toward its rapid gloaming, my concerns were more immediate,
closer to panic.

From the air, the city seemed so small and leafy that it barely stood
out at all among the vastness of the bushlands that spread to infinity
all about it. Blink, it seemed, and you'd miss it. What kind of place
had I come to that seemed to have no roots below the rich, red earth
of the great Central African plateau? In Turkey, societies had left their
memories layered like rock formations awaiting inspection: Hittites,

Persians, Romans, Greeks, and the Ottomans themselves. Here was a town invented as a center of colonial administration; the landmarks seemed to be the Intercontinental Hotel and the Cricket Club. So what or where was the real Africa amid the confusion of bush wars and foreign ideologies? And where was my niche, my security, in this huge alien continent? It was a big, frightening question a long way from what had been home.

My suitcase was heavy. So was my heart. Night had settled by the time I cleared customs. Crickets chirruped. There were too many stars in too much darkness, too much unlit emptiness, too many distant prickles of fire. I was too far from anywhere. I was driven into town in a rattling Fiat—the office car—to find, opposite the ramshackle showgrounds and riding stables on the potholed Great East Road my new home. It was a small bungalow with old furniture (the sofa collapsed under my first guest, a notable Zambian newspaper editor prone to ill-temper, alcohol, and quixotic behavior). There was a banana tree in the yard and at the gate a watchman who chased and ate flying ants at the beginning of the rainy season. A telex was in an office converted from a garage, and in the backyard was a small, two-roomed home where Eni, the maid, lived, and, it later transpired, ran a flourishing marijuana business in conjunction with a policeman who visited her.

"Hello, Bwana," she said.

Suddenly, at the age of twenty-nine, I was the Bwana, the master of my modest domain. The mantle of the White Man in Africa had settled on me willy-nilly, as if by some imperial order they forgot to amend when independence came in 1964.

"Call me Alan," I said.

"Yes, Bwana," she replied, and smiled, as if contemplating a wisdom totally beyond my grasp.

It was an odd sort of a beginning. Like much of the continent that had molded her, Eni expected no miraculous changes in the order of things. When I traveled north, to Zaire, the country Joseph Conrad had called the heart of darkness, I began to understand why.

PART ONE

BUSH LAW:

From Zaire
to
Zimbabwe

1.

Black Magic:

Living by the Sword

in Zaire

Then I saw the Congo, creeping through the black,
Cutting through the forest with a golden track.

VACHEL LINDSAY, "The Congo"

"The horror! The horror!"

JOSEPH CONRAD, *Heart of Darkness*

Just back from the Memling Hotel in Kinshasa, the traders sold monkeys, parrots, marijuana, fetishes, herbs, cures—routine fare in a land where you could also buy women, officials, army officers, and bank notes so worthless that they were traded by the shoebox.

It was also possible to purchase what, at first glance, seemed to be watercolors of women clad in bright and intricate robes. The figures were gaudy, exuberant, robust, but the appearance of inner strength was deceptive because they were made of the frailest of things—butterfly wings artfully composed to give the impression of wholeness.

At once, they evoked the weakness of their raw materials, the cruelty of those who hunted and gathered them (I wondered how they wrote their job description: butterfly-plucker?), and the great vigor of the final product. They were striking not only because of their inner juxtapositions but because they offered an uncanny metaphor for the entire country: like the butterfly-wing paintings, Zaire was a collage of frailties without individual strength beyond the illusion of nationhood.

Since 1965, when he came to power, President Mobutu Sese Seko, one of Africa's most durable dictators, had juggled and rearranged the country's fragments to keep the illusion alive. He presided over one of the continent's most ruined, paradoxical lands, a place that seethed with energy yet was febrile with collapse. He contrived to perform this legerdemain with all the skills and panache of a three-ring-circus master. At once, he was the pointman of Western interests in the Great Game of post-colonial influence and the emblem of corrupted, personalized power.

Alone he ruled a country seventy-seven times larger than Belgium, the colonial power that once ran it, and the same size as all of Western Europe. Its borders were so long that they were contiguous with nine other African countries. Zaire's access to the Atlantic seaboard of West Africa was small, but it blew into Africa's heart like a vast, misshapen balloon that filled half a continent. It was—and is—a place of evil, decay, and fascination, run by one man whose personal wealth—by no coincidence—was always the same size as the country's crippling national debt. Mobutu—tall, handsome, bespectacled—*was* Zaire, the master practitioner of the political alchemy that transmuted a single personality into a national emblem. He was the nation; his words were the nation's truth, propagated by slavish newspapers that placed his picture on every front page, and by servile TV and radio stations that made his every doing the first item of news. To question him was to deny the very essence of nationhood, to commit treason. His wizardry lay in the fact that he cast his spell so wide and so long over a land never made for cohesion. And, for me, he summed up one of the great paradoxes of Africa's struggle against white minorities: from bases such as these, freedom's incongruous banner was lofted to legitimize leaders who had perverted liberty's very essence.

The place was so big and fecund that, when an American construction company built a powerline from the north to the south, by the time they finished it in the south, the jungle had overgrown the pylons they had planted in the north. The place was also so mean and broke that, when engineers began repairing the powerline, they discovered that whole sections had been removed by villagers too poor to procure building materials and copper wire for personal adornment from any other source.

It was a land of accelerated decay, high-speed entropy. Kinshasa, the hot, moist capital, expired around broad cracked boulevards and warrens of slum. The countryside was a story of wilful neglect. Its provincial cities resembled the lost garrisons of a fallen empire, distant outposts, forlorn and beleaguered, forgotten. The bush grew over the Belgian-built roads so that no one could even find them. There never was a single highway or railroad connecting north and south. The best route to the interior was by a river ferry laden with whores and traders who dabbled in parrots and monkeys and booze and dope. Somewhere, out there, were pygmies and rebels, diamond smugglers and jungle. Zaire was the dark side of the African moon.

If you asked how Mobutu's magic worked, people would tell you about his secret police, the personality cult surrounding him, his obsessive attention to personal security. But there was more to it than that. He had discovered, as many dictators do, that fear turns myth into reality and lies into truth.

According to his propaganda, Mobutu Sese Seko was the "sole guide" of his people, the "cock who goes from hen to hen knowing no fatigue," "the warrior who fights battle after battle but is not tired." He embodied the personality cults of a generation of African leaders in the first flush of independence. His loyalists wore lapel pins bearing his portait on suits designed by him as a break with the colonial past— a blend of Mao jacket and pinstripe that he called the *abacos*, from *à bas le costume*—"down with the suit," a rallying cry that blended the ideological with the sartorial. His portrait was everywhere. So were his policemen and spies. As his magical emblems of power, he wore a leopard-skin hat and carried a stick carved to show women entwined around the shaft. When he dropped out of public view for a while in 1978, the "radio trottoir"—Kinshasa's effervescent sidewalk rumor mill—reported that his hat had been stolen and his magic with it, so he did not dare venture forth. His airline, Air Zaire, broke its unpredictable schedules whenever he or one of his wives wanted to shop in Europe and needed a DC-10 for the trip. When you entered his palace, you did so through an arch created by the biggest pair of elephant tusks most people had ever seen. The country's ideology was called "Mobutism" and its devalued currency, the Zaire, bore his portrait.

Zaire was all Africa had to be and should not be, a cornucopia of callused foreign hubris and home-grown decay. All the worn truths about modern Africa—its fake frontiers and myriad tribes, its recourse to tyranny and the defiance of accountability—seemed to tumble together through the streets of Kinshasa. The jungle was reclaiming the place, pushing up through cracks in the paving. Secret policemen in dark glasses tortured people in cells behind rusting steel gates. Legless beggars staked out turf on the sidewalks of the grandiose boulevards named for the benchmarks of freedom, swept by the dusty airstream of passing Mercedes. The cobwebs in the telegraph office, a friend told me, had been there since 1960, the year the Belgians precipitately went home and abandoned the country to its predilection for chaos. And beyond all that lay the tentacles of a tyranny that brooked no opposition.

"I solemnly declare that from now on I will be without pity for all attempts of this kind," Mobutu proclaimed on television after a show trial of thirteen purported conspirators supposed to have plotted his overthrow in March 1978. "Whoever tries again to use the sword will perish by the sword."

The plotters, convicted on evidence as flimsy as the butterfly wings, were shot at dawn.

No one could accuse Mobutu of fudging the ground rules. After all, he had written them with the express purpose of maintaining power and wealth, drawn from people who had nothing.

La Cité, Kinshasa's great, reptilian slum, its open sewers clogged by debris, had filled up with those who had left the countryside for relatively bright lights. This might not be much—an old man in a sick woman's yard told me—but at least it was something. Back home, in the village, under the thatch in the bush, there was nothing. So they came and settled and brought their ways with them to a city the Belgians had once named for their avaricious King Leopold. Women pounded wooden mortars by meager stands of corn. Money was so unreliable that people bartered with such trivia as a foreigner's jettisoned empty whisky bottle. Belgian missionaries pulled on monkey skins and waved spears in the aisles of the great colonial churches, performing a liturgy originally devised to deny—or at least balance— the hold of the ancestral spirits. Once, as I drove through La Cité, a woman laughed hugely at my shock when she hoicked her skirts to pee on the dark banks of a sewer right in front of me. The semblance of Belgian order had long given way to improvisation and spontaneity.

Zaire defined Africa's underworld. Water hyacinth floated down the Congo River like a shipwreck's corpses. Upstream, the vast, dark mass of the interior glowered, restored to the impenetrability Henry

Morton Stanley had found when he came here on the Belgian monarch's ticket as his colonial agent a century before. It was no coincidence that Joseph Conrad chose this place to write about as the core of evil.

The poor were so poor they earned less than it cost to eat. And the rich were so rich it was staggering, blessed by a president who gave them access—in return for loyalty—to the state coffers from which he siphoned his own billions. When we correspondents wrote stories about him, we called him "pro-Western," or "anti-Soviet," as if the labels imparted some fictitious legitimacy. But the baffling question was why those he oppressed in La Cité never simply rose up and said no more. The idea of 3 million people marching on the presidential palace was Mobutu's nightmare. He permeated the great slum with agents whose task was to ensure that it never happened. Even by the most sympathetic account, he was a man beset by insoluble problems that he confronted by recourse to the jiggery-pokery of autocracy, lured by the siren call of megalomania. But Mobutu was not alone in personalizing his dominance.

In Zambia, President Kenneth Kaunda devised "one-party participatory democracy," and put his face on the money supposedly to hold the nation together. In Guinea, President Ahmed Sékou Touré put his face on the money, too, and called it the *syli*, by an awkward linguistic coincidence pronounced "silly"—a frivolity that did not reflect the harshness of his bloodstained rule. Julius Nyerere in Tanzania became "The Teacher," although the lessons were only in how to run an economy into the ground. Hastings Kamuzu Banda in Malawi—"The Conqueror"—waved a fly whisk and had big-bottomed women dance around his diminutive figure so that all the spectator could see at his festivals was the fly whisk—the wand of power—held magically, quiveringly, irrepressibly aloft. Jean-Bédel Bokassa in the Central African Republic had himself enthroned as Emperor, even as he maintained a cold room at one of his villas for human flesh to satisfy his cannibalism. (He also maintained a buxom Romanian mistress to satisfy other needs.) Idi Amin in Uganda killed his own people and had himself carried above the crowds in a throne borne by white expatriates, just to show whose continent it was. And when he attended an Organization of African Unity meeting, he received a standing ovation.

One easy issue that united these fragile despots was South Africa and the battle against apartheid. In their pronouncements, African leaders cast themselves collectively as the rear base of the struggle against white minority rule, hiding their own iniquities behind the continent's last, great racial epic.

Yet black-ruled Africa seemed such a frail encampment, with its tattered economies and nebulous polities. That very weakness demanded that the strategy of black resistance further south should be guerrilla warfare: for, in conventional terms, black-ruled Africa had no chance in confronting South Africa militarily. In the early 1970s, Idi Amin summoned journalists and diplomats to observe his air force going into action against an island in Lake Victoria which he had labeled "Cape Town" for the purpose of the exercise: the pilots missed their target, the bombs fell in the lake, and one airplane disappeared. Indeed, at one time in Zambia, the country's modest fleet of Soviet-supplied MiG warplanes achieved such a reputation for inefficiency that the term "air force" entered the street-corner argot to denote anything that was broken, useless, or as Zambians like to say, "buggered."

While Africa faced the great confrontation with white rule in the south, its leaders avoided applying the same standards to themselves as they demanded of the white Rhodesian minority, or the Afrikaners in Pretoria. Instead, they continued a tradition of dictatorship, hypocrisy, and megalomania that made their pronouncements hollow and denied a new start to a continent that had manifestly been misused. The old dictum has it that people get the governments they deserve. But, patently, people in Africa got governments they did not deserve and yet could not get rid of, even as they slid into ever-deeper poverty. Paradoxically, Africa's economic mismanagement often served rather than threatened the one-man shows that passed as governments because it forced most people's energy into the daily grind of simply getting by. And, in the era of the Cold War, the men at the top flourished, encouraged by one superpower or another in the interests of the wider game of ideological competition, not so much because Africa's assets were critically important, but simply to deny the other sides' access to them. Far below, others lived small lives fraught with worries. Dictatorships do not function solely because people fear the dictator; they function because they teach people to fear their neighbors, and to crave any small release. Saturday night in La Cité showed how.

I had made friends when a hired car bogged down in sand in a dark place. Someone offered to help me push. We met up with others. We partied. All night we talked, danced, drank—strangers pushed together haphazardly, moving from place to place, though the narrow, sandy alleys, the sprawl of gimcrack homes pressed close together, mud to mud, zinc to zinc.

Music throbbed. Drumbeats haunted us down darkened byways lit by the pinpricks of kerosene lamps that spread white pools on vendors' wares—cigarettes, kebabs.

We halted a while at an open-air night spot. You paid the entrance fee by handing cash through a slit in a concrete wall. The clientele was all African—outsiders generally did not come here. You sat on an upturned beer crate. You talked and listened to the music and drank Primus beer from big, cold bottles. You smoked marijuana with a punch like plastic explosive. But suddenly, my hosts lowered their eyes in deference when a self-confident, spruce young man with gelled hair and plum velvet jacket arrived. His wife accompanied him, regal on his arm. The place bowed to them.

He was, they told me, the owner. More important, he worked in some minor function at the presidential palace. I fancied he might be the president's valet, the man who pressed and ironed the presidential hosiery, privy to the mysteries of the boudoir. Whatever his job, the man drew power and position from the association—enough to open a night spot of his own, buy loyalty with largesse, and spread the grip of the palace in his own small backyard.

The president was the fountainhead of patronage and co-option. The nightclub owner was the last rivulet, trickling from the palace to his kin in La Cité. If you came from his tribal lands, up in the north, where the president came from too, my companions explained to me, the nightclub owner would be your godfather. If times got hard, he would help you, with money, medicine, a word in the right place.

Back at the palace, the man was probably a virtual nonentity. But on his own small turf, in his own nightclub, he was a lesser god, stroked with the blessing of the almighty. I wondered how many other emissaries the president had stationed in La Cité, offering the deal: a little something in return for quiescence.

Most people hated the president, they told me as the night and the beer wore away inhibitions. He was a thief. He had ruined them. His policemen and spies were everywhere. But the hatred was not incompatible with subservience, with bowing to his viceroy, the nightclub owner. The faded signboards called the president the Sole Guide. He was strong, too strong to even contemplate challenging. And when the people did challenge him to embark on reform in 1991, it was largely because he had broken faith with his most important constituency—the army. Back in the 1970s, in La Cité, after a night of partying, the realities were different.

One minute, we had been revelers, my newfound friends and I, companionable comrades in the quest for a fast time. Then came Africa's rapid dawn and we were a sorrier assembly, blinking in the new day, taking stock. Africa does not waste much time on the transition from dark to light.

The sky was still pewter, too new for heat, the palm trees gray and mournful like the feeble loam that nurtured them. The fronds arced as if defeated by the sheer burden of these dawns and dusks that brought no change or respite and came and went with such predictable rapidity.

We were at someone's home—two rooms and a small courtyard paved in concrete, ornamented by the discarded rear seat of a defunct automobile. A woman lay on it, listless, moaning occasionally without much hope of attracting attention. A baby curled in her arms.

She was suffering, they said, from malaria, although no one in those days had found the label of AIDS to describe the inexplicable, wasting diseases that had settled on La Cité. She lay there in a grimy red tanktop, a patterned brown-yellow kikoyi wrapped about her loins. There had been money for beer, great liter bottles of Primus consumed without the fuss of glasses or cups, as we sat around the open dance floor of the nightclub. But, it seemed, there was no money just yet for medicine, or maybe there was no medicine to be had beyond the witch doctor's bones.

(Money seemed to come and go like a stream prone alternately to drought and flash flood. One minute it would be there in a wad of bills from someone's uncle or cousin, thick with frequent handling, emblazoned with the portrait of the president in his leopard-skin hat. Then it was gone, just as suddenly as it had appeared.)

The woman stirred, sighed, turned. "Elle est malade," my new friend, Eli, told me, shrugging at the superfluity of the explanation. She was his sister, he said, but the definition of such relationships always seemed elastic.

Nothing could be done about it. She was sick. That was all. She would live or die, depending on the whim of some unseen hand, and there was very little point getting too upset in advance about the outcome. She was dark and pretty, her hair plaited into checkerboard squares. Even in her illness, she stirred with a hint of the voluptuousness that had infused the night's music. Her almond eyes flickered over the people gathered about her in a semicircle—her family and me, the outsider—but registered no surprise or interest. Then they closed again. The baby slept through it all.

"Elle est très malade," Eli said.

In the West, many people believe intuitively that they can translate will into action; that is one of the unwritten assumptions of life in the First World, so ingrained as to be unspoken, a social ethic. The Victorian Englishman Samuel Smiles had written: "I will, therefore I can." It is the guiding principle of ambition and doing well, the fundamental belief that enthuses those young people bustling along the streets of London and New York and Frankfurt: they only have to want it badly enough and work for it and it will come true. Grocers' daughters can become prime minister of Britain if they want it badly enough. B-movie actors can be President of the world's mightiest nation.

Most of Africa knows that the opposite is true, that life simply has too many encumbrances to permit freedom of volition. The stasis cannot be budged. The leaders do not want it to be budged, either.

At dawn in La Cité, people stirred to the prospect of a life as predictably difficult as yesterday's. Children awoke in close intimacy with their parents' intimacy, cramped in small homes, in the bosom of families too big for sustaining. People cast aside thin blankets, pulled on threadbare clothes.

Here it was—the continent's secret, its back lot, the "real" Africa.

This was it: Africa, laden with magic, brought low with hopelessness.

I looked for Eli and his sister during another visit a few months later. He had gone, new people in the small house told me, but they did not know where. And the girl? What had happened to the pretty, teenage girl and her baby, curled on the automobile seat? They did not know that, either.

I thought of her a few months later, as I sat beside a private swimming pool situated above the broad sweep of the Congo River. Giant cacti framed a sunset daubed in layers of orange and bright red and magenta. My Belgian host played tennis on a private court with floodlights. A large black dog gamboled on an expansive lawn of kikuyu grass. The hostess slid through the clear blue, chlorinated water, a perfect form surfacing where she had left champagne to chill in an ice bucket. Dusk settled on the red roof of her villa.

"In Zaire," my friend Jo-Jo Mallel—a Kinshasa businessman with wide and arcane interests—once told me, "everything is possible, everything is impossible."

President Mobutu had come to power in 1965 in a coup supported by the CIA. He paid his dues—as both a creation and a beneficiary of the Cold War. He mortgaged his great slab of Africa to the Western strategic interest; and the West in turn gave him free rein to pursue his visions and to act without mercy in the name of power. He proved a useful, if quixotic, asset in a cynical relationship. By ignoring his excesses at home, outsiders contributed to the miseries of his people, but maintained access to his tawdry offerings: air bases, here and there, but mainly the denial of Soviet influence. They did so with feeble excuses: well, this is Africa, Western diplomats would say, what do you expect? How could anyone run this place? Doesn't the chiefly tradition demand a tight hand on the tiller? And, finally, it could be worse.

Mobutu's dictatorship, it is true, was not the most excessive in Africa, and, looking at what had come before, it was not out of character. Zaire's modern history was written in folly and cruelty, a modern chronicle that began in the late nineteenth century when a Belgian monarch craved an African domain and seized on Zaire.

King Leopold II achieved a unique distinction in the annals of colonialism. From 1885 until 1908, the entire country had been his personal fiefdom, run through a trading association established by royal decree—probably the most preposterous form of foreign domination Africa has ever known. The king set its boundaries, decided how it would be administered, and milked it of its wealth. Henry Morton Stanley, the Welsh-American journalist, soldier, and explorer who had found Dr. Livingstone in 1871, had been his agent, signing treaties with local chiefs that bound them to the distant, rapacious monarch.

In the scramble for Africa, Stanley beat the French to most of the Congo basin. At the Berlin conference of 1884 and 1885 the European powers—Britain, France, Belgium, and others, but no Africans— partitioned an entire continent into spheres of influence. The gathering simply awarded Zaire—then called the Congo Free State—to King Leopold. Under his remote tutelage (he never did visit his domain) the urge to loot the continent reached proportions of unequaled horror. Tribesmen who did not fulfill their quota of rubber for the bosses were maimed and disfigured by the king's men as a punishment. Some versions have it that the population actually shrank by 8 million people during Leopold's reign. The only way the gang bosses could prove to their managers that they had exacted the punishment for inadequate tapping of the rubber trees was to show them the amputated limbs. And so, to preserve them for display, some of them were smoked, and baskets of cured, human hands were presented for inspection. Such practices inspired Mr. Kurtz, the central figure of *Heart of Darkness*, to sum up the Congo in four words: "The horror! The horror!"

In 1960, the Belgians precipitately furled their banners, withdrawing an entire bureaucracy without provision for a successor, in response to the clamor within and the dawning of an era of African decolonization. It had begun three years earlier with Ghana's independence, laden with promises of freedom, hope, and renewal. But in Zaire, freedom led only to five years of rebellion, secession, and war. Outsiders mingled freely in the trauma—Belgians and Americans, Russians and Chinese. The United Nations sent troops to put down secession in the southern province of Katanga, now called Shaba. Revolt broke out throughout the country. Within months of independence, the place boasted at least four rival administrations. Once, Belgian rule had somehow contained Zaire's centrifugal forces—250 tribes bound by frontiers delineated by the king, brought haphazardly together under the Congolese flag. At independence they reasserted themselves, as if to avenge a cruel history of neglect: eighty years of colonial rule had left no expertise for government at all.

By the time Mobutu finally took over in 1965—it was his second coup since independence—any sense of order was a relief. That was the American diplomats' argument: if you thought Zaire was bad in the late 1970s, you should have seen it in the early 1960s. Mobutu, they said, had brought a measure of stability. He had ended the chaos. And, in any event, the bottom line was that there was no viable, pro-Western alternative.

The reason for relative tranquility and the absence of alternatives, of course, was that the president himself had eliminated or co-opted all challengers through trickery, torture, and outright repression.

When, at the height of a crisis, Uganda's Idi Amin flew in to offer moral support, the two dictators dined under a thatched pagoda over-looking the Congo River. Beside them, sleek leopards prowled in a cage, the very symbols of Mobutu's power. The tables were set with solid gold cutlery—the trappings of wealth and power exercised without mercy.

Only a few months before the show trial in March 1978, men from Mobutu's elite personal guard had gone to the Bandundu region to confront members of an obscure religious sect who had turned against the authorities. The president's men flew there in American-supplied C-130 transport planes and carried American M-16 rifles. But the result would have been the same if they had flown in Russian Antonovs and fired Soviet AK-47s. At least 800 people were slaughtered—some said 2,000 was closer to the mark—as the president's men displayed loyalty to their leader by mowing down their countrymen. The event—so remote, so typical—went largely unreported outside Zaire. It was insignificant. Who cared? It was the Congo. After all, it was only blacks killing blacks.

A year earlier, Zaire had drawn brief and sarcastic headlines with a comic-opera war in the region of Shaba that was later to be seen as a rehearsal for bloodier events. Disaffected Zaireans living in exile in Angola, men from the Lunda tribe, marched back into their own country on the straight dirt road that runs from Dilolo on the border to the copper and cobalt centers of Kolwezi and Lubumbashi. They encountered no real resistance, until President Mobutu called reluctantly on his friend and ally, King Hassan II of Morocco, for supplies and soldiers to aid his own forces, who had, until then, fought a curious campaign.

Pygmies—official communiqués reported—had been sent to the front, men of the forest armed with bows and poisoned arrows. To assist them, Idi Amin sent Coca-Cola as military aid and promised to lead a suicide platoon in person. But when we correspondents finally got to what was termed "le front"—a broken bridge on a small stream called the Lubudi River—we found the president's men fighting among themselves over a great vat of beans. The enemy had long departed, not because it had been beaten, but because its supply lines had run out. Also absent were Idi Amin's suicide platoon and the much advertised pygmies.

"Où sont les pygmées?" we asked. The soldiers looked bemused. Pygmies?

A spokesman hastened to explain. The pygmies, he pointed out, averaged 4 feet in height. The elephant grass, by contrast, was about 10 feet tall. So the pygmies could not see to fire their poisoned arrows at the rebels of the Congo National Liberation Front, so they had been sent home, back to the forests, where the light was not so bright and the grass not so tall. (Editors had a fascination about these small men and it became imperative to locate one for an interview. When, later in the campaign, in the town of Kasaji I found a man of no great stature clad in Mobutu's uniform, carrying a bow and poisoned arrow, duty obliged me to ask him: "Are you a pygmy?" "No," he replied, politely but firmly, and with wry dignity, "I am a small Zairean.")

By some magical process, it became the wisdom that the decisive battle of the conflict would be fought at Mutshatsha, a dusty railway stop suddenly elevated to the status of a strategic crossroads. No one, except its residents, had heard much of Mutshatsha before, but now it became an objective of the war, because that was as far as the rebels had got before they ran out of supplies. As Mutshatsha, thus the nation.

On April 26, 1977, Mutshatsha fell to Moroccan forces and Mobutu arrived for a visit.

He sat below the blue-gum trees in his general's uniform posing for the photographers, munching American C-rations, while an aide knelt before him to buff up his paratroop boots. Men from what was called the elite Kamanyola Brigade—trained by North Korean advisers—

goose-stepped by him, singing war songs. Those who sang were rewarded with a pack of American rations, and so, as the singing trailed
off in the indistinct bushlands, the word went around that there were
prizes. The singing duly swelled again as more men joined the triumphant homage to Mobutu and more cardboard packs of C-rations were
handed out: the spoils of war.

There had not, after all, been *grandes batailles en Afrique.*

But the real message came from Washington: on the day Mutshatsha
fell, the International Monetary Fund in Washington announced an
$85 million loan to Mobutu, with economic conditions attached but
no pressure for political change.

"We will do our best to prevent Soviet influence in Africa," Mobutu
duly proclaimed, interpreting the rebels' bloodless withdrawal as a body
blow to Moscow's encroachment in Africa. "If Europe trembles every
time Brezhnev coughs, it is not for me," he said. The bargain remained
the same as it had always been—a tough stance toward the Russians
in return for dollars and a free hand at home.

The insurgents, however, were no aberration. They drew on a
profound disaffection among the people of Shaba Province, who saw
the country's wealth pulled from the ground and shipped away, never
to return. The money went north, to Mobutu and his kin from the
Equateur Province, light-years away from those who mined it for pitiful
wages. A whole tribe felt dispossessed, and their anger was not directed
only at the president and his henchmen.

The expatriates, the French and Belgian engineers, lived off Shaba's
riches too, in their villas walled with frangipani and bougainvillea,
and their social clubs for tennis and their flying school at Kolwezi
Airport. (Their life was one I recognized, for it was not much different
from Lusaka, and my own.) And so these outsiders, the whites, came
to be seen as Mobutu's agents, no less privileged than during the
colonial days, and as aloof and scornful of Africans as they ever had
been. Independence seventeen years before had brought nothing, and
neglect had nurtured a rage that was to turn bloodily against everything
associated with the regime. In May 1977, we charted the last of the
loyalist victories, and left. A year later, almost to the day, we were
back again to chronicle a conflict that sent shockwaves across Africa.

2.

Drawing the Lines:

Bringing Africa South—

Shaba

"Marxism-Leninism was in the air."

ROBERT MUGABE, as a guerrilla leader, to the author, December 1976

For weeks before their second invasion in 1978, Shaba's rebels had infiltrated supporters into La Cité Manica—Kolwezi's slum—and many people knew something was afoot. Zairean army officers decamped Shaba, closing their bank accounts as they went. Loyal servants whispered to longtime employers that they ought to think of leaving. But the warnings went largely ignored by both the Zairean authorities in distant Kinshasa and their Western sponsors.

The rebels were led by Colonel Nathaniel M'Bumba, who had been a policeman in Katanga, as Shaba was formerly named. He had taken part in the region's attempt at secession in the 1960s, but when the breakaway state collapsed, had fled to Angola. Now, he was coming home. His men, slicing across a remote and unpoliced corner of Zambia, pushed from Angola into his tribal homeland. The Western intelligence agencies who broke the first word of the invasion reckoned there were 3,000 to 4,000 of them, under the ragged banner of the Congo National Liberation Front with its hodgepodge of Marxist jargon and nationalist rhetoric. Their victory was short-lived and grisly. On May 13, 1978, Kolwezi fell to them, and on May 19, they melted away again as paratroops from the French Foreign Legion dropped from the skies.

If President Mobutu had been slow to call for foreign help a year earlier, this time there was no delay. Two thirds of Zaire's hard currency came from Shaba Province and the place was a tinderbox of resentment and anger. But more than that, the invasion had raised Africa's ghost: secession.

"Every African country has its Shaba," one Zambian official told me, by way of explaining the continent's numbed silence, its inability to condemn or restrain the actions of either side. Colonial frontiers, such as the long, geometric border dividing Zambia and Zaire, had taken no account of Africa's old empires and tribes, running through the lines, assembling disparate tribes in unfamiliar nation-states whose central authority did not extend to the peripheries. The frontiers, African leaders acknowledged, were an insane legacy. But, at the same time, they were sacrosanct. When newly independent states established the Organization of African Unity in Addis Ababa in 1963 as the emergent continent's supposed political voice, it was a founding principle that the colonial boundaries remain intact. If an unraveling began, no one would be safe. Zaire's Western patrons had no wish to see their fiefdom disturbed. If the invasion succeeded in igniting revolt across the rambling land, then their investment would have been in vain, the Congo's madness would be reborn, and no one could guess who, at the end of it all, would occupy Mobutu's palace on the Congo River, or where the challenges to other clients would end. No one, at the time, seemed to consider that a sterner approach to Mobutu's excesses might have averted the buildup of frustration and disaffection that enabled the invaders to march as the liberators of the downtrodden.

There was another imperative, a political imperative in France, Belgium, and the United States, too. Around 3,000 foreigners were caught up in the revolt. Most were Belgians, but there were also French, American, and British nationals. No government in Europe wanted to contemplate the charge that their kith and kin had been abandoned to the forces of mayhem and savagery. Yet the very effort to rescue them, with hindsight, probably caused the bloodiest killing of all.

When I spoke to the survivors of Kolwezi's occupation, their traumatized memories were all pretty much the same. For the first couple of days, the rebels had run an administration with relative order. Then, alarmed by the fact that their triumph seemed to find no echo elsewhere, and anticipating a counterattack on a large scale, they had armed the ragged lumpenproletariat of La Cité Manica. Then the looting and the witch-hunt for fictitious French mercenaries and foreign spies began. The liquor stores went first, and the alcohol ignited the great blaze of rage, anger, vengeance.

The killing started in earnest on Wednesday, May 17, with all the detail the Congo was expected to produce—women raped in front of their husbands, capricious slaughter, summary executions against the wall, servants avenging themselves in blood for years of indignity and subservience. The first, rough tally of the dead listed one hundred foreigners and at least eight hundred Zaireans, some felled sickeningly by bullets in the back. (Many days after the rebel withdrawal, I came across a line of undiscovered corpses, ten or twelve of them, along a narrow path in high grass, neat and lifeless as toy soldiers. All lay face down where they had been shot from behind. The bodies had swollen in the heat so that it seemed, at first glance, that they had all been wearing clothes too tight for them. In the shock of the moment, no one seemed to know what to do with them, so they just lay there like forgotten garbage.)

On May 19, the French Foreign Legion, stealing a march on the Belgian paratroops still assembling back home, dropped into Kolwezi by parachute after a twenty-hour flight from their bases in Corsica. Angered by this coup de théâtre by the French—rivals for influence and business contracts in Zaire—the Belgians had leaked word of it to radio stations, newspapers, and news agencies. So Colonel M'Bumba's men knew they were coming.

The French lost the element of surprise and the rebels wisely decided to withdraw, their trucks piled high with loot. But in the chaos of the moment, something happened that surpassed in its pure horror anything I or most of my colleagues had witnessed.

There were twenty-eight of them, all Europeans—men, women, children—herded together in a villa on the outskirts of Kolwezi. The numbers were not so important, however, as the way they died.

I arrived on Saturday, May 20, in an American-built C-130 transport of the Zaire Air Force, flown part of the way by Mobutu himself from a co-pilot's seat draped in leopard skin: the photo opportunity was too good for him to miss. The French Foreign Legion held the town and, by then, the Belgian paratroops had arrived too, albeit a day late. A great airlift of over 2,000 white survivors was under way, and the

French told us that if we wanted transport from the airport we should simply hot-wire a car from the many abandoned by the fleeing ex-patriates.

The evidence of slaughter was everywhere. The streets were littered with corpses, shot by the rebels, the loyalists, the French Foreign Legion. Dogs gnawed at bodies. Outside a looted supermarket, a store-front mannequin lay in the dust like some cruel parody of the human dead. Shards of discarded uniform stained the red earth. Here and there, a lone boot testified to someone's precipitate shedding of military gear and subsequent flight as a civilian. (Lone boots always seem one of the most enigmatic of battlefield visions, because it is never totally clear how they were lost, or by whom.) In the bright, fierce sun that left no detail unexposed, around homes that looked just like mine on the Great East Road in Lusaka—with high gates and illusions of security—bodies lay in the curious abandon of violent death, all dignity stripped away. The villa, when we came upon it, was much worse.

In a corridor, a woman crouched in a corner, her hands to her ears, the final scream frozen in a rictus of sheer terror. In what had been a living room, the bodies were piled two or three feet high in a chaotic tangle. A child peered from them with unseeing eyes. Belgian intelligence officers said they believed a grenade had been thrown first, then the room had been sprayed with rifle fire, then the assailants had gone in to administer the coup de grâce. What lingered was the in-timacy of it, the sheer cruelty, the knowledge that whoever had shot the woman had seen the terror of her scream and felt no pity; that whoever opened fire had seen the child's small face amongst those to be executed.

This had not happened in the heat of battle. It had happened as the result of some atavistic urge that corroded the common humanity, that cheapened life and callused the souls of those who witnessed it. It took a while to absorb the notion that this was no film set and these were no extras. No one would get up and wipe off the make-up when the cameras stopped rolling.

But the horror did not end there. Although the rebels melted away into the camouflage of the bush and the foreign survivors were evac-uated, the residents of La Cité Manica were left to face the retribution of the French Foreign Legion and the wrath of Zairean soldiers out to avenge their humiliation.

As the foreign soldiers departed, Zaire's own ragged army resumed its despotic rule of Shaba, loosing off salvoes at shadows. For all the trauma and bloodletting, nothing had changed. The soldiers stole from the cooking pots in La Cité Manica and swaggered with an exaggerated bravado that fooled nobody into thinking they were the saviours, the brave. Returning from a final visit to Kolwezi, a Zairean bishop drove me to the airport and we came upon an army roadblock. He introduced me as a father, a missionary, and we passed through safely. If he had not dissembled and pretended I was a man of the cloth, he said, the soldiers would have stolen my watch.

Only a few months before, an American diplomat in Kinshasa had told me, "We are simply no longer going into the business of propping up regimes, particularly discredited ones." The promise was short-lived: the United States provided the logistics of the Western rescue operation, ferrying men and kit in C-141 Starlifters and C-5A Galaxies the length and breadth of Zaire, offering salvation not only to the white survivors of Kolwezi but—yet again—to Mobutu. At the center of the Great Game, though, something had been torn in Shaba's sense of its own humanity.

In *Heart of Darkness*, Mr. Kurtz scribbles a postscript to his idiosyncratic thesis on Africa: "Exterminate all the brutes!" That found its echo in Shaba, too. "I'd like to see all the blacks shot," a survivor told me. He was a priest.

Many Westerners perceived the uprisings in Shaba as the linear descendants of the Congo of the 1960s, the relief of Stanleyville replayed in a slightly updated setting, provoked by Mobutu's neglect and greed, but drawn from the same somber wellspring of violence. That certainly was part of the story. But there were other potent dynamics at work.

The rebels who pressed across the frontier could not have done so if the Portuguese had still controlled Angola, because Portugal's interests coincided with the maintenance of a status quo favorable to the West—and to South Africa—and disrupting Mobutu was not part of the game plan in Washington or Pretoria. But Portuguese rule had begun to collapse with an officers' coup in Lisbon in 1974 that flowed from the imperial soldiers' frustration with the tribulations of empire. Of all the events that have changed Africa in recent years, that distant upheaval in Lisbon, far from the continent's shores, was possibly the most pivotal.

While Portuguese rule was in force in Mozambique and Angola, South Africa was strategically safe. The ruling white minorities of Rhodesia and South West Africa completed the ideological palisade that sheltered apartheid, and the black-ruled states caught up in the equation—Botswana, Swaziland, and Lesotho—had no strength to challenge raw, white power or the geography that placed them adjacent to or surrounded by it. South Africa's borders were sanitized. Until the Portuguese let the side down, that is, and crumbled.

The coup of April 1974 led rapidly to independence in Portugal's colonial possessions—Guinea-Bissau in September 1974, Mozambique in June 1975, and Angola in November the same year. It was the weariness with the guerrilla wars that prompted the officers to end the dictatorship in Lisbon. And it was those same guerrillas who now claimed victory in Portugal's former territories in the name of ideologies that troubled both South Africa and the West.

In Mozambique, Samora Machel's guerrilla organization, Frelimo, took power after some skirmishing with right-wing whites in the capital—then called Lourenço Marques, soon to be renamed Maputo—in the name of a Marxist ideology that took years to shed. The Portuguese left in large numbers, stripping the store as they did elsewhere in Africa, not only taking trucks, light bulbs, and expertise with them but also sowing destruction, even pouring concrete into the toilets.

Angola was a greater strategic and economic asset, with its coffee and diamonds and oil. Like Mozambique, it became a fulcrum of outsiders' rivalries, and wars would persist into the 1990s, in part as offshoots of the Cold War, in part as expressions of the region's own tensions.

For years, China and the Soviet Union had vied for influence among Africa's liberation movements. And, after Vietnam, in the shape of Henry Kissinger, the United States had begun to show unaccustomed—but in the end fleeting—interest in Africa, casting it as the new cockpit of rivalry with Moscow, a place where America might reassert its power.

Ethiopia had "gone" to the Soviets when Emperor Haile Selassie was deposed in 1974. With policies that ultimately brought it few benefits, Moscow, moreover, was sponsoring liberation movements identified by a dizzying array of initials and acronyms—the MPLA in Angola, Frelimo in Mozambique, SWAPO in Namibia, ZAPU in Rhodesia, the PAIGC in Guinea-Bissau, the ANC in South Africa itself. All of those groups had assailed pro-Western regimes.

So pervasive was the superpowers' contest that the Organization of African Unity—the supposed repository of Africa's freedom from dependence on outsiders—was neatly divided into camps looking to Washington or Moscow for succor, brandishing competing ideological labels to support their claim to superpower benefaction.

As the Portuguese prepared to scramble out of Africa centuries after they arrived, bequeathing nothing of much value to those they had colonized, the Angola war of independence became the center of these rivalries. And Angola, a vast territory on the Atlantic coast, would decide which way the balance tipped. Or so the theory went.

In Angola, three separate liberation movements were in the field. One—the MPLA of Agostinho Neto—was supported by Cuba and Moscow. The other two—the FNLA of Holden Roberto and the UNITA of Jonas Savimbi—drew sustenance from a more complex and bizarre coalition: the CIA, the Chinese, white mercenaries, British big business, and, of course, Zaire's President Mobutu.

Portugal's precipitate departure was bound to leave a vacuum. As Angola's independence approached on November 11, 1975, the struggle intensified.

In early 1975, all three armed factions were encamped in Luanda, the capital, all claiming different constituencies. Fighting between them broke out almost immediately. The FNLA, backed at that time largely by Zaire and the Chinese, was militarily the strongest, politically the weakest. China's embroilment, however, started a chain reaction.

Moscow intervened heavily in support of Agonstinho Neto's MPLA, which it had backed in a lesser way for many years before the Portuguese coup. By July 1975, the MPLA, with major Soviet and Cuban support, had expelled its two rivals from the capital.

That, in turn, added a new urgency to Washington's plan to mount a huge covert operation with Zaire and South Africa in support of Neto's adversaries—the FNLA and UNITA—and against the Soviet-backed regime. It was the beginning of a war that would preoccupy southern Africa for the next fifteen years, bringing Cuba and South Africa into direct conflict, and pitting competing visions of the future against one another in the wider ideological duel—a duel that was seen to have been folly when the Cold War came abruptly to an end.

Events tumbled on one another with a speed and passion that touched the entire southern chunk of the continent.

In October 1975, as independence approached, fast-moving South African mechanized units pushed five hundred miles north from the South West African border to within striking distance of Luanda, carrying Savimbi's UNITA guerrillas with them in a power play so audacious—even by Pretoria's flawed standards—that word of it was censored from all South African news media. The white folks back home were not supposed to know what mischief and mayhem their leaders had gotten their conscript sons into. The black folks were not supposed to contemplate the Afrikaners in direct battle with the continent's newest champions of black power. And the world was supposed to believe the fiction that Pretoria was not involved at all.

With massive support, the MPLA triumphed to hold the capital on the day of nominal independence. And, for the purposes of African recognition and a nebulous legitimacy, holding the capital meant winning the nation. Yet, to the south, Savimbi's men with their CIA and South African supporters still held a string of towns across the country's rich Central Highlands along the Benguela Railway. Dislodging them might have been a far greater challenge had not the United States defeated its own strategy to win Angola for the West: on December 19, the Senate voted to withhold all funding for covert operations in Angola; the effect on the recipients of CIA support was instantaneous.

By January 1986, Roberto's FNLA with their Zairean and white mercenary supporters were falling back to the Zaire frontier. In February, Savimbi's men lost their last redoubt in central Angola after the South Africans pulled back, blowing the bridges behind them. Savimbi, facing the Cubans and his Angolan adversaries alone, limped back to the inhospitable southeastern bushlands that the Portuguese called "the end of the earth."

The palisade that had once protected South Africa and Rhodesia became a launching pad for their adversaries. Using Mozambique as a base, the guerrillas fighting white rule in neighboring Rhodesia could now open a second front across a long, porous border of bushland and tea estates and mountains. Nelson Mandela's supporters in the African National Congress, living in exile far from South Africa's borders, could now be brought to the perimeters of the Afrikaner stockade from staging points in Maputo. And Sam Nujoma's men in SWAPO now had access from Angola to a lengthy frontier with Namibia—the object of their long and often feeble guerrilla war.

These were heady days for those who called one another "comrade" and relied on violence as their principal tool of political change. This was also a time of black self-confidence; long reviled by white adversaries as cowardly and inefficient, black guerrillas had brought down the last remaining European empire in Africa. White rule was not, after all, invincible. And, in backing the winners in Portugal's erstwhile possessions, the Soviet Union had shown itself to be a reliable supplier of the means of forcing change—the AK-47 assault rifle, the RPG-7 rocket launcher—all in the name of spreading an ideology that would redeem colonialism's inequities: socialism was on the march.

Back in the 1960s the insurgents of South Africa, the Portuguese colonies, and Rhodesia had concluded that violence was their only recourse. Now in the 1970s they had been vindicated, legitimizing not only the strategy of guerrilla warfare but a fundamental way of thinking: if white minority regimes enforced their writ with violence, then violence was the only way to end them; if the enemy would not listen to talk, it would have to listen to gunfire.

It was the beginning of a chronology that sculpted southern Africa's history, emboldening the forces of change in Rhodesia and South Africa. But it did not go unchallenged. The growth of black power injected a new resolve into Pretoria's effort to rebuild its fortress, through proxy wars and economic pressure, and to create a "constellation" of pliant states to replace what the Portuguese had abandoned. If the citadel was to be surrounded by black-ruled countries, then at least those countries should be taught to toe Pretoria's line.

And, since Pretoria's adversaries and its new, black-ruled neighbors without exception embraced socialist dogma, the Afrikaners dubbed their effort a fight against a "Total Onslaught" by communism—a

notion designed to legitimize a total response, within and beyond their
frontiers. The Afrikaners had no doubt that they were the ultimate
target, the greatest prize of all.

The alarm bells that had sounded with the Portuguese coup in 1974
rang inside South Africa itself on June 16, 1976, when the Soweto
protest erupted, ostensibly over the use of Afrikaans as a language of
instruction in segregated black schools. If the Mozambicans could
shake off an empire, then surely the South African majority could
challenge the white minority.

The irony—and the hypocrisy—lay in the deliberate myopia of the
black struggle. In Lusaka or Kinshasa—and soon in those new stan-
dardbearers of revolutionary rule and "people's power" that had replaced the Portuguese Empire—one-party states ground themselves
and their people to a standstill, untouched by the same demands for
renewal as confronted the white regimes of the south. Coup d'états
might reshuffle the elite, as had happened in Zaire, but nothing offered
a style of rule that changed the lot—or the status—of ordinary people.

By the mid-1970s the first dance of freedom from the 1960s was
played out, eroded by a greed for power, by tribalism and corruption.
A foreign wizard had been chased away, and a home-grown sorcerer
had replaced him; that was the overwhelming impression of Saturday
night in La Cité, or any other of the gimcrack sprawls that surrounded
African cities from Lusaka to Nairobi to Lagos.

Notions of parliamentary rule had given way to one-party states and
military dictatorship. The effort of ruling these ramshackle lands,
where authority beyond the capital was often no more than a chimera,
had worn away whatever good intentions existed in the first place.
Westminster could not be simply transplanted to Africa's otherwise
fertile lands, and a body of lore and contorted ideology made the point.
"You cannot have two bulls in one kraal," they said in parts of black-
ruled southern Africa, meaning that there was no tolerance of opposition, that the very nature of the continent demanded a single, strong
focus of power.

In Zambia, the system called "one-party participatory democracy"
meant that, if you had a grievance, you expressed it through the sole
party. But, since the sole party was often as not the object of grievance,

there was not much chance of redress. President Kenneth Kaunda, an otherwise benevolent figure prone to emotion and public tears at the continent's plight, led his followers in a chorus that embodied Africa's political logic. "One Zambia," the president would cry at public gatherings. "One nation," came the response from the assembled gathering. "One nation," the president resumed. "One leader," came the reply. "That leader?" a crony would call. "Kaunda," everyone would chorus. The president would smile bashfully. The opposition benches that the British had left behind in their colonies gathered dust. The man became the nation, until, in 1991, the changes that flowed from the collapse of Soviet communism reached Zambia, too, and "K.K.," as he was nicknamed, bowed out after an unprecedented election defeat. It was to his credit that he did so with grace. But by then, and not only in Zambia, the damage was already done.

If Africa's first generation of post-independence leaders betrayed the trust of their people and the promises of freedom, it was partly because the challenge was great and humanity is frail. It was one thing to talk of parliamentary opposition in Britain, African friends would tell me, but how did you equate that with an opposition rooted in tribe and greed that would see you dead rather than relegated to a temporary sojourn on the other side of the parliamentary divide? And what of those artificial, colonial frontiers that had lumped disparate tribes together in the new nation-state? How better to produce the notion of unity and cohesion than a one-party state, the symbol at least of a national authority? The people needed the vanguard to guide them.

All those arguments had a validity, if only by reference to history's unfolding. The European colonialism of the nineteenth century was only the latest in a succession of intrusions that had disrupted the continent. Slavers had preyed on the nation-tribe for centuries, taking away men and promise. Missionaries, anticipating and cementing the intrusion of colonial rule, had brought a foreign God to lands where other spirits had prevailed. In the nineteenth century, particularly, adventurers had roamed with guns and treaties across southern Africa. Outsiders' banners had risen over lands that were not theirs by any conceivable right. For centuries, the vast continent had been prey to usurpation and invasion. By comparison, freedom was a new and untested commodity.

But where the first post-independence rulers really betrayed the trust of their people was the refusal to acknowledge failure. One-party states derived a kind of legitimacy from Leninism, and the notion that revolutionary times demand revolutionary methods. But even before the Soviet Union under Mikhail Gorbachev came to the conclusion that those revolutionary notions did not make economic sense, Africans knew in their hearts that something had gone hopelessly wrong, that the imported ideologies were not working for them. That was something the old guard of African leadership could not accept without acknowledging its own demise. To suggest there could be no economic renewal without a new political debate and openness meant that the old orders would not endure. If the charitable interpretation of Africa's malaise was that the task was too great for mortals, then the cynical riposte was that the individual greed for power and status and wealth was overwhelmingly greater.

Over the years, one-party rule and dictatorship bred their own reflexes, setting higher values on loyalty and obsequiousness than managerial talent. Michael Holman, the wise Africa editor of the *Financial Times* of London and a good friend, once told me of an incident on an airplane leaving Uganda's Entebbe Airport. A government minister was aboard the plane, and, naturally enough, the ministerial delegation took up the front rows of the aircraft. Toward the rear, a large lady from the minister's party who had apparently been excluded from these arrangements was protesting loudly. "I am part of the minister," she cried, suggesting an almost organic relationship between boss and crony. To be "part of the minister" was what power was all about, conferring status, privilege, the front-row seats at the pillage of the nation. But it was a status rooted in tribe and loyalty, not skill or ability. Across Africa, the traveler would come across the continent's bright young men striving with their computers and fax machines to break the mold. Blocking their path were those who were "part of the minister," enjoying the largesse that spread from the leader to the supporting cast that sustained the supremacy of the clique.

The schools had no textbooks, the hospitals no medicine, the future facing the children was blank. There was no work, food was scarce. And there was no escape, either. So who would not rather be "part of the minister"?

This phenomenon, more than anything, eroded Africa's fabric because it denied those very managerial talents needed to cope with the complexities of debt and decline that were the legacy of freedom's first generation. Instead, graft and elitism became the self-perpetuating talismen of political power, unrestrained by any sense of political accountability. One-party states—whether in Eastern European countries or in African states that borrowed the seductive idea from them—did nothing more than isolate unworthy leaders from the demands of their people.

People in Western democracies might wonder why and how people lived as long as they did under the despotism of dictators like Mobutu. The answer is that, above all, they want to live, even if being "part of the minister" is the only visible path of advance.

Further south, however, as another war unfolded, Mobutu's example played into a central argument that drove southern African wars: if freedom brought only injustice in places like Uganda, or Zaire, or Kenya, or Zambia, why should its fruits be different anywhere else? The answer, in Rhodesia, depended on who you asked.

3.

Holding the Line:

Whites at War

in Rhodesia

"It was a privilege to make a stand against communism.
We held the line back."

FORMER RHODESIAN PRIME MINISTER IAN D.SMITH to the author, August 1984

At midnight on April 17, 1980, in a crowded soccer stadium, the British colony of Rhodesia ceased to exist and the new, independent republic of Zimbabwe came into being. Bob Marley and the Wailers played some rasta music, and one or two disgruntled policemen from the old times lobbed tear gas over the wall, just to remind those assembled where they had come from. The Union Jack snagged briefly on the pole before Zimbabwe's new banner replaced it, so freedom came a couple of minutes behind schedule. But after so long in the gestation, liberty's brief delay was bearable.

Rhodesia was Britain's last African colony, an idiosyncratic chunk of bush and rich farmland in Central Africa, ruled by a cantankerous and defiant white minority that had seized independence for itself in 1965 to staunch the flash flood of black freedom washing through the continent. The white declaration, renouncing Britain's theoretical control and parodying the black independence in vogue elsewhere in Africa at the time, won no international acceptance; indeed, the United Nations imposed economic sanctions as a punishment. The Unilateral Declaration of Independence—UDI, as it became known—propelled the land toward a guerrilla war that lasted from 1972 to 1979. In that year, a peace conference at Lancaster House in London drew up the terms for a cease-fire and lawful independence with a government elected by all the people. For the black majority, Lancaster House was the greatest of victories. For many whites, it was a cruel defeat; by their lights, they had not lost on the battlefield but in the treacherous eddies of international diplomacy, where expediency came before what they liked to depict as honor.

When the fighting stopped, 30,000 people, most of them black, had lost their lives. (The conflict, like many others in Africa, seemed to prove the point that the best way to stay alive in these wars was to join the army. Most of the dead were civilians, "caught in crossfire.") Many more people had been herded into protected villages or had fled as refugees. Zambia and Mozambique—the guerrillas' rear bases— had suffered the depradations of a spillover war from Rhodesian re- prisals that left their economies in far worse shape than that of the newly created Zimbabwe. The losses seemed cruel and futile. But Ian Smith, the man who led the whites in their rebellion, the scion of a Scottish settler family that ran a butcher's shop, had a different per- spective. After the war was over and the victors had allowed their old white adversary to stay on, I visited him at his farm at Shurugwe in the center of the country and asked him whether the death toll had been worth it.

By then, Smith, a former Spitfire pilot in the Royal Air Force, was in his sixties, craggy-featured, lantern-jawed, his face slightly lopsided from a crash in air combat during World War II. He retained the guarded, ruminative manner that he had deployed against the many British and American emissaries who, over the years, had tried to overturn his stubborn rebellion. Before he would answer questions, he required visitors to inspect his fine stock of bulls, as if they were evidence of white viability in Africa, of power and vigor. Then we sat on his porch below a stuffed tiger fish mounted on wood, and I raised the question of the 30,000 dead, and he said, well, you know, the dead "were mainly terrorists, weren't they," and only 450 people from his rebellious minority had succumbed. The whites, he said, had won "fifteen years extra"—from UDI in 1965 to independence in 1980— of running their show, of the life in the sun that the settlers craved. So, all in all, the balance sheet did not look too bad. Most of all, he said with a pride that brought a brief fire to his eyes, Rhodesia had held the line against communism, an ideology indistinguishable for his followers from black majority rule, and little more than a euphe- mism for it.

Smith had not been in attendance when the flag was lowered in Rufaro Stadium, and that was not surprising for, from his point of view, it symbolized the final breaching of the line.

For his adversaries, the spoils were easily discerned—the whole country was finally theirs again, ninety years after British settlers colonized it in 1890. The losses and the passions of the white minority were more difficult to gauge. What Smith and his followers had seen themselves defending was not simply land, but an identity that glamorized their mundane lives and imparted a sense of purpose; Rhodesia, after all, had built the region's second most sophisticated economy, with farms and mines and factories that mocked both Africa's decay and international sanctions. And it had provided the prelude to South Africa's battle—a fight that would again be cast by a white minority as part of the great, global contest of the twentieth century between communism and the West.

From the comrades' perspective, the ceremony in Rufaro Stadium again vindicated the decision of many nationalist movements in the 1960s—including Nelson Mandela's—to turn to "armed struggle" in alliance with either the Soviet Union or China to unseat the recalcitrant regimes of the Portuguese Empire, Rhodesia, and South Africa. The lesson was the same as had been established in 1975 in Mozambique, Angola, and Guinea-Bissau: violence achieved aims that no amount of talk could fulfill. But, in the process, it raised a question of competing legitimacies: if the guerrilla armies could justify their recourse to violence by reference to the "just Cause" of democracy and freedom, then their enemies justified their resistance by reference to "holding the line" against communism in the broader conflict of the Cold War. For Rhodesia's whites there was an evocation, often spurious, of Victorian values, an attempt to justify racial distinction by reference to those same, elusive standards of civilization and Christianity that Dr. David Livingstone had sought to bring to what, in the nineteenth century, had been called a savage and barbarous continent.

Rhodesia posed the same question for its white minority that would preoccupy South Africa: Could whites maintain a cherished and elitist lifestyle without political control of the land and people that sustained it? During the war years, the very unfolding of a conflict that pitted armed guerrillas against a settler army seemed to say the answer was no. But when peace came to Zimbabwe, the land provided an object lesson for some South Africans in racial harmony and tolerance—despite all the bloodshed and hatred that had gone before.

The whites had fought the war with a dogged tenacity, not only against the guerrillas of Robert Mugabe and Joshua Nkomo but also against a hostile world that had imposed economic sanctions. In the end, the war had exhausted them and their neighbors: 95 percent of the country was under martial law, and it was unsafe for anybody to travel outside the cities as dusk approached. Civilian airliners had been shot down by Nkomo's guerrillas, landmines freckled remote tracks. Even South Africa, Rhodesia's ally, had come to see the conflict as a dangerous source of instability and was pressing the whites to compromise.

The easy interpretation of white motives was to ascribe their very existence in Africa to racism and greed. But to understand it from their point of view, it was necessary to go back to the beginning of their line and the man who gave their country its name—Cecil John Rhodes, the most renowned of those young Victorian men who sailed for Africa and molded an unsuspecting continent to their will and whim. Rhodesians still saw themselves as the linear descendants of the nineteenth-century pioneers who tamed a continent in an era that attached no shame or guilt to the projection of British power across the globe. The results—farms and Bibles, "civilization"—were the justification of the means. Zimbabwe, the new name for Rhodesia, was not simply another title for the same piece of land; it was the antithesis of everything the founder intended and a statement of an identity regained after ninety years of white domination.

Rhodes was an extraordinary phenomenon whose shadow cast itself far beyond his time. But he was also the product of an extraordinary period of history that could never be duplicated, a century in Africa that never stood still for long enough to see far beyond the next campaign. Events seemed cast in an epic mold. Everything was larger than life. Everyone was on the move. In that era, the lines were drawn for Africa's modern wars as the outsiders spread the economic and political latticework of their dominance across a continent that fell easy prey. And it was in that period of motion and claim-staking, adventure and derring-do, that later white Rhodesians saw their roots. Yet their twist of history was only one of many in a century of upheaval.

In 1818, Shaka Zulu, warrior, nation builder, and despot, came to power in the area now covered by Natal Province and KwaZulu homeland in South Africa, expanding the fiefdom of his tribe with such ferocity that other tribes fled before his depradations to the farthest reaches of Central Africa, hundreds of miles to the north—a diaspora known by its Zulu name, the *Mfecane*, which translates as "the crushing."

Among the fugitives were the Ndebele who, under their chief Mzilikazi, arrived toward 1840 in what is now Bulawayo, western Zimbabwe, to subjugate the Shona peoples, an event that was to shape the nation's destiny and that was avenged in blood only after Zimbabwe's independence.

Starting in 1835, moreover, Afrikaners at the Cape of Good Hope, chafing at British hegemony and what they perceived as racial liberalism, decided to move northward, away from the inhibitions of alien dominance, to settle the Transvaal, arriving at Pretoria in 1838 after many bloodstained adventures now woven into the mythology of Africa's only white tribe.

Further north, history records even greater movement and intrusion. For decades Arab slavers had pillaged the continent; now missionaries invaded to "redeem" the animist tribes. A map of Central Africa in the nineteenth century showing "the routes of the early European Travellers" resembles a child's scribble across a blank page, with lines heading willy-nilly back and forth, distinguished one from the other by the names of the white men who presumed, with that inherent self-confidence of Victorian Britain and Imperial Portugal, to change a continent, to implant a way of life that would determine the very God to which the people prayed.

Colonialism was one of history's greatest and most ambiguous invasions—not so much military as emotional, a technological and spiritual assault that pried people loose from whatever their lives had once been, preying on a region already enervated by the slavers and its own internal conflict.

Marching to their own drums and pennants, whole empires and kingdoms that predated the missionaries and the adventurers in the savannah of Central Africa were in a state of flux. The chronicles of the time speak of a seemingly endless tally of wars as pretenders came and went and frontiers between one tribe and the next ebbed and flowed. Those conflicts enabled the outsiders to win their treaties and concessions, offering protection in return for mining rights and land, exploiting division to establish rule.

In 1884 and 1885, the Congress of Berlin sought to freeze the continent in place, carving out the spheres of influence allotted to the British, the Portuguese, the Belgians, the French, and the Germans—the colonial powers, not the Africans, nor, indeed, the Afrikaners. That seemed to settle the scramble for Africa. But only one year later, an event occurred that was to have consequences that further reshaped the entire region, sundering families, setting the markers: in 1886, gold was discovered on the Witwatersrand—the reef of white water—that runs below what are now the Transvaal and Orange Free State provinces of South Africa. The event galvanized the struggle between Englishmen and the descendants of the Afrikaners who had arrived at the Cape 234 years earlier, and the pickings gave Rhodes part of the wealth and wherewithal to finance the most grandiose of his dreams.

Gold made South Africa the continent's wealthiest, most powerful land. It was the magnet that drew the claimants to Africa's riches. The mines changed lives forever. They brought black men from villages to work far from their families; and they were central, thus, in weaving the strands of migrant labor and township dwelling that in the next century became the geography of apartheid. Dominating this period was the unlikely, ailing figure of Cecil John Rhodes, third surviving son of a wealthy clergyman from Bishop's Stortford in Hertfordshire, England, who came to South Africa in 1870, supposedly for reasons of health, and stayed for reasons of power and fortune. Rhodes started his life in southern Africa as a cotton farmer in Natal, then went on to the diamond fields at Kimberley, and then got into the gold boom. He ended up reshaping the entire region.

Rhodes was an enigmatic colossus, driven by enormous energy, yet undermined by a heart defect that was to kill him at the age of forty-nine, a man of ambivalent sexuality in an era that had difficulty acknowledging sexuality at all, capable of charm and corruption in the same breath to secure the paramount goal—the assertion of a vision that verged on megalomania. His fortune grew initially from the diamond fields of Kimberley, where his brother Herbert staked out the claims that were to lead to Rhodes's near monopoly of the entire business. In 1887, at the age of thirty-four, Rhodes was said to be earning at least half a million English pounds a year.

Rhodes privatized colonialism. He won a royal charter to develop and occupy the lands north of the Limpopo so that his British South Africa Company might govern untamed lands for which the charter set no northern limit. With the Belgians moving south into Katanga, and the Portuguese seeking to link their much older possessions in East and West Africa, Rhodes was Britain's point man, pressing the wedge of British rule into the heart of Central Africa. The result was the Rhodesias—North and South—spanning the Zambezi, bounded to the west by what is now Botswana, to the east by what is now Mozambique, and to the north by the Belgian Congo, now Zaire.

Rhodes sent his agents to strike dubious treaties with equally dubious chiefs. He made promises of gold to white pioneers where no proof of gold existed. He offered them land that was not his to give and the prospect of riches that were, at first, a chimera. And, in 1890, he ordered the Pioneer Column forth across the Limpopo in a cavalcade of covered ox-drawn wagons, guarded by British government forces, carrying with them, among other things, a huge naval spotlight that scanned the hostile bushlands at night to scare off those whose dominion predated their arrival and to show the magical power of the new wizards.

Rhodes's grave is located in the Matopos Hills, just outside Bulawayo, where in the 1880s the early colonial bounty hunters wrangled with Ndebele King Lobengula to win a mining concession that offered Rhodes the pseudo-legal right to create the land named for him— Rhodesia. The grave is a low, granite plinth capped by a heavy metal plate with the inscription "Here lie the remains of Cecil John Rhodes." I clambered up to it once, after Zimbabwe's independence, just as Rhodes himself had done long before to choose the site and supervise his own posterity. It was still there, unmolested, free of graffiti, despite its potent symbolism—facing north as he had planned it, along the route of empire its occupant sought but never achieved, from the Cape to Cairo.

His legacy shaped attitudes for decades and established economic ways that simply would not be undone. When, in 1980, the new black authorities decided to remove Rhodes's statue in central Harare—as

Salisbury had been renamed—a crane hoisted it from its base and laid it on the ground. A great mass of newly confident, newly enfranchised Zimbabweans set about the massive bronze with rocks and steel bars. I looked on, imagining the passions being unleashed at this act of erstwhile heresy that would once have brought great retribution—the vandalization of white history, the denial of its wellspring. But when the crowd had moved on, released from the furies, I took a closer look at the statue: the attack had barely left a scratch, just as the belief in his rectitude endured among whites for years. (The statue now stands, re-erected, in a quiet corner of the garden at Zimbabwe's National Archives.)

When the Pioneer Column moved northward in 1890, Rhodes was prime minister of the Cape Colony of present-day South Africa, with the wealth and power to win over Whitehall to his ambitions as much as he bamboozled the African chiefs who stood in his way. Most of all, to his spiritual heirs, he embodied the notion of the "can-do" Rhodesian: anyone could be "squared," everything could be fixed. It was part of the Victorian ethos that individual will knew no obstacles. It remained part of the ethic of white Rhodesia that no problem was insoluble: if there were sanctions, you slid by them; if the world denied you guns and technology, you made your own. You could make a plan for everything—guns or butter. It was no coincidence that the lyrics of one of the most popular Rhodesian songs of the bush war proclaimed: "We're all Rhodesians and we'll fight through thick and thin/To keep this land of ours a free land, stop the enemy coming in." The song was called "Rhodesians Never Die." Vainglorious though it was, it epitomized the notion that Rhodesians were special, a breed apart, the inheritors of Rhodes's omnipotence and of a legitimacy nurtured in colonial conquest. It was that view of themselves that enabled Rhodesia's whites to argue that they had built the land, not the blacks who worked under them, that they had molded it in their image, established it as a European outpost. What it had been before was of no consequence.

That was the heroic perception. The reality was not so colossal as Rhodes's visions. The land he established reached its zenith as a repository of British settlers only after World War II, when the white population numbered its highest—270,000. What inspired them to come was partly the weather, partly the easy life, and partly, too, the sense of a new start. No one, then, told them they would come to be seen as pariahs.

With the postwar white population swollen by demobilized British servicemen in the late 1940s—the belief among many whites was that the officers went to Kenya and the lower ranks to Rhodesia—Rhodes's heirs flourished in their second home. They ran the farms, the mines, the factories, the filling stations, the shops, carving out their lives in the sun, seizing by legislation the best land for their spreads, disenfranchising the majority to whom the land had belonged before their arrival.

They brought their baggage and sense of suburban style with them: fake Tudor cottages dappled Africa; matrons in white played lawn bowls on billiard-smooth lawns. At Troutbeck, way out in the east, a white could stroll through pine forests, cast a fly for trout, ride horses, and play golf—a squire's life molded on a barrack-room dream of escape. In postwar Britain, exhausted by the long struggle with Nazi Germany, you dealt with cold, unemployment, and ration cards. Here, the sun shone and the locals called you "boss." Taxes and laws and edicts relegated the majority to a secondary status as cheap laborers, cooks, and servants. At their zenith in Rhodesia, 270,000 whites dominated 7.2 million Africans, and took a delight in their ability to do so. When the winds of change began to blow in the 1950s and 1960s, they sent a chill vision scudding through this far-flung outpost. It would not, could not, happen here.

During the late 1950s, Rhodesia had formed a federation with Zambia and Malawi, then called Northern Rhodesia and Nyasaland, respectively. Britain, with greater influence in those territories, had granted them independence under black majority government in the early 1960s. But Rhodesia's whites, by contrast, had wielded significant powers of self-government since 1923, and would not be treated like their former federal partners. No colonial power would sell them out to black chaos.

On November 11, 1965, thus, Ian Smith, the unchallenged voice of the white minority, set the land inescapably on the path to war. Invoking values that smacked of America's Declaration of Independence, he announced that, unilaterally, Rhodesia had renounced the last vestiges of British rule and rejected Whitehall's writ. In doing so, he drew on and reinforced the notion of a special white Rhodesian identity that countered the oratory of African nationalism. "We have struck a blow for the preservation of justice, civilization and Christianity, and in the spirit of this belief we have this day assumed our sovereign independence," he declared on the radio as homes fell hushed and traffic drew to a halt across the land. "God bless you all."

Three years after Zimbabwean independence, in an ex-servicemen's meeting hall in Durban, South Africa, I snuck into a reunion of ex-Rhodesians, who had headed south with their goods and chattels rather than face the perceived rigors of Zimbabwe and the indignity of living under the black government that came in 1980. The conversation was depressing. "We had twenty-five years," one man said of himself and his wife, as if that brief tenure were some badge of office. Even the oldest Rhodesian stock could boast only three or four generations. By comparison with the Afrikaners, who traced their African past to 1652, the roots were shallow indeed. When they gave out the prizes for the raffle that night in Durban, the winner got a copper plaque depicting an AK-47 rifle, the very weapon that had brought the white minority down. At first I did not understand this odd choice of a first prize when, it seemed from the miseries and complaints of Rhodesians who had fled to Durban, life had cheated them and provided them with a poor consolation prize indeed in South Africa.

But then it dawned on me that the weapon was a symbol of the war itself, of the conflict that somehow glamorized mundane lives, casting these fugitives from postwar Britain in the front line of a noble fight, against communism, falling standards, black savagery. The war had transformed them from exploiters to freedom fighters, and it was easy to live with that self-image until the late 1970s when two things became clear: the war was not glamorous at all, and they would not win it without help from an outside world that had turned its back on them. The replica AK-47 represented the distorted memory of a heroic struggle in a good cause. But in reality it was the AK-47 that signaled the end of their time and relegated them to the drafty meeting hall in

Durban with its faded portraits of Queen Elizabeth II—the monarch whose sovereignty they had rejected in 1965.

When the peace conference got under way at Lancaster House in 1979, the war had debilitated the guerrillas' black African sponsors, and the white minority was gradually hemorrhaging from the twin wounds of white emigration and the economic sanctions imposed as a punishment for unilateral independence in 1965.

The British, seizing one of those moments when history's strands suddenly coalesce, convened the conference, and pledged to reassert their lawful authority for a brief period in Rhodesia so as to end it in the creation of Zimbabwe. The mechanisms of change were the time-honored, post-colonial devices—a new constitution guaranteeing democracy, elections, a new nation. For British diplomats, it was an uncharacteristically bold and audacious move. Rhodesia's whites never could understand why the British would not subscribe to their world view that equated whiteness with rightness. Neither did they really grasp that Whitehall simply wanted to be rid of a vexatious problem that consumed time and energy with no prospect of reward. But the puzzle was how this notion of a white identity, a separate specialness, had been formed. In one way it was defined by default, by its own converse: black rule did not work.

In their quiet, private moments, even the most avowedly liberal of Africa's whites will say shocking things about what they consider to be black inadequacies. And, in Rhodesia, they said them publicly to win elections among the white minority: whiteness implied an inherent superiority. If black people took power, then "standards" would fall, inefficiency would creep in, things wouldn't work any more, and the sunlit idyll would become difficult and unhappy for all. Look at the Congo, they'd say. Look at Tanzania, or Zambia, or just about anywhere to their north. Black rule meant chaos, nepotism, corruption, collapse. That was empirically true, if places like Zaire and Uganda were any yardstick. but it did not justify the corollary that Rhodesia's whites attached to it: that the white minority—the biggest on the continent north of the Limpopo—should continue to exercise real controls and be rewarded with a privileged life in return. Blacks, the argument ran, were "not ready" for democracy or self-determination, and so should be guided by the benevolent white minority. Rhodesia's blacks, Ian Smith once remarked, were the happiest in Africa, which did not at all explain why so many them were ready to take arms against those who dispensed this happiness.

The two separate guerrilla armies of Robert Mugabe and Joshua Nkomo offered the counterargument, buttressed by the whole ethic of the post–World War II Western world: the majority of the people should exercise full control of the instruments of power, so the whites should come to terms with that and either go away or support the new, majority-ruled Zimbabwe that was to come. If the British had fought the Nazis to secure the spirit of freedom, how could they deny it to their colonies? Was European freedom somehow a different commodity than African freedom? The whites would simply have to take their chances in this new world like everyone else. In the end, that was precisely what many of them did.

A cease-fire—the precursor to peace, elections, and independence—finally took hold in Rhodesia on December 21, 1979. Although a war had ended, white despair was at its deepest, because peace, for them, was surrender. (The sense of betrayal and incredulity among the white minority taught me another lesson about them: their sense of their own exclusivity was not easily breached.)

I had traveled to the country club of Centenary, a white redoubt in the northeast of the country, where the guerrilla presence was said to be more threatening than anywhere else, and where the slightest hint of doubt about white motives translated as treason. I tried to strike up a conversation in the bar, but my drunken interlocutor, having established that I was a reporter and therefore not "on sides" with the war effort, ordered me off the premises and told me to go fend for myself, out there, with my "comrades." This man was a Special Branch plainclothes policeman wearing a bush jacket and shorts; he supported his edict with a 9mm pistol. His hope, he said, was that I would be shot by the guerrillas, because that would provide a delicious irony: white liberal shot by black gook. I had seen this attitude elsewhere in southern Africa's racial conflicts. Whites at the sharp end of the conflict loathe the whites who sympathize with their foes far more than they hate the adversary itself. A black guerrilla is the enemy. A white sympathizer is a traitor.

In Namibia, just before independence in 1989, extreme right-wingers assassinated Anton Lubowski, a white lawyer who had openly supported the SWAPO insurgent movement. But Sam Nujoma, SWAPO's leader, was left untouched. In Port Elizabeth, on South Africa's Indian Ocean coastline, the person who incensed the police far more than black activists was Molly Blackburn, a middle-class white woman who had joined forces with black protesters and invited them to her solid and spacious house in what was supposed to be a white area. Afrikaners had a word for people like Molly—*kafferboetie*, which translates literally as "black brother" and, in spirit, as far worse. There are many severe profanities in the Afrikaans language, but *kafferboetie* ranks among the worst.

That night at the Centenary Club was like many others I spent in Rhodesia, trying to explain my credentials to incredulous settlers who had no patience or sympathy for what I had to say. To them, I was no more than a convenient target for all the rage and frustration associated with an unjust defeat resulting far more from betrayal by kith and kin than from the effectiveness of the guerrillas.

Once outside the clubhouse, I discovered, too, why many whites were incredulous at the notion of defeat by such a ragtag adversary as the guerrillas opposing them. I was rescued from a night in the wilderness by two white soldiers who told me I could sleep at their place inside the settlement's security fences once they'd completed a last little item of business. Sandwiched between the two of them on the front bench of an open Land Rover under a starry sky, we set off, headlights blazing, moving briskly across the cricket pitch and then into the bush. The soldiers loaded rounds into the chambers of their FN-rifles, knocked off the safeties, and thrust a cocked and heavy .357 Magnum at me for safekeeping. One of them was a German from Namibia who found this war more interesting than the one back home. I asked why he kept the headlights on as we turned through the bush, close to the very homestead where a guerrilla rocket attack in 1972 had started off the whole thing. He explained it to me, with a Germanic edge to his Rhodesian argot, like this: "We keep the lights on so the gooks can see us. Then they open fire on us. Then we see where they're firing from. Then we shoot back and slot them." It never seemed to occur to him that a gook might be skilled enough with a rifle to slot him first. That was one reason why defeat hurt so much. And if the logic of white perceptions was extended, it meant white Rhodesia had been defeated by an adversary barely worth the fighting.

I can recall a score of conversations in country clubs and homes that began with the words: "Listen, Alan, I understand these people. I grew up with them." What followed was invariably an explanation of why black people could not be trusted with power, responsibility, or even an electric kettle.

Central Africa's robust elder statesman, Roy Welensky, had set the tone of this form of rationale when he said that, as a child, he had swum "bare-assed in the Macabuzi River with the picanins," as if this implied some closer knowledge denied those of us who came from afar, from the naive land of the Great White Queen, where we swam in overchlorinated public baths. Yet, patently, you could argue that whites did not understand "these people" precisely because they defined them as "these people," assigning to blacks a collective identity easier to define or strip of humanity. Whites would not say that because they had swum in their own, chemical-blue pool in their own backyard with a white neighbor, they understood their own race all the better. The notion of black ineptitude served white privilege: without the superior, guiding hand, there would be chaos. If there was one refrain that exemplified this attitude, it went something like this: "Now, Simon, here's the new lawn mower, and don't break it." The imprecation might apply to anything from a combine harvester to a pair of scissors: whatever it was, don't break it. I often wondered whether the late Lord Soames, when he handed Zimbabwe over to Robert Mugabe with its shining new constitution and its farms and riches, thought privately to himself: "Here it is, Robert. Now don't break it."

White Rhodesia suffered from that peculiar disease of perception I came to think of as "enclavitis"—a world view as deeply held by Lebanon's Maronite Christians as it is by South Africa's Afrikaners. It starts from the notion of a threat, a terminal, all embracing threat, menacing a beleaguered outpost. It defines a sense of shared identity and it produces its own morality: we are threatened, our very survival is threatened, so our response to the threat is justified, however brutal it might seem to those outsiders who are not privy to our special

knowledge, who have not been initiated by daily, constant exposure
to threat. Once the world is defined in the apocalyptic terms of survival
and extinction, then the response is justified. But it goes further: the
threat is not of our making, and others outside the world of our Masonic
symbols, our initiation rites, must understand this. We have a right
to demand the sympathy and protection of those outsiders, even though
they do not understand us, because we are encircled and deserving of
help, and, whether they know it or not, we are fighting their war for
them; we are the distant garrisons of their civilization.

Most people, at some stage, need to belong, to feel they are among
others who share their values and will not threaten or destroy the
familiar icons of their day-to-day existence. For many, the reference
points may be no more than an apartment or home or street, a neighborhood where you grew up with the kids along the block. But, for
some, transposed from dimly perceived ancestral roots and living on
the pioneering edge in alien lands, that is not enough. Enclavitis
demands that the identity must be vaunted, guarded, embellished, and
above all nurtured as a frail thing facing ever present danger. The
enclave, too, demands its protectors, its godfather, the sense that,
lonesome though we may be, someone back there cares.

All that helped explain the embitterment of white Rhodesia: kith
and kin, the folks back home, had betrayed them, had brokered their
defeat at Lancaster House. And it was not their fault. They had built
this land, made it what it was. Without them, there would be no
district commissioners, no rule of law, no schools or clinics, dams
or bridges or railroads. One-man, one-vote could wait. Rhodesia's
Africans were the happiest on the continent, Ian Smith had said.
They had good food, good jobs. And when they were ready for democracy—in twenty-five, or a hundred, or a thousand years—well,
they'd get it.

Look, the whites would say, pointing to the neat city streets lined
with jacaranda, the supermarkets filled with locally produced food in
good supply, the great spread of their estates laden with corn and wheat
and tobacco. Look, we have built something good here. But they
avoided the glimpse over the horizon into the black reserves, the
shanties, the souls of people whose color denied them access to the
riches the whites cited as the emblems of Rhodesia's success. They

did not acknowledge that this great gulf of wealth made their downfall inevitable, because they saw the requirements of blacks and whites as being intrinsically different: a black needed a hut, a white a house with pool and court. Only by taking a disproportionate slice of the wealth could the house be roofed and the pool chlorinated. That was what was meant by "standards."

4.

Bush Rules:

The Spoils of Victory—

Zimbabwe

"You cannot have two bulls in one kraal."

MATABELE PROVERB

The Lancaster House conference struck a deal. There would be a cease-fire and elections. The guerrillas from Nkomo's and Mugabe's armies would return from their bush hideouts and congregate at so-called "Assembly Points"—distant encampments where they could do no harm. The Rhodesians would go to their barracks. British policemen in their distinctive hats would oversee the voting to ensure fairness. And a force of Commonwealth soldiers, drawn mainly from Britain, would monitor the disengagement. For the period of transition to independence, Lord Soames would formally reassert British authority and the Union Jack would flutter again over Salisbury. Then Prince Charles would hand over power to whomever had won the election, and, its job as umpire and arbiter done, Britain's flag would come down again. It took a willing suspension of disbelief to accept that it would all work, but, miraculously, it did, defying the passions and hatreds and unleashed emotion that threatened from the beginning. And it ended, sometimes, in innocuous ways, more with a whimper than a bang.

I had been waiting for several days when the guerrilla commander sauntered into the clearing in the bush known as Assembly Point Lima. He did not so much appear as seem to materialize from nowhere.

He was twenty-three years old, he said, a one-time accused car thief from Bulawayo who had fled the land for training in East Germany and Angola, and then joined the forces fighting white rule. Now he held the notional rank of colonel so as to claim parity with the foreign commanders he would encounter. The other comrades were out there—he gestured—in the bush, six hundred of them or so.

His camouflage fatigues were too new, his AK-47 assault rifle too pristine for a man fresh from or really familiar with recent combat, suggesting that he was a showcase guerrilla, selected for his ability to make contact with the foreigners. He was too neat and clean for this war. (A second man, more ragged, meaner and leaner, had accompanied him, then slipped back into the bush.) But the colonel's appearance held electrifying significance, for it meant that, in one corner of the country at least, the war was over.

Across the country, 22,000 nationalist guerrillas were at large, armed and nervous. The terms of the cease-fire engineered by the British required them to report quietly and in an orderly manner to the Assembly Points, where, under the supposedly benevolent gaze of British and other Commonwealth monitoring forces, they would await the final peace and the political prizes of their struggle—independence, majority rule. But many of them could scarcely believe that victory would not turn into a cruel and terminal trap, luring them from their sanctuaries only to face extinction from their adversaries, the white Rhodesians and their co-opted black allies.

Meanwhile, the newly arrived peacekeeping forces were asking a similar question: Would the guerillas turn the peace into a trap for them? The 2,000-some monitors had deployed early, before anyone could be sure that the bush fighters would heed the orders of their leaders, Robert Mugabe and Joshua Nkomo; they were hopelessly outnumbered, adrift in alien, unfamiliar, and inhospitable terrain, isolated on the home turf of potential adversaries.

Assembly Point Lima, where I and two other journalists had been accredited as pool reporters, was an open space, a flat clearing deep in the bush of Matabeleland near a place called Madhlambudzi, seventy miles northwest of Bulawayo. Looking out from its openness into the bush, all you could see was the impenetrable tangle of mopani scrub. Looking in, all you could see was easy targets with no cover. Six hundred guerrillas, the intelligence reports said, were out there somewhere, surrounding a platoon of soldiers and three journalists. If there was a miracle to Madhlambudzi and places like it, it was that all six hundred of them would, in a space of days, trickle in from the bush, believing the promises of a cease-fire that meant victory.

Yet the cease-fire was only the beginning of a perilous process laden with challenge. The guerrilla commanders and their political leaders returned from exile to black jubilation and white menace. Robert Mugabe himself narrowly escaped death when a huge bomb went off in a culvert as his motorcade drove by. Rumors of a white coup abounded, fueled by the sudden apparition of soldiers from the elitist Rhodesian Light Infantry at strategic locations on election day. The guerrillas were uneasy in their Assembly Points, fidgety with their weapons, occasionally spilling out so that once, on a quick visit to Assembly Point X-Ray, near Mrewa in the east, I suddenly found myself driving between armed Libyan-trained guerrillas, crouched in the roadside drainage ditches, their AK-47s panning my hired car.

Worst of all, the potential for bitterness and vengeance was almost limitless.

Both Robert Mugabe and Joshua Nkomo had spent over a decade in Rhodesian prisons, detained without trial as agitators and terrorists. Some Rhodesian units—notably the Selous Scouts—had achieved a reputation for violence and ferocity that drew charges of torture and cruelty with awesome and credible frequency. As a counterinsurgency force, they built on British tactics honed in Malaya and Kenya, and their commander himself, Ron Reid-Daly, had served as a British Special Air Services operative in the Malayan jungles.

Conventional warfare was not for the Selous Scouts; neither was the notion of winning hearts and minds. Clad informally in shorts and bush boots, using the weapons of their choice—usually their adversaries' AK-47 assault rifles—they roamed the bush, white men with blackened faces and black men under their command, tracking guerrillas to their camps, intercepting, ambushing, killing, penetrating far beyond Rhodesia's borders. Some of the photographs of the era show them in a bush encampment in Zambia, grinning at a camera, wolfing down tinned food next to the body of a slain guerrilla. Whatever atrocity was committed in the bushlands, the nationalist commanders would blame the Selous Scouts. Their reputation was superhuman and sub-human at once. Everyone feared them, even some whites.

If black perceptions of Rhodesian ruthlessness were molded by the

Selous Scouts, however, white perceptions of the guerrillas found their own counterpoint: white nuns had been raped and children slaughtered at Elim mission station in the east of the country. Two Viscount airliners carrying civilians had been shot down and Joshua Nkomo had taken responsibility, his nervous hesitation and throat clearing as he did so in a radio interview seeming to the whites to be the most bloodthirsty of chuckles. In the months that surrounded the British-supervised elections and independence, passions ran deep and ugly. Dirty tricks were a specialty of the war, and would not disappear overnight.

Early one morning we drove east to Rusape to find a bus that had been ambushed during the night with rocket and heavy machine-gun fire. The bus had been blown over onto its side by the impact of an RPG-7 anti-tank rocket that had sliced the driver in two. Then its black occupants had been raked with bullets. A little girl lay amid the carnage, her face the very image of serenity, a small dark hole in her back showing why she no longer moved. The authorities tried to blame the massacre of these sixteen people on rogue guerrillas from Robert Mugabe's army. But the story did not fit with the evidence, and the man from the white-run Information Ministry seemed to deliberately belie his own credibility by wearing a baseball hat that showed a skull with a bullethole between the eyes. The motto read: "Cheers, gook." The man's name was Miller. His nickname was "Killer Miller." No one suggested that he was personally or directly involved in the ambush, but no one believed his version of events, either.

In the passions of the time, the event was not so unexpected because there was craziness in the air. In the townships around Salisbury where the black majority lived, jubilation ran high; the moment of peace was nigh. In the smarter parts of town, whites partied with a frenzy that said this is our last chance before Armageddon. At some point in the high drama of it all, a white soldier blew his brains out, playing Russian roulette in the bar of a city center hotel. That did not raise many eyebrows either. As the elections approached in February 1980, white anxiety grew febrile. The years of wartime propaganda had taught whites that the enemy, Robert Mugabe in particular, was the devil incarnate, the embodiment of Godless communism and black chaos. Now he had flown back into the country and Satan was loose among those who cherished their standards and civilization. Worst of all, he was on the way to winning. It was not surprising that someone tried to blow him to smithereens with a culvert bomb.

What happened next, however, became a benchmark of relations between black and white—and a grim augury of relations between black and black—that offered an ambiguous message of hope and despair for the rest of southern Africa.

When the election results were announced, Mugabe's Zimbabwe African National Union, rooted in the Shona tribes, had taken fifty-seven of the eighty parliamentary seats contested by the black majority (the other twenty were reserved for whites under the Lancaster House agreement). Bishop Abel Muzorewa, promoted by white Rhodesians and South Africa as the acceptable face of majority rule, won three seats, and Joshua Nkomo, the burly patriarch of nationalist struggle, won twenty, reflecting the demographic breakdown between his minority Ndebele tribe and the majority Shona tribe. It was a clear sweep for Mugabe. For the whites, Beelzebub was loose upon the land.

But then something remarkable occurred. Mugabe went on national television and addressed his one-time adversaries, telling them everything would be fine, that he would seek national reconciliation, that he would heal the wounds of war. His reasons were essentially pragmatic, urged on him by the late President Samora Machel of Mozambique, who had suffered from the precipitate flight of Portuguese expertise. It was President Machel, too, through his artful young adviser Fernando Honwana, who had kept up the pressure on the guerrillas to negotiate a settlement at the Lancaster House conference. Even though it fell short of the revolutionary victory Mugabe and his advisers saw as their ultimate goal, the Mozambicans insisted that their own country, battered by Rhodesian attacks and a doomed economy, could no longer sustain the struggle—a point the Zambians made to Nkomo, too.

For most whites, Mr. Mugabe's first television address was a revelation. And, suddenly, through the suspicion and hatred, some began to believe him. The can-do Rhodesian reemerged: if sanctions and war could be survived and turned to advantage, then, hell man, so could black rule.

But in Zimbabwe, the end of the fight against minority rule was not the end of the struggle. The nation had established the broad outlines of its new identity as a majority-ruled African nation, yet the way state power would be exercised was still unresolved.

The fighting that pitted Shona and Ndebele guerrillas against one another in November 1980, and February 1981, long after the white adversary had withdrawn, was the final phase in the inevitable struggle for identity and power that had started with Rhodesia's creation. Unlike many African countries, Zimbabwe's geographic frontiers make some sense—the Zambezi to the north, the Limpopo to the south, the deserts of Botswana to the west, and the mountains of Mozambique to the east. But those were accidental frontiers that happened to coincide with the way the continent was divided in the late nineteenth century, and, like all of Africa's boundaries, their delineation ignored tribe and history.

The white man's frontiers sliced across tribal boundaries so that, for instance, eastern Zambians and western Malawians speak the same language and have the same history, but carry different passports and bear loyalty to different regimes. The Ndau of eastern Zimbabwe trace the same roots as the Ndau of Mozambique, but different capitals demand their loyalty. In Kenya, the street vendors used to sell maps of Africa made into jigsaws. It always struck me how easily the pieces came together, because there were no awkward wrinkles: Africa had been divided by European notions of geometric neatness where no such neatness existed on the ground. Indeed, just about everywhere that European interests have settled foreign frontiers, it is easy to imagine distant cartographers drawing straight lines on blank maps and saying: "Well, this ought to do it."

Rhodesia brought together two hostile groups of people, whose sense of separate identity was deeply rooted in the way they saw their own histories and in their distinct and mutually incomprehensible languages. When Robert Mugabe addressed his countrymen in the west after independence, he needed a translator—a bellicose firebrand called Enos Nkala, who embroidered the new prime minister's words beyond recognition. If Mugabe could not even make himself understood in their own language to a fifth of his people, how would his message of reconciliation to the whites ever be extended to the Ndebele?

Mugabe had once been Nkomo's press spokesman, but had broken away from the Ndebele leader in the early 1960s to form a rival party with a far stronger tribal appeal. During the war with the white minority regime, Mugabe's Shona guerrillas had borne the brunt of the fighting, suspecting that Nkomo was holding back his far better equipped forces for a lightning push to take power once white resolve faltered. Nkomo, known as the wily *Mdala*—the old man—secured financial support from Britain's Tiny Rowlands, a mining and commercial tycoon in the tradition of Rhodes, and military support from Moscow. Mugabe looked to China for the limited weapons he got, so the Sino-Soviet rift drove its wedge into Africa. Nkomo was regarded by Moscow as one of the "authentic six" liberation leaders; the rest, as far as the Soviets were concerned, were relegated to the scrapheap. It was one of the Kremlin's biggest miscalculations in southern Africa, and it deepened the personal, ideological, and tribal differences between Mugabe and Nkomo. While they had formed a loose alliance called the Patriotic Front during the war with Ian Smith, they had not brought their two armies together, and their political relationship was uneasy.

The withdrawal of the outsider exposed rivalries that would not easily be settled. As cynics liked to say, there were no second prizes in the region's politics. The sense of winner taking all enhanced the expedient notion of one-party rule, and that, in turn, as I had seen in Zaire and elsewhere, became the cloak for nepotism and corruption.

Within the relatively new countries, three forces conflicted: the nation, the state, and political power to rule the state. The white state of Rhodesia did not coincide with the nation's identity, so the state faced two options—to be changed, or to impose itself on the nation by force. The war changed the nature of the state, bringing it closer in line with the nation, but it unleashed new forces because the nation itself was divided. So Robert Mugabe faced a new problem. To imprint the political authority of the state, part of the nation had to be brought into line. Brute force overcame initial resistance so that Nkomo's party was obliged to merge with Mugabe's party on unfavorable terms. Effectively, the result was one-party rule, cementing Mugabe's authority.

Robert Mugabe, Marxist ideologue and political pragmatist, had the consensus of the Shona, but not of a troublesome, sizable Ndebele minority. Zimbabwe's early years were bloodstained because the lines of the triangle of state, nation, and political authority simply did not join up and could only be made to do so by force.

Just outside of Bulawayo, in the township of Entumbane, rival guerrillas had been housed close to one another. Under the terms of the cease-fire, they were supposed to be merged with their old adversaries into a new national army. But it was only a matter of time before the profound tribal animosities erupted between the Shonas, who regarded themselves as the rightful heirs to Zimbabwe, and the Ndebele, who had usurped that right and enslaved them in the nineteenth century. Bloody fighting began in November 1980. Hundreds died. Whites, looking on with a sense of self-satisfied vindication, arranged for the bodies to be store in refrigerated railcars usually used for transporting meat, so that the families could come and identify them. The bodies piled up and began to decompose. The families lined the railway sidings, awaiting a turn to inspect the noisome cargo for relatives. A sudden wail of grief from within one of the cars denoted the discovery of a son. The whites, in general, were left on the sidelines of all this, except for those who still commanded units of the new army. What mattered now was to set the parameters for Zimbabwe's future, and that was a question solely for the victors.

The conflict produced odd visions. At one point, I accompanied a platoon of black soldiers under the command of a former American mercenary who had stayed on at independence to join the new national army. These soldiers had fought the war on the side of Ian Smith as the Rhodesian African Rifles. Now, under the terms of the cease-fire, they were redesignated as a battalion of the new Zimbabwe Army, into which they were supposed to be integrated. So Mugabe ordered them, his former foes, into action against Nkomo's guerrillas, his former allies, to clean up the mess at Entumbane, where his own guerrillas were losing. One of the black soldiers, who told me his name was Lieutenant Max, beckoned to me to come join him as he crouched behind an armored vehicle, aiming his rifle at a tree in an open field. Behind the tree was a guerrilla from Nkomo's army. "I hate these fucking gooks," Max said, and loosed off fire that chipped bark from the tree. The response came in a blast of unnervingly accurate AK-

47 fire that pinged off the steel plating of our cover: black guerrillas were fighting an adversary that included black soldiers "on sides" with the authorities. All that had changed, it seemed, was the nature of the authority.

Under the rules of the cease-fire, both guerrilla armies were to fuse with their erstwhile adversaries in the new army—a feat that was eventually achieved. But revolts by Nkomo's ZIPRA men re-erupted the following February, again centered on Entumbane. This time the whites were ready: they had already gotten the railcars prepared for repeat action and, on one, had painted the word "DEAD." Hundreds more corpses duly filled the cars, and relatives fumbled through them, looking for their own. What was at stake, and what underlay Mugabe's response, was that same fundamental notion about bulls in the kraal. He had taken power in an election that had been fair and free. Now he had to run the country at all its levels—as a nationalist ideologue, as the nation-state manager, and as the center of absolute power. All three came together in the notion of a one-party state, with himself as president (an ambition initially thwarted by the Lancaster House agreement). Africa, the rationale went, could not afford the luxury of a multi-party democracy when adversaries took that either as a sign of weakness or as an opportunity to express opposition through the gun barrel. And, to develop the land, a strong center would act as the vanguard of progress. But underlying the rationale was a profound sense of insecurity. The winner had to be acknowledged.

Demography had guaranteed Mugabe's electoral success. But Nkomo's followers did not easily abandon their belief that he was the rightful heir, the veteran of the struggle now denied its fruits. And their reluctance to abandon the quest for supremacy led to yet more killing in Zimbabwe's first years of freedom. The fighting at Entumbane reflected the harshness of the rivalry but did not resolve the issue. If anything, it showed only that the recourse to violence had become reflexive, as it would later in South Africa in similar circumstances.

In 1982, the authorities unearthed weapons on a farm owned by Nkomo, substantial caches that his supporters said were for defensive purposes. The discovery triggered a crackdown on Nkomo's followers and that, in turn, convinced some of them to again take up arms. And so yet another small and nasty war gathered momentum in the cattle-raising reaches of western Zimbabwe—Matabeleland—the home base of Nkomo's supporters.

Many of his guerrillas melted into the bush, and for years into Zimbabwe's freedom they roamed Matabeleland, harassing anybody related to the government, even slaughtering British and American tourists. Their presence offered a direct and intolerable challenge to Mugabe's ability to run the state, to extend his writ throughout the land. To resolve not only the rebellion but the future of the state he wished to mold, Mugabe finally sent in the brutal forces of the North Korean–trained 5th Brigade, whose effort to crush the dissidents produced yet another new crop of stories that began: "The soldiers came to the village. . . ."

The campaign brought the same impossible choices, too.

The villagers of Matabeleland belonged to the same tribe as the rogue guerrillas, but they were ruled by their tribal adversaries, the Shona. Any suggestion of support for the guerrillas met with harsh reprisals, torture, and killings from the government's 5th Brigade. And any support for the government invited equally vicious treatment from the guerrillas. Bodies were found in shallow graves. "It was better," an old man in a village near Bulawayo told me, "when Ian Smith was in power." Race, ideology, and the whole notion of freedom had become irrelevant; all that had happened was that one wizard had replaced another. The Ndebele, this time on the receiving end, had another saying for the battle that raged for ultimate power: "When elephants fight, it is the grass that is trampled."

The elephant fights, in Zimbabwe and elsewhere, were to play a crucial role in the next unfolding of southern Africa's tortured history, because the accumulation of power at the center naturally excluded those denied access to it. And that, in turn, provided a pool of disaffection that South Africa was to adopt as part of its arsenal against black rule on its borders. What made the campaigns all the more urgent was that the juggernaut of majority rule was rolling south, and the Afrikaners stood square across its path.

5.

The Road to Nkomati:

The Empire Strikes Back—

Mozambique

"I take full responsibility for the actions of our security forces. I congratulate them."

STATE PRESIDENT P. W. BOTHA the day after South African forces struck at three African capitals simultaneously in May 1986

"Never underestimate the Boer."

AFRIKANER JOURNALIST DEON DU PLESSIS to the author, December 1985

It was the face of the girl that struck me, much more than the litany of suffering I was supposed to be listening to.

She wore a green and faded shift, crisp from frequent washing. Her hair was plaited in small, tight squares, in the style of many parts of Africa, and her eyes were clear and big as a doe's. She exuded peace.

Beside her, in the living room of what had once been a Portuguese civil servant's villa in Mozambique, a party commissar was reciting the statistics of all the losses that war and calamity had caused, how much food they needed, how much they would get, how bad things were in general. Everything had been tabulated in ballpoint in a large notebook he carried like a chain of office, the emblem of order in chaos and of the party's supposed grip on a situation that was beyond all control. But the girl's face seemed to glow with some secret, inner serenity, as if she knew the recitation was futile, and had come to terms with a life that foresaw improvement or deterioration with equal acceptance. Her tranquility was total. Given her dependence on forces she could not control, that was probably the best response.

When I met her, in late 1985, at Chicualacuala on the border between Mozambique and Zimbabwe, near their convergence with South Africa, she, like everyone else there, was waiting for a train to arrive in town. But it was no ordinary train. It carried no freight, no food, no passengers. It did not run from station to station and appeared in no timetable of arrivals and departures. And until it arrived each day, there was nothing to do but wait.

All the train carried was water, drawn from a borehole fifteen miles away in a game reserve in Zimbabwe on the safer side of the frontier. The town's own water pump had been blown up by Rhodesian insurgents during the Zimbabwean war many years before, when Rhodesian forces struck regularly into Mozambique to weaken the already frail rear bases of Robert Mugabe's guerrilla army. Now the pump lay in disrepair, twenty miles away on a riverbank. There was no point fixing it, the commissar said, because the newer insurgents from the Mozambique National Resistance—sponsored by South Africans to undermine Mozambique's avowedly Marxist government—would only come and blow it up again. And there would certainly be no spare parts to fix it, no one to tackle the job, even. So why bother?

Each afternoon, thus, at around 4:00 p.m., people waited for the train to chug in through the blue-gums along the bush frontier and pump its precious supply into Chicualacuala's cistern. Then, for a couple of hours, the people would wash, drink, hoard. After that the supply would run out again until the train came the next day. And if the rebels attacked the train, or if it broke down somewhere along the line, then there would be no water until it came. The crazy schedule helped me understand the girl's serenity: out there, miles from help, light-years from the city, there was nothing to be done, no control over destiny. The commissar's statistics represented the vanity of the helpless, the pretense that something could be done according to some Cartesian principle where there was none. But the girl had come to terms with the war the commissar and his comrades refused to admit they were losing.

Chicualacuala was one halt on a day's journeying with relief workers, distributing food by airplane to places that had suffered not only from the conflict conducted by the Mozambique National Resistance but also from four years of drought. The plane was a Twin Otter, flown by Canadians, loaded with sacks of cornmeal that were dumped off on isolated strips before flying back to Maputo, Mozambique's capital.

In Chicualacuala, our arrival forced young men to abandon a soccer game on the dirt strip, and brought out hundreds to greet the saviours from the sky. We unloaded the sacks of corn and walked to the small town, where 12,000 people had sought refuge from the insurgency.

Outlying villages were completely unsafe because the tracks leading to them were vulnerable to ambush by the South African-armed insurgents. So people left for town, abandoning the villages to the rebels, whose control thus spread, making it yet more difficult to distribute the West's food donations to those who really needed them.

That was not the only problem. Only one third of Mozambique's available fleet of 8,000 trucks was operational, even by the most optimistic assessment. Foreign relief workers had, in some parts of the country, withdrawn from remote areas to the relative safety of provincial capitals. Or they had left Mozambique altogether.

So the food arrived in the small towns that boasted airstrips, and went very little farther. Even the word "town" was almost a misnomer, for it held connotations of order and services that barely existed. At some time in the colonial era, the Portuguese had come and implanted the visible symbols of municipality—villas, offices, roads. But then, with the Portuguese departure at independence in 1975 and the endless conflicts and confusions, the settlements had eroded. Some of them were no more than points on old maps, gathering places for the relief effort and the army and the fugitives, but, as real towns, no more than Potemkin facades, notions, memories.

Earlier, in Chokwe in the same region, relief workers had told us that food donated from the United States and elsewhere was being distributed to townspeople who did not really need it because they could get it no closer to those who did. And even there, the presence of relief workers, distributing corn under the limp pennant of the Red Cross, had drawn the rebels to attack the people clinging with their goats and bicycles to the pretense of safety.

In one needy settlement, the relief experts said, somewhere between 16,000 and 20,000 people were so desperate that they had cleared the bush by hand and, literally with their bare feet, stomped out a strip for the plane to bring them food. But by some tangle of bureaucracy and worry about security, the authorities would not certify the crude strip fit for landing. So, out there, somewhere, sitting beside the home-made airfield at Dindiza, the people still went hungry, awaiting the apparition from the sky that never came.

It was impossible to know if the authorities were simply being in-sensitive or oversensitive to the insurgent threat. But there was no doubt that the guerrillas had the upper hand. We landed at a place called Massangir and unloaded the allotted sacks of corn to the care of soldiers at the thatched hut next to the strip. The local commander exchanged words tersely with the pilot, who said the brief conversation had been to the effect that the relief workers should not return for a while because the insurgents had taken up position at the far end of the runway—something we had not known when we landed. The takeoff was the shortest, quickest, steepest I had ever known in a fixed-wing airplane. Barely had we started to roll than we were airborne. And barely were we airborne than the pilot put the Twin Otter into a dizzying bank. He had no way of knowing whether the Mozambican commander had been exaggerating the threat. But he was not prepared to take chances, accepting the potential for disaster easily and stoically.

The whole episode provided one more strand of craziness and un-certainty woven into a nasty war that had spread across the land, to within a few miles of the capital, marking its path with brutal muti-lations and killings by the guerrillas of their very own people.

The soldiers, once again, had come to the village, and the villagers, ragged, hungry, their children pot-bellied and terminally sick, barely knew the answer to the question: why? And even if they had known the answer, they could have done nothing about it, because a large part of it lay far from their borders, in Pretoria.

With Zimbabwe's independence, South Africa's white leaders con-fronted black-ruled and mostly hostile countries on all fronts, corridors for guerrillas from the African National Congress to filter into the sanctuaries of the segregated black townships, to plot sabotage and bombings.

This was the Total Onslaught, Pretoria liked to say, the cutting edge of Soviet encroachment in Africa. In the space of seven years, the safe buffer of Portuguese colonial rule had gone, replaced by a ring of hostility, by black nationalism that Afrikaners found easier to translate as a Communist conspiracy than as a yearning for freedom as natural as theirs had been when they confronted, and ultimately confounded, the British. Africa, moreover, helped provide the labels.

The African National Congress—the principal guerrilla organization—operated in alliance with the South African Communist Party, so slavishly loyal to Moscow that it supported the Soviet invasion of Afghanistan even as it fought for its own freedom. The Soviets, moreover, supplied the SWAPO insurgents in Namibia. In Angola and Mozambique, Soviet arms and advisers bolstered weak regimes that professed adherence to Marxism-Leninism and spoke of Moscow as a natural ally. Over the years, tens of thousands of Cuban troops rotated through Angola.

Even within South Africa, the prophecies of Red advance had become self-fulfilling: apartheid was so closely identified with capitalism in the minds of black radicals that the ideology had a visceral appeal. The Communist lands, after all, supplied guns and diplomatic support to the ANC, and they played no role in the great powerhouse of an economy that was seen as the source of apartheid's strength. The West, by contrast, signaled its presence in the advertisements and billboards that, until the onset of divestment and disinvestment in the mid-1980s, dotted the land and confirmed the unwritten alliance of Western capital and the apartheid state: Ford, General Motors, Mobil, IBM, Citibank, Chase Manhattan, companies that provided jobs for some and political symbols for others.

Total Onslaught demanded a Total Strategy in response. By depicting its adversaries as part of a global conspiracy, Pretoria sought to legitimize a projection of power well beyond South Africa's borders.

From afar, it may have seemed as if South Africa's military strikes into neighboring countries, and its support of surrogate armies, was no more than a sometimes panicky reaction to the southern advance of black rule. But in the minds of Afrikaner military and political strategists, the ambitions were much greater. Total Strategy did not see South Africa and its restive, black majority in isolation from the rest of the continent. Rather, it represented an all-embracing concept of political and military management that sought to deal with domestic problems within a safe cocoon created by the neutralization of threats from beyond the frontiers.

Total Strategy depended on strength and the will to use it in whatever way seemed appropriate, convenient, or effective. Economically, militarily, and through covert operations, South Africa's neighbors felt Pretoria's great weight pressing upon them.

Botswana, Lesotho, and Swaziland were closely tied to the South African economy by a customs union that provided essential revenues and thus enforced a measure of docility. Their currencies—supposed emblems of sovereignty—were backed by the South African rand, once the all-powerful coinage of the gold and diamond fields. If they stepped out of line, then retribution would come: a commando strike on Botswana, say, ostensibly against ANC safehouses; or, in Lesotho, an economic blockade that succeeded in toppling the leader, Chief Leabua Jonathan, and replacing him with a more malleable regime.

Zimbabwe, the newest potential adversary, the last piece in the jigsaw, was offered the same options.

When Rhodes and the others built the railroads, they had done so with South Africa at the center of a communications web extending to northern Zambia. Alternative routes—the Benguela across Angola, the lines that traversed Mozambique—fell early victims to southern Africa's turmoil and South African–inspired sabotage, forcing the landlocked black-ruled countries of Central Africa into reliance on South Africa for their access to the sea, to markets, to the sources of spare parts to keep the mines producing the minerals that sustained their failing economies. Even Zaire, far to the north of South Africa's Indian Ocean ports, depended on routes running south because its own internal lines of communication—a circuitous combination of old railways and creaking river barges—barely functioned. Zimbabwe was even more reliant on trade routes through South Africa and long-standing commercial links with apartheid's economy. So Robert Mugabe's new administration faced an economic stranglehold that placed his politics in a tourniquet.

Ideologically, he was a fierce opponent of apartheid, an advocate of punitive sanctions to press the white regime toward change. From his own fight against white minority rule in Rhodesia he knew that, however flawed sanctions were as a punishment, and however unequally they were applied, their long-term effect was to sap the adver-

saries' will, and force the contemplation of alternatives that would not
be considered from a position of total strength. But Mugabe made
clear from the start that his own government could not apply them.

Pretoria controlled his ability to build an economy essential to keeping the promises he had made during his own war: if no wealth was
produced, there was none to distribute; without earnings, the visions
of land reform and enhanced education could never be fulfilled. He
was not about to commit economic or political suicide. So Zimbabwe
had warned the ANC from the beginning—one of Mugabe's most
senior lieutenants once told me—that it could not deliver the same
kind of support its nationalist armies had won from Zambia and Mozambique during the seven years of the Rhodesian conflict.

The situation was different, the argument went. Zimbabweans had
fought a largely rural campaign from rear bases in neighboring countries, undermining the countryside that produced most of the nation's
wealth. South Africa's insurgents were fighting an urban war, from
the black townships located near Pretoria's motherlode of economic
power—the mines. The ANC's weapons thus had to be drawn from
a different arsenal: not just AK-47s and landmines—the symbols of
armed resistance—but the black labor movement, black numerical
strength, and their ability to paralyze the white-ruled state and its
economy. Therein, the Zimbabweans said, lay the true strength of
South Africa's revolution. Strategically, the argument meant that Pretoria was relatively safe from infiltration across the Limpopo River
border. But relative safety has never been enough for Afrikaner military
planners.

Shortly after independence, one third of Zimbabwe's air force was
sabotaged on the ground at a military base in the Midlands, and there
was strong evidence that South African agents, using die-hard white
Rhodesians as co-conspirators, were behind the attack.

Zimbabwe learned the narrow limits of Pretoria's tolerance in other
ways, too. By allowing the ANC to open what was called a "diplomatic
and political" office—effectively an embassy—in Harare, it invited a
South African commando attack in the center of its own capital. The
point, from Pretoria's view, was not simply to do it, but to show how
easily it could be done. Black-ruled neighbors had to learn the same
lesson as apartheid had sought to drum into South African blacks for

decades: that white power was awesome and could be deployed with impunity; that black resistance, therefore, was futile.

On the same day in 1986 that South African airborne troops hit Harare, other units struck simultaneously into Zambia and Botswana. Many in those countries said the white soldiers had attacked the wrong targets, that their intelligence had been wrong. But the real message was that they had done it, and returned home, without losing a single airplane or taking a single casualty, with the nonchalance of a training exercise.

It was a calculated impression meant to daunt black majorities everywhere and reinforce white sentiments of invincibility. South Africa's black-ruled neighbors had to know the perils of supporting the ANC and its guerrilla force *Umkhonto we Sizwe*—the Spear of the Nation. And they had to reach the logical conclusion: a quiet life, and freedom to develop, would not be achieved as long as the ANC maintained a presence on their soil. Total Strategy fused physical and psychological warfare. Pretoria's military considerations became so closely embroiled with political goals that the two, under P. W. Botha, were indistinguishable.

The South Africans had learned much in the ways of counterinsurgency from the experiences of the British, the Israelis, the Rhodesians. But, by some accounts, the most telling analysis originated, of all places, in Indochina and the experience of a French general, André Beaufre. His study, *An Introduction to Strategy* (1963), according to the South African political scientist Phillip Frankel at Johannesburg's University of the Witwatersrand, became a principal text of staff college training because its message most closely approximated South Africa's concept of the totality of war. It was no coincidence, either, that the principles enunciated by the French strategist should have achieved such prominence under P. W. Botha, who had been defense minister for many years before becoming prime minister in 1978, and executive state president in 1984. Botha was, by personality and persuasion, a military man's man.

His nickname was "Piet the Weapon." He kept model tanks on the desk of his den at the Tuynhuis, the residence allocated to South

African leaders in Cape Town—itself a former home of Cecil Rhodes. It was under Botha that military thinking became inseparable from the exercise of political power. He created a State Security Council of senior politicians and generals that had far greater influence than the cabinet. When Botha took over from Balthazar Johannes Vorster in 1978, the influence of the civilian intelligence service—the Bureau of State Security, known, appropriately enough, by its acronym, BOSS—gave way to Military Intelligence. State Security Management Committees were set up throughout the land, bringing the military into decision making and policy planning at all levels of white administration. The intention was to marshal white strength behind the overriding goal of securing Afrikaner survival against the same threats of black numerical strength that had haunted the Afrikaners throughout their tenure in Africa.

It was the sheer number of blacks far more than their skin color that haunted the Afrikaners. And Botha himself, by personality, style, and political education, became the embodiment of the iron fist that would open only when the adversary acknowledged its dominance.

War, according to Beaufre, is "a dialectic of wills, where a decision is achieved when a certain psychological effect has been produced on the enemy: when he becomes convinced that it is useless to start or alternatively to continue the struggle."

Therein lay the very essence of Afrikaner thinking, not because the French said so, but because its echo was so resonant—it had been a way of life from the very beginnings of Dutch settlement in the Cape. What Boer farmers and trekkers had achieved with the *sjambok* whip of rhino hide on recalcitrant black workers, and what the practice of apartheid had sought to stamp on black perceptions since 1948, were what the French general proposed on the wider canvas of modern conflict. Yet there were refinements, too, that Botha sought to embrace with his program of political changes in the late 1970s and mid-1980s.

"The concept of strategic action necessarily stems from political analysis," Beaufre says. "By thoroughgoing reforms we must cut the ground from under the feet of the malcontents."

Botha thought he understood that. The iron fist always held the promise of an alternative, inside and outside the country: accept our way of doing things, our promises of a changed relationship, domestically and internationally, and you will find peace. More than ever, what happened outside South Africa was entwined with what happened inside South Africa, and military strategy became a sustaining force of political action.

The paradox was that Botha never could bring himself to introduce "thoroughgoing reforms," so he never did manage to cut the ground from under the malcontents. But he never underestimated the urgency of what he and his followers saw as a battle for survival.

Throughout the decades of decolonization, South Africa had placed itself in a state of undeclared war with the rest of the continent. What unfolded north of the Limpopo was the antithesis of the Afrikaner vision. Yet the "time of the comrades" in Angola, Mozambique, Zimbabwe, and within South Africa itself had brought the war to its very frontiers. Worse still, these huge geopolitical changes coincided with the acknowledgment within Afrikanerdom's innermost conclaves that the apartheid orthodoxy implanted by D. F. Malan and Hendrik Verwoerd had become unworkable: it had sought to separate black from white, but the pressures of demography and a growing need for black skills in the white economy had blurred the lines. Above all, it had not brought peace, credibility, or respectability, and did not guarantee Afrikaner survival. Apartheid was never a monolith. As a label for white domination, it endured; but as a policy constantly twisting and turning around the central imperative of white survival through control, it failed at every turn. The Afrikaners acknowledged, as Beaufre had taught, that there had to be change of some kind. Yet change needed management, it needed an environment in which no external forces could upset the processes initiated and implemented by the Afrikaner minority. The need to neutralize the external threat thus became all the greater as Pretoria sought to establish a new accommodation—what Botha called a "new dispensation"—with the black majority at home.

Change demanded control of events throughout the region.

The rules of engagement were never even: the black-ruled governments made no secret of their commitment to ending apartheid violently by supporting the ANC guerrillas fighting for majority rule. But, militarily, they could never challenge Africa's best-equipped, best-trained, and certainly most self-confident armed forces, who were only too ready to demonstrate their superiority.

South Africa's adversaries had another word for Total Strategy—

"destabilization," a policy whereby no black-ruled government should sit easy with itself until it accepted Pretoria's dominance and fiat. The weapons Pretoria deployed were various, but they drew on a long tradition of nurturing ethnic and political dissent, of sponsoring and building surrogate armies, of turning Africa against itself.

The Mozambique National Resistance—known by its Portuguese acronym, RENAMO, or by its initials, the MNR—had been formed, initially, under the tutelage of white Rhodesian intelligence officers in 1976 and was drawn from an assemblage of Portuguese businessmen and disaffected black Mozambican soldiers who had fought alongside Lisbon in the effort to maintain imperial rule. Rhodesia's intelligence supremo, Ken Flower, conceived it as a force to go behind the lines in independent Mozambique, undermining the rear base of Robert Mugabe's guerrillas, harassing his supporters and supply lines.

Then, shortly before Zimbabwe's independence in 1980, South Africa's military planners grasped its potential and Britain looked the other way while South Africa transferred this hodgepodge army from central Rhodesia to the Transvaal. If there was a stain of shame on Zimbabwe's birth, it spread from Britain's failure to halt this transaction, which became the death warrant for tens of thousands of Mozambicans.

The MNR dovetailed perfectly into South Africa's strategy of using surrogate armies who owed their very existence to the exclusivity of power in their own capitals: these were the other bulls, seeking entry to the kraal. They were cheap to sponsor, unlikely to take power, and thus unlikely to draw Pretoria into any long-term financial commitment to propping up a new regime. Their function was defined by negatives: to ensure that Mozambique remained in a state of turmoil and collapse under its revolutionary government.

The idea behind South Africa's support for the MNR—as Mozambican officials often told me—was not to get rid of President Samora Machel, but to display him as weak and ineffective, to show South Africa's own black majority that the dreams of fire and revolution that suffused his oratory were false, that his ideas of Marxist advance were so much nonsense.

Elsewhere Pretoria's tactics were stamped by the same urge to choreograph a dance of division.

The surrogates spread far and wide, in perception as much as fact, reinforcing the notion of Pretoria's devious omnipotence. When dissidents supporting Joshua Nkomo roamed western Zimbabwe, the Zimbabweans said South Africa was supporting the insurgency, as if to legitimize their harsh response to it. Across southern Africa, Pretoria abrogated to itself the right to steer and manage the doings of its neighbors in pursuit of a long-standing goal: the creation of what Afrikaner leaders called a "constellation of states" with South Africa as its sun. "Destabilization" was one way of pursuing that goal by blackmail and coercion. But there were other methods, too.

In Namibia, Pretoria sponsored countless efforts to counter the political strength of the militarily limited SWAPO guerrilla movement by creating not only puppet regimes but also one of the most ruthless of counterinsurgency forces, known as *Koevoet*—the Afrikaans word for crowbar. Technically a black police unit under white command, it achieved much the same reputation as the Selous Scouts had done in Rhodesia, and through much the same methods.

Even impoverished and distant Zambia, feeling perversely slighted by the lack of South African attention, claimed to see Pretoria's hand in the activities of Adamson Bratson Mushala, a disgruntled game warden who had taken to the bush at independence from Britain in 1964 when President Kaunda declined to offer him a ministerial post. Now, he roamed the distant lands of northwestern Zambia, half Robin Hood, half incarnation of evil, allegedly possessed of magical abilities to melt bullets and to make himself disappear or metamorphose into an array of fauna. When the authorities finally tracked him down and shot him in 1983, the decomposing body had to be carted around the country and put on public display so that people would know that, finally, Mushala was dead.

Mushala was an odd sideshow, but for the nations South Africa saw as its principal adversaries, destabilization meant a daily battle in which there was no prospect of victory.

The Mozambique National Resistance caused untold misery and agony in its own country. Tales of mutilation, rape, and pillage were routine. The soldiers indeed came to the villages and left them with the women violated, the men dead or dragooned into the rebel army or horribly disfigured by the gouging of lips and ears. By the late 1980s, the fatalities numbered over 100,000. More than a million Mozambicans had become refugees, rootless, shifting, starving, fleeing to Malawi, South Africa, and Zimbabwe. Mozambique never had an even break from independence onwards.

For many years, Mozambique refused to talk to the MNR, calling them unprincipled bandits—which they were—but failing to acknowledge a tragic irony.

One reason President Machel's forces emerged victorious from the war with the Portuguese lay in the capability of an elusive guerrilla force to withstand conventional attempts to eradicate it. Now, Mozambique made the same strategic mistake as its colonial adversary. Relying on Soviet advice and assistance, the Mozambicans sought to convert their guerrilla army into a conventional force that found itself as impotent in the face of an insurgency as the Portuguese had been.

Mozambique's rationale was that the strategic threat lay in conventional attack by South Africa, so Mozambique needed the facilities to counter such aggression. But Pretoria, chastened by its experiences in Angola in 1976, had no intention of committing its own forces to a battle that could just as well be fought by a cat's-paw band of dissidents. Mozambique, thus, faced unique miseries. During the Zimbabwean war it had suffered greatly because it provided a rear base for Mugabe's bush fighters. Now it faced its own bush war without the resources to strike at the MNR's rear bases in South Africa. So it lost, both as a supporter of one bush army and the enemy of another. And it discovered another hard fact of life: it was of no avail to try to win the hearts and minds of its own people by high-principled promises of betterment through scientific socialism when those same people were peering down the wrong end of an MNR rifle, their lives becoming more tenuous and marginal by the day. Now, the one-time guerrillas of Frelimo held the towns the Portuguese had once occupied, while their adversaries roamed the bushlands where most of the people lived, just as Frelimo had once done. Then, with the peculiar capriciousness of many African tragedies, drought stripped the land of the last vestiges of hope. Destabilization surpassed its designers' best hopes: Mozambique was ruined.

Although barely into her teenage years, the girl in Chicualacuala, where the train came only to bring water, drew her serenity from acknowledging the hopelessness of her plight. And the craziest thing of all was that, at the time I met her, the war all around her was not even supposed to be happening at all.

On March 16, 1984, in the no-man's-land on the Mozambique–South African border at Komati Poort on the Nkomati River, Presidents Botha of South Africa and Machel of Mozambique had signed what was called a treaty of nonaggression and good neighborliness. But it was a full sixteen months after the signing of the agreement that I visited Chicualacuala and watched the train pull in with its load of water. So why had the war continued when Mozambique had already acknowledged defeat?

The Nkomati Accord obliged both parties to refrain from sponsoring the other's adversaries. In effect, it was a crude trade-off: the MNR for the ANC. The South African insurgents fighting in the name of Nelson Mandela knew nothing about it in advance. The cruel blow came from the least expected quarter: they had been sold out by the man who cast himself as Africa's great revolutionary.

President Machel arrived on the banks of the Nkomati in an old black Rolls-Royce, trying to salvage some dignity. He and Mr. Botha talked in a railway car that had been used for an earlier, treacherous meeting in 1975 of black and white adversaries on the bridge at Victoria Falls between Zambia and what was then Rhodesia.

Most of the press corps was flown in by South African Air Force C-130 Hercules transports: the authorities did not want the world to miss this momentous event, the first of its kind. The South African military had thrown up a village of tents around a shaded podium where the treaty would be signed. They offered the reporters field telephones that linked easily with computer modems, dark rooms, and picture wires.

For the South African leader, the event represented a diplomatic triumph of near-unimaginable proportions: black-ruled Africa's charismatic revolutionary had been brought low, low enough to sign away his protection of the ANC in return for a South African promise to rein in the MNR. For Machel, it was a humiliation, and for the ANC itself—the oldest, most active of South Africa's liberation movements—it was a crushing strategic blow, the severance of its guerrillas' principal infiltration trail into South Africa.

Never, so publicly, in southern Africa's recent history had a black-ruled nation been obliged to eat such crow. The moment by the Nkomati River was the model of *Pax Pretoriana*, the fulfillment of South Africa's response to the Total Onslaught.

Within days, in Mozambique, ANC figures were being rounded up and deported to Zambia and elsewhere by their own African allies. And within months of the signing, P. W. Botha was feted in Western Europe as a statesman who had lowered the region's plateau of violence. He even got to see Margaret Thatcher, though at Checkers, her country residence, not at 10 Downing Street, Britain's center of prime ministerial power. Machel's aides sought valiantly to depict the agreement as evidence of a long-term strategy that would enable Mozambique to regenerate, to build new strength for the struggle against South Africa by persuading Pretoria to abandon the MNR. But they did not sound convincing, even to themselves. Everybody knew that destabilization had achieved a prime goal. What was not so obvious at the signing of a piece of paper that hot day by the Nkomati River was that the deal would be critically flawed.

First, President Botha did not keep his side of it. South Africa had committed itself to reining in the MNR and it had not done so. Pretoria offered many explanations: rogue Military Intelligence units, it was said, refused to go along with the terms of the agreement; supplies to the MNR, in any event, had been greatly increased in the months leading up to the Nkomati agreement, so the rebels were able to continue fighting. The reality was, however, that the war had continued and so, according to senior Mozambicans, had South Africa's supplies to the MNR. The Mozambicans seemed ready to accept some of Botha's explanations, but that did not solve their problems: they were still locked in a war with no absolute winners but with one big loser, the entire country. Paradoxically, though, Botha's diplomatic coup was to have momentous repercussions at home that he had never envisaged.

A couple of days after the agreement was signed, I went to Soweto and talked to whoever wanted to talk about what the Nkomati Accord was supposed to mean. I did not understand their full import at the time, but the responses all followed the same line: Botha had not addressed the issue. The issue was apartheid. It was not an issue that could be solved in Mozambique or Angola or Zambia. It was an issue, here and now, in Soweto and all the other segregated black townships. That was where the problem lay, and that was where it should and would be resolved.

In Lusaka, where the ANC was headquartered, the response was similar, although it sounded, at the time, more like a gloss on bad tidings: the Nkomati agreement had shifted the onus to those inside the country. Severed, temporarily at least, from the ANC's externally based guerrillas, the people themselves would feel the pressure to take matters into their own hands. Once they realized that the cavalry would not ride over the hill, they would have to look to their own resources.

What the Nkomati Accord had inadvertently achieved was to narrow the diffuse focus of a decade's violent black nationalism to a single point—the very laager South Africa had erected to thwart it. Years later, Joe Modise, the ANC's military commander, told me that the organization's military operations—sabotage and bombings—were never designed to be more than a catalyst for uprising at home, messages to the oppressed that they were not alone. With the Nkomati Accord, President Botha had taken the catalyst away and hoped, thereby, to create a climate in which his reforms would take root among the black majority. Total Strategy, moreover, had sanitized South Africa's borders. But Botha had underestimated the desperation of his adversaries and the fury of their response to what little he was offering. Within months, protest would erupt on the streets, a spontaneous combustion of rage. Nkomati had raised the temperature, not lowered it.

The South African president had chosen to ignore the central tenet of Beaufre's theory. He did not offer "thoroughgoing reforms" because he equated such reforms with surrender and the annihilation of Afrikanerdom.

For the "malcontents" inside South Africa, his gamble represented an invitation to battle. And, beyond South Africa's borders, Total Strategy raised the stakes to ruinous levels, from forlorn spots like Chicualacuala and its trainload of water to equally bereft places across the continent in Angola.

6.

Savimbiland:

Chaos in Angola

"I am not offering UNITA as a pawn in the game of the superpowers."

JONAS SAVIMBI to the author, November 1985

"To kill the snake, you must first crush the head, then the children."

AFRICAN PROVERB

In Angola, South Africa confronted its greatest theater of external conflict, and in Angola, too, the notions of East-West conflict and superpower rivalry seemed most entwined with modern African conflict.

Angola was a key to southern Africa. It had oil, diamonds, and the land to feed half the continent. It provided bases and training facilities for both the ANC and the SWAPO insurgents fighting their slow war against Pretoria's control of Namibia. Its strategic position athwart rail links to Africa's interior weighed heavily in Pretoria's thinking and in the calculations of the superpowers. And it was there that the ambiguities glared most brightly in the person of Jonas Savimbi, the leader of the UNITA guerrillas who had lost in Angola's civil war and now, with South African and American backing, sought to recover what history had taken from him and given to an adversary armed by and allied to Moscow and Havana.

It is easy, now, to forget the extent to which emergent nations were influenced by that great division of the globe into spheres of rival ideology. Even while communism was failing as an economic and political regime in Eastern Europe and the Soviet Union, black-ruled nations were energetically embracing its teachings. Angola's leaders called themselves the vanguard of the worker-peasant alliance. Robert Mugabe subscribed to what he called "Marxism–Leninism–Mao Tsetung thought." The monopoly of power suited tradition and ambition. Western capitalism, after all, had been the motor drive of colonialism as well as apartheid, its progenitor and defender, so various shades of socialism had been woven into the pennants of national liberation across the continent.

The ideology filled a vacuum. Decolonization changed the relationship between the state and the nation, but it did not yield a specifically African blueprint for the future, leaving some of the new leaders dependent on the borrowed ideas of Marx and Lenin. If there was no food in Poland, no freedom in the Soviet Union, well, that was no fault of the ideology. It was just that it had not been properly applied. As the methodology of political and economic rule, Marxism-Leninism, initially at least, was the only answer. Its basic principles sat uneasily on Africa's landscape of peasant farmers and urban, wouldbe capitalists, but for new leaderships eager to cement their hold on fragile new nations, the appeal was irresistible. And it came complete with a promise of protection.

Southern Africa's Marxists clung to the notion of a great socialist fraternity across the globe, from Cuba to Vietnam. They were part of it and they were paid for their allegiance in Soviet helicopter gunships, tanks, radar systems, Cuban troops, East German intelligence advisers—benefits they were then supposed to repay in a not so fraternal way from their own meager resources. In Angola, Gulf Oil Corporation's installations in the enclave of Cabinda were guarded by Cuban soldiers so that their earnings would continue to flow as the prime source of financing for the Cuban military presence itself and the Soviet arms supplies that came with it—a rare symbiosis of Marx and capital. In Mozambique, it meant the people of Maputo scrambled for leftovers in the tawdry markets while Soviet trawlers took the prize catch of king-size prawn and abundant fish from the Mozambique Channel, according to the terms of a commercial fishing agreement that obliged Moscow to give only 10 percent of its catch to the Mozambicans. The Russian fishermen chose which 10 percent to give, too.

Yet many conversations with those who called themselves "comrade" in Angola, Mozambique, and Zimbabwe left me with a clear impression that the people I was talking to really believed in this ideology that was to be so widely discredited by the late 1980s—another cruel trick played by the north on the south.

Protestations of faith shoe-horned conveniently into Pretoria's depiction of its conflict as a crusade against Godless communism and Soviet advance. And when, in the early 1980s, Washington's diplomacy established a link that effectively made Namibia's independence conditional on the withdrawal of Cuban troops from Angola—a tie that set the very parameters for South Africa's eventual withdrawal from Windhoek—it also legitimized Pretoria's unstinting effort to ensure that the Marxist regime in Luanda could never extend its writ across the country it was supposed to govern.

The MNR of Mozambique was a creation of outsiders, South African and Western officials both argued. UNITA had a past and credentials of its own. It had been formed during the anti-Portuguese struggle and had been recognized by African supporters as a central player. But when defeated in the civil war, it had refused to die. Savimbi bucked the realities of African politics, he refused to accept that there were no second prizes. He wanted a rerun of the contest, another chance at the first prize. And he was not overly concerned if he took Pretoria's help in pressing his cause. Since 1975, South Africa had sponsored him to weaken the avowedly Marxist regime in Luanda. And white officials in Pretoria drew a clear distinction between the MNR and UNITA. MNR was not viewed as a potential government. UNITA was.

UNITA stood, according to its slogans, for Liberty, Negritude, and Socialism. The inclusion of Socialism in the slogan was a throwback to the anti-Portuguese struggle. What it stood for most of all was a quintessential struggle for power.

Savimbi's supporters talked of him as if he were some kind of great, black god who would bring light and justice to a dark continent. Savimbi, they said, had charisma and vision and principles; he would break the continent's tradition of despotism, implant enlightenment, Western values. Savimbi was different—that could not be disputed.

His adversaries reviled him in equal superlatives. He was that worst of opportunists, a stooge of South Africa, apartheid's handmaiden poisoning the chalice of Africa's freedom, a messenger carrying the bullets of white oppression beyond the laager, to the continent's heart. Probably, history will judge him as a little bit of both. My own feeling, after several visits to his bush headquarters, is that no one who erects 60-foot banners of himself above his force's parade ground should really be expected to blaze a new and shining path for democracy. But, as the South Africans and Westerners said, he did have a history.

Initially, he had fought alongside the Zairean-backed Holden Roberto, then, in 1963, had broken away to establish his own movement. He set up headquarters in Lusaka, Zambia, where he befriended and bedazzled President Kaunda, whose independence from the British had come rather more easily than Angola's freedom from Lisbon. At some stage along the way of a long career as a political activist and guerrilla leader, he had attended, but not completed, medical courses at Switzerland's Lausanne University. He nevertheless assumed the title of Doctor. Early on, he once told me, he had gone to the Soviet Embassy in Cairo to seek support and military training. The Soviets ignored him. So, he went round to the Chinese embassy and they gave him a ticket to Peking and enrolled him in a military training course. Moscow's insult rankled deeply.

Some people called him a Maoist, but in reality he was closer to Hollywood—the very image of an African guerrilla leader. He was bearded and barrel-chested. He carried a silver pistol on his hip and an ivory-handled swagger stick in his grip—a magical totem of power, like Jomo Kenyatta's fly whisk or Mobutu Sese Seko's walking stick. He spoke fluent English, French, and Portuguese, along with the language of his tribe—the Ovimbundu, the base of his support, who accounted for 40 percent of Angola's population, principally in the center and south of the country. The MNR had no one of his stature to wheel before foreign reporters. And Savimbi represented to the South African leadership some of their basic ideas about authentic African leadership—legitimated through a tribal base, chiefly in style, ruthless when pressed. He was their kind of black man. They could do business with him, while others demanded their surrender. That was another reason for unstinting support.

After his defeat in Angola's civil war, Savimbi and the remnants of his battered army retreated from the Central Highlands that had been their fiefdom. In their mythology, they liken their trek back into the bush in 1976 to Mao Tse-tung's Long March. By the time I met him in the early 1980s, Savimbi had set up a string of fortified encampments in southeastern Angola, connected by dirt tracks. From there, his men pressed far to the north, beyond the Benguela Railway that had been closed since the civil war, and on toward the diamond fields of the northeast, attacking government garrisons, often seizing foreign hostages and marching them back to the south for well-publicized release to the Red Cross.

Not all his campaigns were so well publicized and, on many occasions, his forces were accused of gross violations of the normal rules of war, of spreading terror and mayhem among civilians deemed to be government supporters, of playing by the rules of the bush. Savimbi himself was accused by dissidents within his own movement of supervising the incineration of his adversaries—a charge he denied.

Africa may not have big battles, as the French attaché in Kinshasa had told me, but it has plenty of small, cruel encounters in areas where there is no umpire, no arbiter to see fair play, in Mozambique, in Angola, and in many other places. Westerners, preoccupied with urban worries, may forget how distance from the center of authority diminishes accountability. No one will call the cops in some remote village, because there are no cops, and if there were cops, they'd be corrupt. The center is unable to extend its writ to some small place where a man with a gun becomes his own authority, freed from any sense of retribution or disgrace, feeding on a power most people never get to or wish to contemplate: the very godlike ability to decide whether life continues or not.

It was simple to denounce Savimbi as a surrogate of the South Africans, but a fundamental dilemma remained that reflected on the legitimacy of both the Luanda regime and Savimbi's insurgency.

Angola had never had the elections that were promised when the Portuguese withdrew, so the MPLA regime in Luanda drew its probity from two prime sources: it occupied the capital and other main cities; and most of black-ruled Africa, Eastern Europe, and Western powers other than America had recognized it. But, collectively, the people of Angola, like the people of Mozambique, never had the opportunity to pass their own judgment on who should rule them, and that gave UNITA a reasonable cause—a "just Cause"—in whose name the battle was ostensibly waged, a fight for democracy. For many years,

Luanda rejected Savimbi and his crusade, clinging to Leninist orthodoxy and knowing full well that, were they to allow him near the cockpit of power, there would be few, if any, second prizes in the contest for control of the nation. The MPLA's standing offer, thus, was that they would talk to UNITA, but not to Savimbi. The idea was as laden with inner contradiction as Savimbi's own quest for democracy. A personality cult had made Savimbi indistinguishable from his movement. So talking to UNITA without Savimbi was like offering to talk to a shadow. To kill the snake, you must first crush the head, then the children, an African proverb says, and that is what the MPLA wanted to do with UNITA. (Ultimately, with the ending of the Cold War and the stalemate of their own war, the MPLA and UNITA had no choice but to talk to one another, and make peace in 1991. Killing the snake is not always so easy.)

However tainted he may have been by contact with the CIA, the South Africans, and British big business, Savimbi and his movement had been participants in the collapse of Portuguese rule; so, in his view, his claim to a place in the kraal was as valid as anybody else's. The main reason he had not been able to press it was that his outside backers—the CIA and the South Africans—had thrown in the towel at a crucial time in 1976, while the Soviets and Cubans supporting his adversaries had shown greater resolve in the name of Marxist internationalism.

After that defeat, Savimbi had set up an odd kind of mini-state in southeastern Angola. Foreign journalists would come to visit by courtesy of a clandestine South African charter outfit linked to Military Intelligence that flew old, unmarked Dakotas at treetop level across the bush, relying on skilled pilots and avionics that had not even been dreamed of when the airplanes were built during World War II. The pilots wore baseball hats and displayed extreme reticence when asked about their names or the airplane's destination. They invited comparison to Humphrey Bogart's Mr. Rick in *Casablanca*, saying they never made plans that far ahead.

The airplanes, dated from exactly the same era as the movie. Ominously, the Dakotas were kitted out with crude heat deflectors over the engine exhaust ports, although no one thought they would offer

much of a protection against heat-seeking missiles. Rather, our principal protection lay in the pilots' skill at navigation at very low altitudes,
north from Namibia, across the Kubango River at Rundu, thence into
Angola. There, at some bush strip, UNITA soldiers handed out immigration forms for Free Angola requiring either a signature or a
thumbprint. Then came the truckrides, overnight, uncomfortable,
and, by some perverse logic, designed to enhance the authenticity of
the message we had been summoned to hear.

Savimbi's "capital" was Jamba, deep in southeastern Angola, beyond, he thought, the range of government airstrikes, close to the
borders with Zambia and Namibia. Its airstrip was thirteen hours ride
away in a Czech six-wheel truck, captured from the MPLA, that
plowed through dirt tracks, deeply furrowed by frequent use, lashed
by overhanging branches, prey to endless sorties by squadrons of mosquitoes and tsetse flies. On one trip, it rained, and rained, and rained.
We found a tarpaulin in the open flatbed of the truck, and Savimbi's
guerrillas supported it with the barrels of AK-47 assault rifles, as a
canopy, but its folds still filled with water in that long, dark night, so
that great bladders of waterlogged tarpaulin settled on the travelers like
shrouds. Savimbi greeted visiting reporters and offered clean beds in
thatched huts, a tour of Jamba, and a military parade in which we,
the foreign reporters, were the ones really being paraded before his
followers, filling the makeshift benches of the reviewing stand as if we
were dignitaries or envoys, come to offer gifts and pledges from distant
chanceries.

Visits to Savimbi showed how well he sensed the inner nature of
many reporters and photographers: provide them with a Boy Scout
adventure, and they will do your PR for you. By contrast, the MPLA
in Luanda displayed a Stalinist aversion to even giving visas. Reporters,
Savimbi sensed, loved assignments requiring sleeping bags, Swiss Army
knives, compasses and rucksacks, khaki trousers with too many outsize
pockets, miniatuarized short-wave radios; reporters loved flying in old
planes 100 feet above the trees; they liked to hear guns fired, see bodies,
drink beer; then they liked to go home and write about the fun they
had had. Visiting Savimbi was designed as a hybrid of summer camp
and *The Dogs of War*, in which, I suspect, Savimbi cast himself as
the warrior and reporters as the dogs.

But part of his dilemma was that his entire fiefdom was, indeed, little more than a summer camp forced into a reluctant semi-permanency. Jamba was called the "provisional capital," pending his arrival in Luanda, located in terrain that did not favor long tenure. The Portuguese had not called southeastern Angola "the end of the earth" for nothing. Tsetse fly decimated cattle. The bush was harsh, uncultivated. In all my journeys there, I never once saw an elephant or a herd of antelope in what the Portuguese had called prime hunting country. But I did see the ivory workshops in Jamba, alongside the other places where they repaired UNITA's lone tank, refurbished weapons, and tailored their own olive drab uniforms. I had no reason to doubt—as South African newspapers reported—that Savimbi's men had poached ivory on a large scale in a scam conducted with the assistance of some members of the South African military.

Indeed, it was impossible to escape the conclusion that without South African support and smuggled ivory, Jamba would barely have existed. The diesel for trucks and the ceremonial tank and the four-wheel-drive pickups that passed as staff cars all came from South Africa. So did most other things. The lines of communication ran south to South Africa and north to the war. From a tactician's viewpoint, Jamba was a long way from anywhere that mattered. The distances were both an advantage and a disadvantage. They protected Savimbi's men from surprise attack or airstrikes, as did the promise of South African radar cover. But they also confronted him with insuperable logistical and politico-military problems. The Benguela Railway, 450 miles to the north, represented the absolute limit of the insurgents' ability to take and hold positions. Yet the strategic government installations—the diamond mines, the oil fields of Cabinda, the capital itself—lay far to the north, beyond the reach of an army that boasted a few trucks, one tank, no air force. It was an army whose strength lay in its soldiers' ability to cover huge distances on foot and still maintain unswerving loyalty to the man who sent them tramping hundreds of miles across inhospitable bush. And it was an army whose principal tribal backing among the Ovimbundu—Angola's largest tribe—automatically placed its roots far from the capital.

Altogther I paid five visits to Savimbi, some in the company of many colleagues, some more privately. "Savimbiland," invariably, had its rites. Visiting reporters were treated to a march-past, not just of Savimbi's well-drilled elite forces. The parade also included floats depicting aspects of the life of Jamba, supposed to show that there was more to "Savimbiland" than men with guns. Here, for instance, was Tailor, working industriously on a treadle-powered sewing machine atop a truck rolling by the reviewing stand. Here was Radio—a float with antenna and wires and men busily talking into handsets. One that always struck me as very bizarre was Hospital. The truck would roll by the reviewing stand with some kind of medical operation going on, surrounded by drips and green surgical sheeting. Then, just as it came abeam Savimbi, a medic would rise from the operation, holding aloft a genuine baby (literally born that very second!), offered to the leader with a flourish that fell somewhere between conjuror-with-rabbit and priest-with-sacrifice. Savimbi would acknowledge this legerdemain with a knowing and slightly embarrassed smile. But how, I wondered, did they always get the timing right? Would the whole parade be delayed until the contractions were at the critical phase? Surely, even Savimbi's demand for loyalty did not extend to childbirth on command.

Jamba had no railroad, no port, no mines, no industry, no paved roads. As in Mozambique, the Western notion of a town had slipped away, leaving only concepts. Mavinga, Savimbi's forward headquarters, two hundred miles to the northwest, for instance, boasted street, post office, villas. But they were all wrecked and empty, and Savimbi's men lived in foxholes near a dirtstrip, too close for comfort to government- and Cuban-piloted MiG-23 aircraft and MI-18 attack helicopters.

In Jamba, as at other centers of what became known as "Savimbiland," the children went to class under the shade of trees, 4,500 of them chanting their way through a little math, a little geography, a lot of propaganda. "UNITA, the guide; UNITA, the people." At the roadsides they were taught to snap to attention when trucks of visitors or dignitaries sped by in billows of dust.

Without UNITA's constant military harassment of the authorities, Jamba would have been an irrelevance, as threatening as some obscure religious sect that had hidden away in the wilderness seeking solitude and redemption. But the military campaign demanded attention. Lodged like a bone in the throat, it offered a permanent challenge to Luanda's authority, to its ability to implant policies that might have improved the lives of Angola's people. It denied the very title that MPLA had won for itself as the Government of the People's Republic of Angola. Savimbi's campaign—and South African strategy—meant that the MPLA did not, could not govern the country. Savimbi's aim was not secession—for the creation of a separate state of southern Angola would have left him with little more than a great, barren tract of bush. Rather, his intention was to ensure that his adversaries could never forget his demand to enter the kraal in Luanda in triumph.

What Savimbi wanted to prove, moreover, was that he was indeed fighting Soviet encroachment in Africa, that he was the front line. The corollary, of course, was that he qualified for a resumption of the American assistance that had been severed almost a decade earlier, leaving him uncomfortably dependent on Pretoria.

"If UNITA is destroyed in Angola, which will take a long time," he told me once in a lengthy conversation at one of his encampments, "the Soviets will make Angola a launching pad.

"I am not offering UNITA as a pawn in the game of the super-powers," he said. "But the situation is so serious that the intervention of the Americans is needed to stop the Russians doing what they want to do."

Savimbi was adept at tailoring his comments and actions to the interests of those he sought to exploit. In response to the protests that swept South Africa in the 1980s, he argued that P. W. Botha was on the right track and should be given a chance—a statement that set him at odds with most black South Africans, but ensured a continued flow of military hardware and even a visit to Cape Town for Botha's inauguration as state president in September 1984.

In his quest for American assistance, he hosted a conclave in Jamba in June 1985 that assembled under his roof the right-wing American lobbying group, Citizens for America, and its leader, Lewis E. Lehrman, along with representatives of anti-Soviet insurgents from Nicaragua, Afghanistan, and Laos. The Americans handed out framed copies of the Declaration of Independence. Dusk presented an incongruous sight: in the African bush, robed Afghani Muslims prayed to the East, their souvenirs of democracy propped in the foliage beside them. Mr. Lehrman read from what he said was a letter from President Ronald Reagan that spoke of "people joining together to get control of their own affairs and to free their nation from outside domination and an alien ideology." The participants signed a document establishing themselves as the "Democratic International," a global alliance against the Soviets that went no further than the paper it was written on. Savimbi himself sounded a somber note, wary of being sold out again by foreign supporters. "From our own experience," he said, "sometimes those who have helped the liberation movements have pushed them to a defeat." But he had again reminded the American right of his cause; nothing short of inclusion in the power structure in Luanda was going to satisfy UNITA and its leader or his principal supporters—South Africa and, from 1986 onward, the United States.

With Savimbi and Angola, South Africa played out the most direct of its destabilization games. While the MNR could be left to ruin Mozambique with a momentum of its own, the presence of Cuban troops and Namibian insurgent bases in Angola drew South African army and air force units directly into combat, far north of their own borders, both to support UNITA when the going got rough and to thwart the Namibian guerrillas from SWAPO who sought to press southward into their own country. Angola had become a patchwork of competing armies and guerrilla movements and intruders; and it was there that, ultimately, Total Strategy collided head-on with Total Onslaught, and the Soviet commitment to the Luanda regime raised the stakes beyond those Pretoria could afford.

When Savimbi's army did not simply wither away in those hot, distant lands, the government took to formal, frontal assaults—armed by Moscow, trained by Cubans, and accompanied, Savimbi insisted, by Soviet and Cuban advisers. Those attacks in turn raised the levels of protection South Africa was called upon to give, bringing Pretoria ever closer to direct confrontation with Moscow and its surrogates.

African wars often run to meteorological rhythms. The wet season—in southern Africa roughly from October to March—bogs down conventional forces and provides foliage that acts as cover from airstrikes. Then, when the dry season comes, tanks and trucks again can move, and the sun strips the bush down to an ochre bareness, exposing the guerrilla trails. The wet season, thus, is when insurgents undertake their main offensives. The dry season favors conventional counterattack by their adversaries. In Angola, that meant year-round fighting in both directions.

In the rainy season, SWAPO guerrillas fighting South African control of Namibia would generally seek to launch what would be billed as a major offensive, spurring the South Africans to press north to intercept them, or hit them in what Pretoria called their bases and training camps, which the insurgents called refugee camps. Then, when the dry season came, the government in Luanda, with its Cuban allies, would try one more conventional thrust to prise loose Savimbi's grip on southern Angola, obliging Pretoria to press north once again to support him. Each year, for almost a decade, however, as the Soviets installed more sophisticated radar and missile shields to guard against South African air attack, and the Cubans were pushed closer to a direct combat role, the battle became more perilous for Pretoria because of one overriding political consideration: support for a black ally could not and would not be financed by white, South African casualties beyond a very low threshold because white opinion at home would not tolerate it.

The perils had been emerging since early 1984, when a push by 2,000 South African troops further west against supposed concentrations of SWAPO insurgents had run into unaccustomed resistance from Cuban soldiers. The Soviet Union, moreover, had sent an unusual message to Pretoria, saying the presence of South African troops in southern Angola was unacceptable. Most significant of all, however, were the casualties: South Africa lost twenty-one dead in that campaign, a higher figure than could easily be explained to white voters long used to the idea of protection by an invincible army.

As in most wars, inconsequential places—places of no apparent inherent meaning or importance in civilian life—achieve great importance as the symbols of conflict because they lie on the fault lines between opposing forces. Thus, in southern Angola, Mavinga, Savimbi's forward headquarters, was important because that was as far north as Savimbi could maintain a permanent presence. It also boasted a landing strip, critical for South Africa resupply.

Around 120 miles to the northwest, Cuito Cuanavale was important because that was as far south as government forces could encroach without taking major risks. And between the two lay the modest stream of the Lomba River, which also became important because it was the dividing line between the two fiefdoms and thus the triggerpoint for escalated hostilities.

Somewhere, in an album, I have a snapshot—taken by a friend

and partner in many escapades, the photographer Mark Peters—of me bathing in a tin tub in a grass shelter in the Angolan bush, reading the late Barbara Tuchman's *The March of Folly*. The title summed up everything Angola's war seemed to stand for. And, during a visit to Mavinga in late 1985, we had realized how high the stakes had risen.

The Dakotas took off late and flew longer than usual, this time under cover of the night, the airplanes' running and interior lights extinguished, the pilots relying on the countdown of a digital clock and the sophisticated compass that provided a heading to bring us to Savimbi's advance headquarters. The instruments showed us to be between 500 and 1,000 feet above ground in total darkness. The idea, one of the pilots told me in a rare foray into loquacity, was this: there was no radio contact with the ground because that would have given away our position to hostile interception, so we had to be overhead Mavinga at an exact prearranged time for the landing to take place; if we were early or late, Savimbi would not guarantee the airplane's safety from ground attack by his own forces; and only if we were exactly on time would his men ignite the kerosene flares that were to provide the sole aid to a night landing on a bush strip by an airplane that was much older than most of the people it was carrying. If the UNITA guerrillas did not light the flares on time, the pilot said, there was a good chance we'd overshoot Mavinga and come within range of government anti-aircraft batteries. All in all, the venture seemed risky.

I stood behind the pilots as the digital clock counted down through the minutes, wondering if they had been exaggerating. The total darkness through the windshield offered no clues, but already the pilots were beginning to shed the little height that separated us from the treetops, displaying a faith in the instruments and their own navigation that I did not entirely share. Then, exactly as the digital countdown on the flight deck hit zero, lights began to come on below us. The pilots banked tightly, lined the Dakota up with the flarepath, and executed a perfectly smooth landing. Five minutes later, the Dakota had gone again, rumbling off into the darkness.

We were left to ponder our fate. The landing flares had been extinguished and we were being assigned to underground bunkers for the night. The style of the operation was, possibly, justified by military concerns. But it occurred to me that the showmanship of the enterprise had succeeded perfectly in building the sense of high drama surrounding what we had come to see: another close call for Savimbi in the crusade against the Communist horde.

The night ride to Mavinga in 1985 was designed to show that UNITA was not about to be defeated, but was nonetheless confronted with a real adversary. Government forces, supported by Cuban troops and Soviet advisers, had crossed the Lomba River in one of their setpiece advances from Cuito Cuanavale toward Mavinga. They had been stopped and mauled. They had withdrawn. Now, we were to be taken to see the evidence of the Soviet master plan for southern Africa, but what we saw said a lot, too, about Pretoria's master plan for the same region.

The government convoy had been stopped in its tracks on the southern bank of the Lomba. The trucks were charred hulks on a dirt road in scrawny bush. A Soviet MI-18 helicopter lay at a crazy angle where it had crashed. The foxholes that freckled the earth were like archeological digs that show the ebb and flow of habitation in the layers of detritus—first a layer of South African–supplied combat rations wrappings, then empty Cuban sardine cans printed in Spanish, then, uppermost, more South African rations.

What had happened, Savimbi's men told us, was that the convoy had been ambushed with mortar fire. But mortars do not generally cause the conflagration that had seized the burned trucks. Neither were there many bodies, suggesting that the occupants of the trucks had already fled by the time the vehicles were hit. In one, though, a soldier had not run in time; in the blackened mess, all that remained of his head was the shining whiteness of his skull obtruding like a boiled egg where the flesh had been burned away by fire. The evidence, both from the visit and from accounts that emerged later from the other side, was that UNITA had been rescued from the painstaking advance by a South African airstrike using napalm. By the time we arrived, there was some desultory fight noise in the distance, mortars possibly, from the north bank of the Lomba River. But the battle was over for that year. The rains would come, and, in the way of things, both sides would rest and contemplate next year's campaign, on the same route, for the same aims, but bigger in scope and hazard.

The spiral was in motion. In September 1987, at another battle for Cuito Cuanavale, the stand-off finally came in a long bush campaign that signified the outer limits of South Africa's ability to sustain the war on Savimbi's behalf.

Initially, government and Cuban troops had pressed south, seeking to oust Savimbi from Mavinga itself. South African support blunted the attack, but in the counterthrust on Cuito Cuanavale, supposedly an important staging post for the government soldiers and the Cubans, Pretoria's men ran into unexpected resistance and were forced to pull back rather than countenance greater casualty figures.

The fighting did nothing to change the military line-up. But it produced some ambiguous conclusions that underscored the futility of the campaign, and spurred Angola and South Africa to acknowledge the long-standing American offer to broker a deal.

By holding on to Cuito Cuanavale, Angolan government forces claimed a victory: that is to say, they had won because they had not lost, even though they had failed utterly in their attempt to crush Savimbi. And, by failing to take the town, the South Africans were forced into a recognition that, while they had not lost in any absolute sense, they could not win without committing far greater forces to someone else's war. The destabilization of Angola—both by supporting UNITA and by challenging SWAPO on Angolan soil—was turning out to be a potentially more costly exercise than had been foreseen, in financial and human terms.

Eventually, these shifts in perception were woven into the agreement of December 1988, long in the negotiation by Assistant Secretary of State Chester A. Crocker, that achieved Washington's prime policy goal: the promise of a phased withdrawal of Cuban troops from Angola in return for a South African withdrawal from Namibia. Finally, Pretoria had realized that it could not pursue the Angolan campaign without unacceptable white losses and without being drawn inexorably toward a direct and bloody conflict with Cuba whose consequences, militarily and internationally, could not be foreseen. When the deal was struck, UNITA was not at the table, but it was still very much in southern Angola, and still receiving American aid.

In 1989, however, South Africa finally relinquished its grip on Namibia under the terms of the agreement brokered by Washington that was also supposed to promote peace between the MPLA regime in Luanda and Savimbi in the south—a peace that did not settle easily. Even at the beginning of a new decade in early 1990, government forces were reported advancing on Mavinga, and reporters were being flown in from South Africa on the old Dakotas, under cover of darkness, to show that Savimbi was still in control. As five years earlier, the night ride over the bush meant that Savimbi had not been altogether abandoned to face his adversaries unsung, whatever might have happened in Namibia and however the Cold War might have ended in Europe.

For the first time, Savimbi admitted losing ground. Stripped of the protection of South African air cover from bases in Namibia, Jamba had come under air attack. In those distant parts, the ripples of change in South Africa, prompted in part by the broader changes far to the north, could not be ignored: with the Cold War's ending, the superpowers were moving their pawns in ways that left less room for manipulation and obliged Angola's warriors to acknowledge what South Africa had already discovered: the war was unwinnable.

One year later, in Lisbon—where southern Africa's most fundamental changes had started with the officers' coup in 1974—the new relationship between Moscow and Washington propelled the MPLA and UNITA toward a formal political settlement. Fifteen years after Angola's independence, the March of Folly had come full circle, a vain campaign that ended, where it began, with a promise of freedom for people raised on war and tired of it. Like Mozambique, Angola lay in ruins.

7.

Reporter's Notebook:

Covering Africa

"Are you journalists—or journalists-plus?"

ZIMBABWE NATIONALIST JOSHUA NKOMO at a 1977 news conference in Lusaka, implying that attending journalists were Western spies

I left black-ruled Africa for South Africa in August 1983, boasting—for my time there—a cabin trunk loaded with notebooks and clippings and the sense that, perhaps, what had appeared in print had not recounted the entirety of my experiences. After all, there had been the adventures and the mishaps, the canoe rides and the panics in remote places where survival itself seemed uncertain. Those were the grist of my memories, more than the dates and events that marked history's slow unfolding. And, beyond every dispatch filed by telephone or telex—even carrier pigeon—from some unlikely spot, there were the logistics, the arrests, the adrenaline of experiences that, at the time, seemed too remote from the mainstream of events to be included in the reports sent to London and New York. Later, though, it occurred to me that those same experiences had provided some insights into how Africa worked, or didn't work, how people coped, or failed to cope, with the issue that consumes many lives in many places—just getting by. And, it seemed, the most basic of a traveler's functions—getting there, finding some place to stay, using the telephone—yielded encounters with Africa's magic and miseries that taught as much about the place as the events supposed to be covered. The lessons began right from the start.

On the map, Lusaka looked as if it should be the hub at the center of a wheel, ideally placed as the crossroads of Central Africa, a base within easy striking range of any number of places. In theory, the spokes of the wheel spread forth through many neighboring countries—

Angola, Mozambique, Tanzania, Zaire, Zimbabwe. But, in those days in the 1970s, the wheel seemed oddly asymmetric.

The border between Zambia and Zimbabwe (then known as Rhodesia) was closed because Zambia had chosen to enforce the sanctions that were supposed to end white minority rule. So there were no direct flights to Zambia's southern neighbor.

Angola and Mozambique had just emerged from several centuries of Portuguese rule, while Zambia had been British until 1964, and the two colonial spheres did not overlap. So there were not too many flights linking these bastions of free Africa, either. Zaire, moreover, had been Belgian, and had so little in common with Zambia that there were no direct flights at all from the capital of one to the capital of the other, even though they were geographic neighbors. (The most regular flights from both seemed to be the European airlines' 707s that roared off for London or Brussels most nights, laden with government ministers in First Class and suddenly cheerful expatriates in Coach.)

Flying the continent, thus, had its own rules. To reach Chad from Nairobi, for instance, the most convenient route was through Paris. There it was theoretically possible to pick up visas for both Chad and its neighbor, Cameroon—where the phones worked when those in Chad did not.

To reach Zaire from Zambia, the traveler set off in the wrong direction, too, heading south, not north. First, a small, propeller-driven Hawker Siddeley chugged its way from Lusaka to Francistown, a diamond-mining stop in Botswana. There, the airplane refueled and pressed on for Gaberone, Botswana's capital, where the flight number changed but the airplane didn't. That was to avoid the impression that, however circuitously, there might be a direct flight between Lusaka and Johannesburg, apartheid's citadel, which was the destination of the renumbered flight. Once in Johannesburg, the traveler switched to one of the European airlines whose wide-bodied jets flew north each night.

Generally, those flights left in the evening, so that passengers heading for London or Brussels or Paris might arrive at a convenient hour the following morning.

Travelers on their way to Zaire, one third of the way up the continent, got dumped off on the tarmac in Kinshasa in the middle of the night—a time when the airport resembled even more than usually a grotesque and not very convincing set for a movie about white mercenaries in seedy, hot places. Large, unidentifiable, and sinister insects buzzed in pools of neon on the darkened, oily apron. It was hot. It was sticky. Soldiers lounged and peered through mirrored sunglasses, fiddling with rifles. At this unearthly, otherworldly hour, a long time after departing Zambia, the traveler arrived to meet the challenge, the initiation rite, of Kinshasa's N'djili Airport.

At the glassed-in booth where passports were presented, the immigration officers glowered, as if no one had ever gotten past them, indeed, as if there were no way at all of getting past them. On my first visit, my passport had no visa. There had been no time to go through the bureaucracy of Zaire's dilapidated embassy in Lusaka; and, anyhow, arriving from Johannesburg, it was supposed to be possible to get one at the airport because Zaire had no embassy in South Africa.

"No visa," an officer said.

It was final, an irreversible fact: no visa, no entry into the country. That was the law. It could not be changed. The punishment did not bear thinking about—held at the airport in some dank cell prior to deportation, haunted by rats and thumbscrews. Even if there had been a visa, I discovered on subsequent trips, the officers would discover some arcane error. "*Visa pas bon* (Visa not good)." An equally heinous crime, with no ready atonement.

You did not, however, lose heart, or abandon the rictus of a smile that cloaked your fury and petulance. "*Chef,*" you said, voice laden with contrition and using the obsequious honorific that foreigners mistakenly believe will stroke egos wounded and prickly from the days of Belgian rule and every other indignity since. "If you could perhaps see your way . . ." The phrasing was unimportant, except as a conversational way of drawing attention to the dollar bills in the passport. "If a visa fee is required . . ." The officer departed, returned with a permit, still glowering, as if this were highly irregular but nonetheless doable. You tottered on to pick up luggage.

Zaire was not unique. Lagos Airport in Nigeria was a comic-opera battle with officials who seem to have composed a chorus of calls for "Five Naira," the local currency, that continued out through the arrivals hall, the taxi rank on the street, and on to the first roadblock on the way into town. Arriving in Madagascar, at Tananarive, there were eleven separate processes to be completed. If the paperwork was wrong at any one of them, the hapless traveler was obliged to return to the very first of eleven booths and start over. At Kano Airport, in northern Nigeria, where I had run a gauntlet of immigration and customs officials, I sank into a seat on an airplane taking me to London and sighed with relief. "Don't relax yet, sonny," said a veteran British expatriate, "we're not in the air."

Several years later in Kinshasa, the system seemed to have been refined to avoid conversation altogether. It worked like this: the glassed-in booth had been whitewashed over, so that it was impossible to actually see the officer. However, a hand would appear on the wooden counter below the impenetrable painted glass. The hand took the passport, reappeared empty, withdrew once more crossed with dollars, and reemerged with a visa. It was all very quick and tidy. At first, I thought the whitewash was some kind of special mirror, enabling the officer to check out the traveler's appearance and manner without being seen himself. But when I peeked around the corner, I realized that the passport officer could no more see the traveler than the traveler could see what happened to the fistful of dollars. The interface had been distilled to a terrifyingly pure, depersonalized transaction.

The name of this form of business was—and still is—*matabiche*, derived for the Portuguese slang for a snack, or drink. Literally, the Portuguese word *matabicho* means "a killer of buck." In Zaire, it translates into a million-dollar business of private surcharges on myriad services. But it does not quite mean bribery because the connotations in Zaire suggest more of a mutually acknowledged need, whether the object to be obtained is a visa or a powerline contract. Words like "bribery" or "corruption" suggest a sense of moral outrage, of aberrant behavior, while *matabiche* is simply the alchemy that transforms the impossible into the possible.

No, there is no room at the hotel, the front-desk clerk will tell you when you arrive at 3:00 a.m., limp and ragged, waving a reservation telex, the rictus smile slipping fast. No, it is not possible to make an international telephone call, says the operator. Then, suddenly, all things change. There is a room, after all; of course, you can call New York, or London, or wherever, and a distant editor is on the line, not really sure why you've called to check in, ransacking the atlas to find out where you're checking in from.

Sometimes, though, *matabiche* was not enough to buy a way out of trouble.

Reporters in many parts of black-ruled Africa were regarded as a hindrance. Visas could take months to be issued. In places where "news" equaled the president's latest utterance, the mission of foreign correspondents was often misunderstood or misinterpreted. Joshua Nkomo, the Zimbabwean patriarch, routinely inferred reporters were spies. Detained by the secret police in Maiduguri, northern Nigeria, I was questioned for five hours by two men—one in Western dress, one in flowing robes—who had finessed the "nice cop, nasty cop" routine to perfection: they were both nasty. There had been religious riots and their questioning seemed to suggest that I was suspected, somehow, of fomenting the fight between Christians and Muslims. The "evidence" that really fueled their suspicions was a cassette tape found in my shoulder bag. A tape player was brought to the interrogation room, and both men glowered at me as the cassette was slowly loaded. Four eyes locked on mine as one of the cops pressed the play button. Eric Clapton filled the room, singing "Lay down Sally." "Ah," exclaimed the Western-dressed policeman. "I like the music, too." He beamed, but did not release me until orders came from Lagos. Later, he wanted to make up and took me on a tour of the night spots. "Have a Chadian woman," he offered, "they're very good." He might have been proffering a box of candies. I declined, but it occurred to me that, though I had raised suspicion because I was a foreigner, a white foreigner at that, I had also been sheltered from real harm *because* I was a foreigner. Rhodesia's whites, my supposed kith and kin, were not always so hospitable.

I had been staying at the Zimbabwe Ruins Hotel when it came under rocket attack by guerrillas under the command of Comrade Nylon, a *nom de guerre* of obscure origin. For months, he and his men had roamed the surrounding bushlands seeking to drive out the last white Rhodesian presence—the handful who ran the Zimbabwe Ruins Hotel, a thatched and rustic place at the end of a narrow road leading nowhere else.

The ruins from which the hotel took its name were a great and baffling collection of chevroned stone and grand, mysterious architecture, towers and enclosures, guardians of the land long before the whites arrived. They, not the modest hotel that squatted nearby, represented the prize, for they were the very symbol of Zimbabwe's African heritage, built by Africans who had founded a great and enduring dynasty centuries before any whites materialized to lay claim to the land. But the hotel also represented the whites' refusal to abandon their custodianship, and that meant that the origins of the historical lore had to be rewritten.

"Maybe it was Arab slavers, or Phoenicians what built it," the trim, peroxide-haired woman in her floral print dress at the Fort Victoria tourism bureau told me as I drove down there in December 1979. "But no way did munts build it." With that wisdom, employing a common and nasty pejorative for Rhodesian blacks, she had sent me on my way, coyly omitting to mention that the access road, snaking through fifteen miles of dense bush, was known as "Ambush Alley"— a grudging tribute to Comrade Nylon.

For both sides, thus, a brief battle in the clear, early light the morning after I arrived, resembled the war in microcosm: black challenge, white resistance.

Across the table in London sat the nation's harshest adversaries— Ian Smith, who led his land in rebellion against the crown in 1965; his black front man, Bishop Abel Muzorewa, the nominal prime minister; and the guerrilla leaders, Robert Mugabe and Joshua Nkomo, who had given the lie to Smith's prediction that majority rule would not come to Rhodesia, "not in a thousand years." On the ground, the war continued.

A few months before, I had spent some time living the murderous routine of Beirut—shelling and sniping in the city, Israeli artillery and Palestinian rockets marching the by-ways of south Lebanon. I had thought it intensely frightening to crouch in some stairwell, tensed for the one that, supposedly, you don't hear. I had lived in a borrowed penthouse with pink marble floors, lots of glass, and a great view of the Green Line dividing the city, which meant the Green Line had a great view of me. One night, the tracer fire decapitated the geraniums I was supposed to be looking after on the balcony, an unsettling end to my brief foray into horticulture. It was no comfort to see the red-petaled heads falling a few feet from my own. Beirut was terrifying.

But Rhodesia held a different kind of fear, rooted in the very unpredictability of it all, fueled by anticipation of the worst—the scratching in the surface of an ochre dirt road that might betray a guerrilla landmine, the sudden rustling in the bush that might foretell an imminent ambush. In Lebanon the calculations were somehow easier, and no one—in the era before hostage taking—took your skin tones as a statement of hostile intent. Here the distinction was impossible to avoid, and there were few ambiguities.

When Comrade Nylon lobbed his rocket-propelled grenade into the grounds of the hotel, I happened to be the only guest, not surprisingly since the place had long been under a capricious sort of siege that kept people away. I had come to write a small story about a small wrinkle in what, after all, was a small war. But I had not bargained with Comrade Nylon, whose actions created two distinct quandaries. The first was that, at the time of the early morning assault, I had been debating with myself whether to swim or shower, and was clad for the latter, certainly not for rapid flight, much less the observing of combat at uncomfortably close quarters.

The second was the kind of question best dealt with theoretically, without the encumbrance of inconvenient reality: What should I do now? In the broadest of terms, I harbored a sympathy for the guerrillas' goals—freedom and independence, the promise of democracy and a new start. In Zambia, I had lived well and happily, a temporary sojourner, it is true, but never really threatened or molested by this specter of black rule that so enraged Rhodesia's whites.

I had never been able to explain to Rhodesians, either, that it was not so bad: a gin and tonic at sunset tasted pretty much the same whether the particular, shaded porch was located north or south of the Zambezi. And I had met the guerrilla leaders often, seen them in their private moments, feted them as guests in my home on the Great East Road. None of them had grown horns and a tail, and they seemed to have a point: they wanted to go home and run their own country, and the whites were welcome to stay in it, but could not govern it. Josiah Tongogara, Comrade Nylon's supreme commander, often greeted me with a bearlike embrace and laughingly called me "comrade"—an honorific that made me uneasy. But the perspective drawn by the morning attack was different. If the battle went the way Comrade Nylon wanted it to, I doubted there would be much time for my protestations of credentials as the attackers breached the security fence and located me in my hotel room. I would be perceived as the enemy. Skin color would almost certainly seal my fate. It was not the kind of war where they took prisoners.

I had spent the previous evening in sometimes nasty argument with the few residual Rhodesian whites who ran the hotel or patronized the bar, and the debate now seemed to have an eerie significance.

The point at issue had been the fact that I tried to cover the conflict and travel in the country without carrying a gun at a time when most of my supposed kith and kin—and some of my colleagues, too—went around armed to the teeth. Anything less was regarded as letting the side down. Being armed was an ideological statement as much as a military necessity.

The discussion turned particularly awkward when I let slip that I had lived in Zambia—Nkomo's rear base in the bush war—before moving to Rhodesia to witness the closing stages of the conflict. That made me highly suspect, and the discussion became unpleasant.

Now, as I hit the deck to ponder my own, more immediate worries, the phone rang. It was Molly, the manager's blond and bubbly wife, calling from Reception, which doubled as a command center in times of strife. The previous evening she had helped out at the bar and participated forthrightly in the debate, coming down strongly on the side of the pro-gun lobby and arguing that my refusal to bear arms in someone else's war was a cop-out because I would still expect their protection when the crunch came. Since the hotel boasted that it had already been attacked on thirty-two separate occasions, the crunch was not inconceivable.

Above the noise of the shooting, she simply said, "You can either come and help us or stay where you are—under the bed." And rang off. Molly had a way with words.

I dressed quickly—without leaving the floor—and tried to work out from the cacophony of gunfire outside the window who was shooting at whom and from where. What frightened me more than Beirut was that, while the weapons were certainly far more modest, so was the cover: there was no impersonal concrete to guard against an impersonal mortar shell. Beyond the door, my morning coffee, brought by a hotel waiter before the fight began, sat cold and untouched on its tin tray. The staff crouched, stoic and miserable, behind the bougainvillea that sheltered the hotel terrace, resigned to these moments of difficulty.

Even the hotel peacocks had fallen silent. Bob Baxter, the owner, and his manager, Doug, were running at a crouch, firing bursts, switching oversized forty-round clips in FN rifles, shouting orders. The hotel's Guard Force loosed off salvos of undirected fire from concrete pillboxes on the perimeter. The bush yielded no secrets beyond the occassional muzzle flash from the higher ground above the hotel. Tracer bullets zipped back in, seeking combustible targets in the thatch and the woodwork.

I scurried to the Reception desk not really knowing what I was supposed to do. I was not much of an ally. But I did not particularly want to be shot on my hotel-room floor, either. And then, with the unpredictability that marked the war—indeed, was one of the guerrillas' principal weapons—events spared me a decision. As I got to Reception to face Molly's sardonic "I-told-you-so" smile, the incoming fire stopped as quickly as it had started. The brief battle was over, the moral decision about bearing arms postponed, even though my reflexes—I had to admit—had overcome ideological worries. The Guard Force preened in Pyrrhic victory.

"We're going after them," Bob shouted, as he and his friend clambered into an armored vehicle made of steel and built onto the chassis of a Volkswagen Beetle. "You're in charge while we're away," he added, to my and everyone else's astonishment, thrusting at me the twin totems of my new command—an imperial German Luger pistol and a radio, neither of which did I know how to operate.

And it occurred to me that it was not only Eni, my maid in Lusaka, who equated whiteness with command: Bob Baxter, a former sergeant in the mounted British South Africa Police, had done the same, leaving me in charge of a Guard Force unit of fifty trained black Rhodesian soldiers and the women and children, too, on the assumption that I would handle the situation adequately. I was thankful that Comrade Nylon decided not to return to press his attack. So, I think, was Molly. My new status had been conferred by reflex, without contemplation or request, just as Eni had appointed me Bwana on my arrival in Lusaka. Just as easily, I had accepted the role, in the heat and haste of the moment, and that gave me pause, for my command derived solely from being white, and, in my case, a tainted white at that. It said a lot about the underlying presumptions of the entire conflict.

"You know we'll probably try to stay on too long, and if we survive we'll end up with nothing but our suitcases," Molly vouchsafed as we sipped morning tea after the attack, the radio and the Luger resting on the linen tablecloth before us in the shade of a great tree. But it never crossed her mind to just throw in the towel and leave, along with the others who took what was scathingly known as the "chicken run" or the "yellow route" to South Africa and elsewhere. It was almost as if the war had become reflexive, a series of encounters that she knew would lead nowhere.

Across Lake Kariba and the Zambezi River, the politics were diametrically opposed, but the terrain was pretty much the same—the hot, dry, dense scrub of the Zambezi Valley where rhinos and elephants once trundled, impervious to war; the high, bright uplands of the Central African plateau where the light seemed so clear that it bathed every individual stalk of tawny grass in crystal brightness.

On both sides, come sundown, the whites would pour tonic over locally made gin (cane spirit with essence of juniper) and sit on their verandahs to watch that brief explosion of flamboyance called sunset before night brought the mosquitoes and the maid with supper. The difference was, of course, that down there in Rhodesia, where the women played tennis and lawn bowls and the men wore shorts and kneesocks and floppy hats, the whites ran the show, while where I lived, President Kenneth Kaunda ran the show. By living in Zambia— I learned when I got to Rhodesia—I had forfeited some of the mysterious essence of whiteness that Rhodesia's white minority nurtured like a fallen bird. No self-respecting white would live under black rule, they seemed to say, although many of them finished up doing just that. Black rule, the reasoning went, was the very antithesis of civilization, standards, Christianity.

The Zambezi Valley, where over the years I fished, canoed, caroused, was the divide. And it was where white mistrust of reporters as fifth columnists gave way to black suspicion of reporters as outright enemy agents. That was something a colleague, John Borrell, and I discovered when we were arrested at Chirundu at the height of the war. Like Mr. Nkomo in Lusaka, our captors accused us of espionage.

The soldiers who seized us separated us, driving John away, and frog-marching me out of sight of the Rhodesians across the steel girder bridge that spanned the Zambezi.

The men who escorted me were a Zambian soldier and a Zimbab-wean guerrilla fighter from Nkomo's ZIPRA forces. As I was marched back from the bridge, the light seemed suddenly very sharp, the silences overwhelming in that hot, languid valley. I became painfully aware of sensory perceptions: the crickets seemed louder, the gaps between their chirruping almost deafening. Ahead stood a great baobab tree that looked ideal as the setting for a firing squad. If I died, no one would know for days that I was dead, and no one in any event would be brought to justice. The Zimbabwean guerrilla drew back the slide on his bayoneted AK-47 with that sickening sound of metal on metal that has preceded many summary killings. I saw him, as if in slow motion, turn the safety lever to the firing position. And I thought the jig was up. "You must excuse my comrade from Zimbabwe," the Zambian soldier said with an inscrutable grin. "He is a little impet-uous."

As at other times in Africa when things could seem no worse, a deus emerged from the machina. A senior officer, seeing our press credentials, rescued us from the comrade's impetuosity, and sent us on our way with a stern warning not to do whatever it was we had done again. But the scene left an unsettling sense of vulnerability: for a brief moment the false patina of security was stripped away by the slide of the AK-47 and my helplessness was total—no umpire would see fair play done. The bush had different rules, and they were the rules of the war that brought power to those who wielded the gun.

In 1978, Joshua Nkomo's guerrillas had shot down two civilian airliners with Soviet-supplied SAM-7 provoking white rage and despair, but not really advancing their cause. Partly in response, the war had been carried far into Zambia and Mozambique with Rhodesian cross-border raids that produced killing, destruction, and humiliation on a massive scale. On October 18, 1978, I had been standing in my garden, outside the house on the Great East Road, when the very earth seemed to shake below me. A dozen miles away, Rhodesian aircraft were bombing a purported guerrilla training facility that the Red Cross insisted was a refugee camp known as Westlands Farm. The raid was in reprisal for the downing of the first Viscount civilian airliner, when Nkomo's guerrillas had shot ten of the eighteen survivors on the ground. The commander of the Rhodesian bombers, under the code name Green Leader, radioed Zambia's ground controllers and told them calmly and firmly that any Zambian warplanes challenging them would be shot down. His tones were almost gentlemanly, insisting that Rhodesia had no quarrel with Zambia. But it gave the lie to Zambia's sense of sovereignty—at will, its airspace could become no more than an extension of Rhodesia's. A tape recording of Green Leader's message was released that night on Rhodesian Radio—a great morale booster for the whites of Rhodesia, a crushing humiliation for President Kenneth Kaunda. Only later did we discover that the tape had been recorded as the Rhodesians were leaving Zambian airspace, and that Green Leader's earlier utterances from the command bomber were far less measured. "Beautiful. Jesus Christ, those fuckin' bombs are beautiful," he had said, inter alia.

The results of the raid were traumatic. Along Lusaka's main thoroughfare, Land Rovers wheeled in from the bushlands with the dead and wounded spilling out in one gory mess after another. The hospitals could not cope. Hundreds died. Armed guerrillas staggered out from the supposed refugee camp, wide-eyed: this was something their commissars had not prepared them for. President Kaunda had spoken frequently and heroically of being on a war footing; regularly, he would burst into public tears at the horror of it all. But few Zambians, including the president, had any concept of what the results of war looked like when seen from close up. Now they did, and the following day whites were mobbed in central Lusaka, the only time I ever encountered racial tension there in two and a half years living on the Great East Road. The Rhodesians had exported their hatreds to the land next door.

In the wake of the attack, Joshua Nkomo's guerrillas broke out of camps near Lusaka, harassing whites, beating and torturing Afrikaner farmers who were settled in a small enclave near Lusaka. Ngwerere, where they lived on widely spaced farms, was a rail stop that boasted a few homesteads and a cricket patch hewn from the savannah. In the clubhouse, during times of peace, wives served tea and cucumber sandwiches on sunny weekend afternoons. The sound of leather cricket ball on willow bat found a counterpoint in the sound of drums from the African village just beyond the boundary, on the other side of a hedge of elephant grass.

The farmers felt their security slipping away and the Zambian authorities offered them no protection from these African comrades, incensed at the Rhodesian attack yet powerless to respond except by the most primeval of reflexes. "Give us the guns and we'll do the job ourselves," one farmer shouted, as he and his colleagues met with a Zambian police chief at a fraught and clamorous meeting held in the Ngwerere clubhouse. Even then, the wives served tea and cucumber sandwiches, though the talk seemed to call for headier refreshments.

One afternoon, I helped a friend who lived near a guerrilla camp in empty and isolated bush dispose of his two guns—a Webley service revolver and a .22 rifle. They were innocuous enough weapons, used only for target shooting, but the guerrillas were raiding white homesteads and searching them for evidence of the spies who had undoubtedly guided the Rhodesian bombers onto their camp. I left my friend's house after dark, steering my open Volkswagen hunting car through the sandy tracks that led back to Lusaka. At an intersection, the headlights fanned over tall grass, catching the glint of bayonets and the gleam of eyes. The guerrillas who had taken up ambush position on the road were probably as much at a loss as I was—should they fire or not? The moment left me incensed, not so much with the guerrillas as with the Rhodesians: they had spoiled my idyll; they had broken the frail tendrils of my African peace.

Journalism requires that historic moments be encapsulated in despatches. These days, that is achieved by laptop computers and modems. In the 1970s, reporters queued, fought, bribed their way to rattling telex machines in post offices that seemed tattered monuments to colonial technology. Covering Zimbabwe's cease-fire in 1980, we took a step further back to pretechnology days and sent our dispatches by pigeon from the bushlands to Bulawayo.

The birds belonged to Alderman Sid Millar, a former mayor of Bulawayo, and they had been presented to us by Sandy Robertson, the last white editor of the Bulawayo *Chronicle*, who had told us there would be no other means of communication once we deployed with the New Zealand contingent supposed to monitor the cease-fire. He was quite right. We were miles from the nearest telephone, or cable, or even runner. The monitoring force radio network was off limits to reporters. For all the modernity of its cities—indeed for all the much-vaunted advances of ninety years of foreign rule—many parts of Rhodesia, like the rest of Africa, lived with communications measured in hours or days or even weeks, not the microseconds of real-time modernity. It was pigeons or nothing. For me, as a correspondent in those times for Reuters News Agency, the birds were especially significant: Baron Julius Reuter had founded his service with carrier pigeons, but time had moved on—through telegrams and telexes to leased, high-speed circuits—and the editorial headquarters in London was switching finally to computers. I, meanwhile, would file by pigeon, confirming the suspicion of those technologically minded people who would see me as a Luddite.

Sandy Robertson had instructed us on the intricacies and protocols of pigeon handling. First, he said, write the story on tissue paper and fold it into a clear, plastic capsule, the sort of container used sometimes for medication. Then tape the capsule to the bird's leg. Then stroke the bird. You hold the bird's legs between the index and middle fingers, he explained, the thumb over the folded wings. It was important—for reasons we never fathomed—to kiss the back of the bird's head and say soothing, encouraging things before gently launching it aloft. The instruction over, the birds were housed in wicker crates, which we loaded into the back of a Land Rover heavy with steel plating to deflect the explosion should we run over a landmine. (Don't think of the bang, a colleague with a taste for the macabre told me once as we discussed the eventuality of hitting a mine, think of the enveloping red wetness.)

Then we set off, tagging along behind the New Zealand column as it trundled into the bush past villagers as mystified by this calvacade as they had been by any number of inexplicable events in the course of the war. The tissue paper from the inside of a 30-pack of Madison cigarettes was big enough for about four hundred words of spidery scrawl. And soon we had an event that merited our first experiment with the birds—the deployment of the New Zealanders at Assembly Point Lima.

A 400-word despatch was duly composed, folded, packed, and taped to the bird, which was held, kissed, and launched aloft, where it spiraled twice and perched in a tree, showing no interest whatever in proceeding. Frustrated, I rewrote the despatch on the tissue from a second 30-pack of Madisons, repeated the procedure with a substitute bird. It, too, spiraled, but then took its bearings and circled. The first bird rose to join it and, together in close formation, they headed off in the rough direction of Alderman Sid Millar's loft in Bulawayo.

This was a wrinkle into which Sandy Robertson had not initiated us: the birds liked company. The lesson was repeated in subsequent despatches. We would compose our four hundred words, tape them to a pigeon, and send it on its way with prayers and caresses. Then it would sit in a tree, awaiting a companion-in-flight. Finally, when yet another pigeon was launched and went nowhere, I grew impatient and scrawled on a second scrap of paper: "This bird is accompanying the bird that's got the story."

The pigeon was launched, and, to our consternation, headed off in solo flight at high speed toward Alderman Miller's loft, while the first bird with the story taped to its leg bestirred itself and shot off in the opposite direction with coordinates that would take it eventually to the Kalahari Desert if it didn't change course. We discovered on our return to Bulawayo that the tactic had caused some puzzlement: a bird had arrived with a message saying: "This bird is accompanying the bird that's got the story." The second bird finally appeared twelve hours later, when it limped home after a very circuitous flight.

I had first visited southern Angola in 1977, when Luanda's control west of "Savimbiland" extended to the Namibian border—even if its ability to feed the country did not. The land was hard and undeveloped and the visit taught me a little about the thresholds of survival in those great, broad swathes of Africa that have yet to catch up with the distant capitals; where you do not move because there is no bus, you do not read because the school has no books or teachers, where the promises of independence remain unredeemed, and where colonialism's legacy is bleak. "What you need here," one of my escorts from the MPLA told me, "is a box of matches and a gun." The same would have held true a century before, when Frederick Courteney Selous, the British big-game hunter, roamed southern Africa. One episode in particular, however, seemed to suggest that, in the early flush of revolution, the MPLA had no concept of the rigors that were to come as they sought to spread their revolution to the south. It took a while for the carnival to give way to the horror show.

Meat was scarce, so one night in early 1977, at around midnight, I set out with the local MPLA and Cuban commissars from the town of N'Giva on a hunting trip. The expedition was not, to British or American sensibilities, exactly sporting, but it showed that no one, in those first revolutionary days, was having it easy.

The lead Jeep occupied by the two commissars and their entourage was equipped with a spotlight, and the hunters carried AK-47 assault rifles, loaded with tracer rounds at frequent intervals in the magazine of 7.62mm intermediate ammunition—the standard Warsaw Pact infantry bullet.

The first target was a hare, startled from the bush at the roadside, transfixed in the glare of the spotlight. Some comradely etiquette obliged the Angolan to offer the Cuban first shot. Clad in a royal blue tracksuit and olive green forage cap, he bounded from the Jeep, stumbled, fell, righted himself, opened up. A round of green tracer zipped by the unfortunate animal, but did not hit it. Several more rounds followed, with an equal lack of accuracy. In confusion, the hare suddenly began hopping toward the Cuban commissar, obliging him to steadily lower his trajectory until he was virtually firing at his own feet. But the animal's apparently suicidal instinct did not waver, and neither did the commissar's aim improve. The hare finally hopped between the Cuban's legs, just as he fired the last bullet in the 30-round clip, spun around, and hurled his empty rifle at the fast-disappearing target. Round one to the fauna.

Other furry things were not so fortunate; as the night wore away, a heap of dead animals—small buck, rabbits, and so forth—built up in the Jeep I shared with other spectators and bodyguards. Ahead of us, the Real Men's Jeep bounced along through the bush, with the Cuban and Angolan commissars and various other comrades blazing away at anything that moved, filling the night with the sounds of advance by undisciplined infantry with unlimited access to ammunition. It struck me that, contrary to Luanda's propaganda in those days, neither the South Africans nor UNITA could be close by if we could embark on this jaunt with such impunity.

At dawn, we headed back to N'Giva, a town that was later to become South Africa's advance headquarters in Angola. First light was an idyll: clear, cool, still. The bushlands were flat, infinite, the new sky a great bowl. We drove past a large pond, tranquil as a mirror—two ducks sat in the middle. The new day was not to be so restful. Tires squealed, hunters loaded up. Various people opened fire with shotguns, AK-47s, and an old Portuguese Army-issue FN. Startled by the opening barrage, one duck flew off. The other sat on the pond, winged or dead, slowly being pushed toward the bank by the flying lead hitting the water. The Cuban's AK-47 ran out of ammunition, so he yanked a 9mm pistol from his belt and blazed away with that. The FN boomed in the hands of a white Portuguese Communist, liberated by the revolution. The MPLA commissar blasted his shotgun.

I vouchsafed to the Portuguese Communist that it did not seem very sporting to open fire, literally, on a sitting duck, and mentioned that, where I came from, it was regarded as the etiquette to try to hit the bird in flight. He scoffed at the idea, pointing out to me that a bird in flight had its wings extended, making it a much larger target. A bird with its wings folded, by contrast, was a much smaller target, and thus a more sporting prey. The discussion came to an end. A bodyguard was sent into the pond, his trousers rolled to his knees, to fish the bedraggled duck from the water, and the sorry bird took a place of honor atop the heap of bloodstained fur in the spectators' Jeep. I estimated that something on the order of eighty-nine rounds of rifle, pistol, and shotgun ammunition had been fired at it.

Much later, when we had all rested, I asked the large and bearded Portuguese Communist a question: who got the duck in the shareout of the spoils? He did, he said. But was it not so riddled with bullets as to be inedible, I asked. Not at all, he replied: it had been stunned by the ferocity of the onslaught, but had taken no terminal hits: it was still alive. This was the army that, according to its own propaganda, had routed imperialism and its flunkies. It did not say much for either side.

Chad was the only place I have ever visited where I had to ask the president, then Goukouni Oueddi, to cut short an interview so that I could catch the last canoe across the river before curfew. Chad was a place where warlords strutted before a muted people, almost inter-changeably. I interviewed Oueddi in 1981, and his capital was so battered by fighting that the phones, the telexes, the hotels—every-thing—simply did not work. The whole infrastructure of a tenuous modernity had literally been shot to pieces. The reason I had to take a dug-out across the Chari River was that the nearest telephone that could raise New York was 180 miles away in another country, Ca-meroon. It was located in the bar of a French-run hostel in Maroua. They served iced champagne with the phone call.

On my last visit, when a new president, Hissene Habre, was in power and the telephones and telexes had been restored, I rose early on the day of my departure and trudged through the unpaved streets at dawn to try to get a phone call through to Nairobi, where my family lived. It would not be easy because trans-Africa phone lines were nonexistent, a legacy of colonial days when communications ran north to the metropolis, not east-west within the competing spheres of foreign dominance, so I would have to reach Paris to talk to Nairobi. The feral dogs that snapped through the night slept in the sand around the peeling, shuttered villas. The heat was building, damp from the Chari River but not yet intolerable. The door to the telephone exchange, surrounded by dark, thick-leaved bushes, was open and I went in to find the international operator deep in a troubled sleep, clad in singlet and shorts, sprawled over the old wooden switchboard.

I roused him and booked the call. He began cranking the handle that supposedly activated the direct line to Paris. No one answered. He tried again and again, but still no one answered. I gave up on the call and headed back to the hotel to pack. In the quiet of the dawn I could still hear him trying to make the connection. " 'Allo Paris, 'allo Paris," he called, a dreadful lament. I thought nothing could be more callous or hurtful than the indifference of the operator at the other end, ignoring a plaintive, distant call from this lonely outpost. But as I headed south, for a new assignment and a new life in Johannesburg, events quickly proved me wrong.

PART TWO

TOWNSHIP RULES:

South Africa

8.

Adapt or Die:

White Choices

"This thing is going to cause a lot of ructions later."

AFRIKANER HOTELIER LEN VAN LOGGERENBERG, to the author, October 1983, discussing racial reform

Moving to South Africa in 1983, to live there as an uninvited, often unwelcome, witness to its turmoil raised in heightened form many of the same questions that confronted me when I first went to Africa in 1976. The easy part was to observe the fault lines. The hard part was to remain aloof. Racial zoning checkered the land, physically and emotionally. Apartheid had succeeded, possibly exceeding the wildest dreams of its creators. The land was splintered not only into separate, racially designated areas but also into separate realities.

In Alexandra black township two miles from my home in white Hurlingham, vendors sold the cheapest of cuts—chicken entrails, even claws—from street-corner containers made of plastic, and the men on the sanitation trucks that collected human sewage in buckets each day tossed the replacement empty buckets on broken streets like casual insults. One mile away, in an enormous, glitzy shopping complex called Sandton City, in "white" South Africa, a sleek man called Dennis Hotz offered different fare—Picassos and Chagalls sold as a hedge against the troubled times. Alongside, other stores were crammed with food, drink, clothes, records, tennis gear, golf clubs, crystal glasses, hi-fis, video cameras, knickknacks.

On Fridays, the vast parking lot at Sandton City filled with new model cars, Mercedes and BMWs popular among them, as whites shopped for the weekend—wine and steak and sausage for the cookout—then went home to neat homes like mine with lawns and walls and burglar alarms and pools. If you were a white and lived in white

135

South Africa, then you shopped, worked, existed in its exclusive embrace. The women who ran the checkouts at Sandton City, by contrast, were black and lived in Alexandra but traveled to "white" South Africa to work. So when they went home, they went home to mayhem and rage and deadly perils that few whites dreamed of, framed by the rule of the comrades and the counterrule of the police.

Apartheid did not just mean separated amenities, housing, schools, buses, but mutually exclusive visions of the same land. Most whites saw no real need to go to the segregated townships and steered well clear of them—a feat easily achieved since urban planning both reflected and bolstered the ideological commitment to apartheid. The highways between "white" settlements looped away from black areas; crossing half the nation on the Blue Train from Cape Town to Johannesburg, you could spend twenty-four hours in air-conditioned luxury and be made aware of black realities only by the signs espied on the station platforms along the journey: *Net Blankes*—Whites Only.

In a chi-chi restaurant in a white part of town (there were no restaurants, let alone chi-chi ones, in the black parts), I asked a group of sixteen young whites how many of them had ever been to a black township; only one admitted to crossing the tracks—during his call-up to the military, on patrol in enemy territory. Conversely, blacks had to come to "white" South Africa for virtually any job at all. They—the maids, the mechanics, the checkout clerks—knew how whites lived while whites did not know how blacks lived. So the blacks also knew intimately and at first hand the cruelties and discrepancies that many whites only sensed with guilt, unease, or indifference. The distinctions cut through the land, while the system maintained the white cocoon that allowed many whites to simply look the other way.

From afar, South Africa seemed like some great and sinister dynamo, whirring with passion and emotion, generating power and drama, sparks crackling from its gigantic superstructure. From close range, though, the gears were not quite in mesh, the machine trembled under its own massive power, and the sparks that flew from it were the paradoxes, the contradictions that threatened self-destruction even as they were accepted as the norm.

In tangled bush each year at a place called Silkaatsnek near Johannesburg, Afrikaner extremists staged a stylized historical pageant depicting the burning by blacks of their ox-drawn wagon during the Great

Trek of 1838. They dressed in the clothes of the nineteenth century. They rode horses. They mimicked rifle fire from the laager. They feigned death at black hands. They sang hymns. Betsy Verwoerd, the widow of Hendrik Verwoerd—one of apartheid's grand architects—arrived in an old Jaguar sedan escorted by horseback riders. No blacks, the organizers told me pointedly, were invited to this tribal rite.

But there was one black there, and his presence seemed to say a lot about what was happening in South Africa. Everyone ignored him and he crouched out of sight, as if not really there at all, a non-person. Yet his job was crucial—to open and close the gas-cylinder nozzles that controlled the simulated conflagration.

White South Africans often accused reporters of distorting the imagery of their land. But, really, the problem lay in perceptions: outsiders saw glaring paradoxes where insiders saw only the norms they had grown used to, drawing solace and redemption from the official conceit that South Africa contained the First and Third Worlds simultaneously.

That was a way of explaining the huge gap between white wealth and black poverty, but the argument omitted a central factor: policies of racial separation since the Land Act of 1913 had nurtured Third World poverty by restricting the majority of the population to a fraction of the land. Apartheid's founders had defined blacks as "temporary sojourners" who were not really there at all in "white" South Africa. So, if their presence was temporary anyway, why encourage them to stay by spending good money on their schools, electric power for their homes, asphalt to cover their dirt roads? Visitors from Latin America said, sure, they knew all about slums and poverty. What shocked them was that South Africa was a very rich country; the slums grew by design and from wilful neglect. This was not simply the result of organic decay in the penurious Third World.

As an outsider, a reporter could delve into both realities and lead a double life, Beverly Hills and Beirut, all in the same day, without breaking stride. Where else could a journalist cover raw, bloody, and terminal conflict two miles from home, then return to find lunch guests frolicking in the pool, beating yellow high-altitude tennis balls on the all-weather tennis court while the smoke rose from the cookout; or arrive for dinner, aquiver with adrenaline from some horror of street warfare, and be asked by a host in a dining room bathed in candlelight, hung with silk tapestries: "Is there trouble in the locations, then?"

The wars in Angola, Mozambique, and Zimbabwe had finally filtered down to the irreducible core: the conflict of the mid-1980s between South Africa's "comrades" and the authorities, between black and white, rich and poor, African and Afrikaner—two nationalisms competing for the same land.

The confrontation raged from September 1984 to early 1987. As President P. W. Botha sought to implant political reforms—and because of the nature of those reforms, first announced in 1983—the battles were fought that would lead ultimately to the freeing of Nelson Mandela and the beginnings of negotiation, of the attempt to reconcile the competing realities that apartheid had so deftly cemented in place since the rise of Afrikaner absolute power in 1948.

Protest on the streets inspired Botha to impose emergency rule—an acknowledgment of political failure. In response, the outside world—bankers and governments—imposed sanctions. American companies shed their holdings. The economy fell. But President Botha's message to those who challenged his writ was no retreat, no surrender. This was the last chapter, the assault on the most powerful and oldest of the alien wizards who had brought their magic to Africa with a Bible in one hand and a whip in the other.

In its ferocity this struggle shook everybody—big business, government, the churches, the black majority. It forced choices on people who did not want to make them. And it showed again that there could be no change without violence.

South Africa demands confession with the insistence of a priest. If you live there, people expect moral acrobatics to justify the fact. And people who care, but don't live there, weep for its sins in vicarious expurgation of other guilts they would rather not confront.

For what it's worth, my confession goes something like this: South Africa brought me up short against the same issues that consumed it—race, identity, and history.

The school atlases in Manchester had told me I was part of it, for it was British Empire, not Afrikaner nationalism, that laid the grid of racial separation in South Africa before apartheid's formulation in

1948. Yet my job at *The New York Times* was to be an objective observer.

Part of me—the parent, the individual, the residual adolescent romantic—told me I was on the side of the oppressed. Another part—my skin color, my passport, my fear, my pool and tennis court—told me that I was not.

I led the double life that produces the hypocrisy of the liberal equation: white privilege plus white conscience equals a very luxurious form of guilt—angst in the swimming pool, anguish on the golf course, righteous anger at the pass raid on the servants' quarters. I was not killing for it, or dying for it, so I was not part of it; it was not my war, but I was drawn to it by covering it, far more intimately than many South African whites, so I could not help but feel the wrench of its opposing forces. I was scorned by the government for supposed bias toward the black cause. But those same people I was purportedly championing threw rocks and gasoline bombs at my car because my skin was the color of the master race created by apartheid.

Racism ran through Africa like an electric current, from the expatriate British mining technicians in northern Zambia who scorned all Zambians to the hooker in Bangui—the land of the cannibal-emperor Jean-Bédel Bokassa—who told me I was a racist because I declined her cheap and statistically hazardous favors. It was implicit in the ideological contortions of white liberals in Rhodesia and in the arrogance of Nigerian cab drivers. It raged openly from the white right in South Africa, and burned in the black left. White liberalism—the desire for accommodation—seemed an attempt to seek racial redemption where none was either needed or likely to be granted.

In the end, as in the countries to the north, I took refuge in the objectivity demanded by my job: reporting on the situation was a clear enough statement of aloofness. But the questions persisted: How could I tell myself I was not somehow to blame for the sins of others when I partook so easily of the privileges they bestowed? How could I rest within the laager without acknowledging a debt to those who constructed it? And how could I then function as a journalist if I labored under a burden of guilt whose impact might cause me to invert the prejudices of apartheid and frame my perceptions of the land between black heroism and white nastiness? Ultimately, I had to remind myself of the message that Archbishop Desmond M. Tutu kept on offering to the authorities. Are we not people, he would say; when you tickle us, do we not laugh; and when you hurt us, do we not cry? Was it impossibly self-deluding, I would ask myself, to apply the same standards to my luxuriant self-questioning, too? End of confession.

In October 1983, South Africa had seemed, misleadingly, to be held in a kind of stasis. The legislation enacted in the early 1950s and onward, the very foundation of apartheid, seemed immutably in place. In a way it had worked even as it began to self-destruct. Interracial marriage or sexual relationships were banned. If you were white, you lived in a whites-only suburb, as the Group areas Act of 1950 intended. If you were black, you lived in a township, according to the same legislation. The schools, parks, buses, beaches were mostly segregated. So were the liquor stores. One, in some small village out in the wheat country of the Transvaal, boasted a low brick wall between the counter and the store window to show where the division lay. Most had separate entrances for whites and non-whites. At birth, you were registered by race, according to the terms of one of apartheid's central laws—the Population Registration Act of 1950 that, in effect, meant that physical attributes (skin color, physiognomy, even the crinkliness of hair) predetermined the life that lay ahead. At death, you were buried in racially pure cemeteries. And the black homelands were separated by tribe. If you were a Zulu, you lived in Zululand, just as the Xhosas lived in the Transkei and the Ciskei, the Tswanas in Bophuthatswana, the Pedis in Lebowa, the Vendas in Venda.

The fundamental premise of South Africa's homelands was that the basic unit of black identity was the tribe, as reflected variously in language, custom, tradition, and geography. Tribal systems and antagonisms predated apartheid, but, in its pursuit of social engineering, apartheid exploited them in particularly nasty way: once he or she became part of a nominally independent homeland, a black South African lost all claim to South African citizenship and virtually all hope of a job except as a migrant or commuter to some distant white city across a frontier marked not by a fence but by economic disparity.

Some of the homelands—Bophuthatswana in particular—were so fragmented among disconnected parcels of land that you could drive in and out and through several times a day on the same highway without changing course; only the contrast between rich, white land and the scrawny soil of the homeland indicated that a frontier had been crossed at all. The homelands were repositories for unwanted blacks denied official residence in the townships. They offered employers cheap labor and blacks false and unaccepted notions of nationhood—tribes with phony flags. Even the legislation that provided for their creation in 1959 bore a title that summed up the underlying hypocrisy: it was called the "Act for the promotion of Bantu self-government."

Their history had been one of cruelty and displacement.

In 1913, the original Natives' Land Act—approved by the British Parliament in London—barred blacks from owning land in all but 7.5 percent of South Africa's surface area. Overnight, 1 million people—a quarter of the black population at that time, and one fifth of the overall population of the Union of South Africa—were made landless and homeless.

Further legislation in 1936 expanded the land available for black ownership to 13 percent. But the black "reserves" were always mean, overcrowded places whose purpose was to provide a pool of labor and to facilitate white settlement of expropriated land.

Neither were the options particularly alluring. Even before the turn of the century, black migration to the cities was hindered by pieces of paper called "Native Labor Passports" held by the white employer. Without such a document, blacks would be sent back to the land— the direct forerunners of the notorious pass laws by which the Afrikaners strove to keep white South Africa white.

But since the Afrikaners' National Party had come to power in 1948, there had been a fundamental demographic shift, and it forced P. W. Botha into what, for him, was an equally fundamental reappraisal— one that would not only have a profound bearing on black lives but divide his own tribe, too.

The economy needed humans to make it work, so that increasingly over the years a category had arisen called "urban blacks," who had special permits and limited rights—residential, not political—under Section 10 of the Group Areas Act to exist in the segregated townships.

From the nineteenth century onward, as South Africa's industrialization and enrichment advanced, the townships had grown as segregated residential areas for the blacks who provided the labor for an expanding and increasingly sophisticated economy. And, as always, there was a catch. While some legislation—the pass laws—strove to limit the size of the townships, other laws, notably the successive Land Acts, ensured that blacks could not make a viable living in the rural areas assigned to them. So they headed for the townships to look for work, braving the pass laws that provided for them to be punished for doing so. Between them, two titans of apartheid legislation contrived to defeat one another.

Geographically, the townships lay apart from the "white" city centers and residential areas. Urban planning kept them that way. Over the years, Soweto, outside Johannesburg, grew into a place of 2 million souls; but the broad freeway curving around it and leading from Johannesburg to other white cities offered only two access roads to this black metropolis.

Apartheid, the Afrikaans word, literally means "separateness" or "apartness," and that was the townships' political significance, too; they were never designed to grow as organic settlements offering blacks a permanent place in "white" South Africa.

The evolution of "urban blacks," forced on white planners by economic growth, defied apartheid's design. Now, as P. W. Botha surveyed his fief, he confronted 9 million black permanent residents of urban areas where apartheid's original design had foreseen only "temporary sojourners."

By the canons of traditional apartheid, their real home was in the so-called "homelands," not in white South Africa. But economic reality and apartheid's dreams had not overlapped. Botha's mission was to somehow synchronize white control and black numbers. What he and his followers had to do, he said as he coined his slogan for the era, was "adapt or die."

Inadvertently, the motto assumed a far more macabre and direct meaning for the hundreds of blacks who did die in the protest of the mid-1980s. But what the South African leader was telling his white constituents was that the old order had to be modified if whites were to maintain what he called their identity—a notion sustainable only by continued control of the way they lived.

In 1983, thus, he unveiled a program of political changes that would give those defined as Indians and those defined as "Colored"—that is, of mixed race—a junior role in Parliament and token representation in the government. They would have their own, separate councils to deliberate their "own affairs"—health care, education, and so forth. They would elect their representatives from among their communities. But on the wider issues of how the country was run, they would remain subservient to the numerically superior white Parliament and cabinet.

The black majority was excluded from the offer of change, whose racial arithmetic suggested that if the whites could co-opt the browns into their system, then, numerically, non-blacks would almost equal the number of "urban blacks" and thus have less to fear. The proposed changes shifted the color bar: traditionally, the distinction lay between white and non-white. Now, Botha suggested that it divide black and non-black. The reforms provided exactly the rallying point that apartheid's adversaries had been awaiting, and so Botha inadvertently sealed his own destiny by embarking not, as Beaufre, the French strategist, had suggested, on "thorough-going reforms . . . [that] cut the ground from under the feet of the malcontents," but on halfhearted and cynical reforms that really gave the malcontents something to be malcontent about.

As the protests unfolded, it became the fashion in the United States and elsewhere to argue that Botha's reform program had raised black expectations that their chance was coming, too, that the hope among the majority for a new way of living automatically implied some upheaval. But from my own conversations with those excluded from what Mr. Botha called his "new dispensation," it seemed that the opposite was true: there was no hope or expectation; Mr. Botha had closed the door, collectively, in the face of 23 million people.

In October 1983, few in South Africa foresaw the extent of the looming upheaval—least of all a newly arrived reporter from the black north. My particular category of person—a white who had lived under black rule—drew different responses than it had done in Rhodesia. Here, in South Africa, I was told by any number of white officials and business leaders that things were much more complex, that this was not a homogeneous society, that the mechanisms of black Africa's decolonization could not be applied, that I should change my way of seeing things to encompass this complexity. Those same conversations also convinced me that many white South Africans were ill-prepared for the changes that would be forced on their way of seeing things.

One of my first appointments was at the great stone monolith of a building that squats at 44 Main Street, Johannesburg—the headquarters of Anglo-American Corporation, South Africa's biggest multinational conglomerate, which owns gold mines and diamond mines and newspapers and, through very complicated cross-holdings, a stake in most other things in South Africa, too. There, in the Chairman's Dining Room, against the backdrop of a tapestry showing hunting scenes, I had lunch with some members of the board—Gavin Relly, the chairman, most prominent amongst them. My suggestion that the answer lay in majority rule was, I seem to recall, pretty well laughed out of court as simplistic, and the conversation turned to constitutional "models": which model should apply for the South African government of the future—the Canadian system, perhaps, or the Swiss, or the Australian?

The conversation seemed to imply a line at the Limpopo between Africa as such and South Africa, altogether a different and separate subcontinent—spiritually, politically, and philosophically. It was easy to understand their point. Sitting among them in the paneled elegance of the Chairman's Dining Room, almost literally atop the great seams of gold that made South Africa so rich, was like sitting in some stratospheric capsule, looking down on a distant world while debating its issues and problems. Anglo's directors were, of course, acutely aware of the perils and difficulties inherent in the land—and in the way they had grown rich from it. But their computations were implicitly based on the notion that their Afrikaner compatriots would hold the stockade while the requisite "model" was located and put into place to secure the future of the free market. Like the African National Congress in Lusaka, and the government in Pretoria itself, they did not seem to include in their calculations the enormous passions that were to burst upon the nation, demanding not models, nor Swiss or Canadian or Australian ways of doing things, but exactly the same as the rest of Africa had achieved—majority rule.

In those first few days and weeks in South Africa, I had to acknowledge that this was indeed a different land than I had known in most of black-ruled Africa. White South Africa was big, rich, efficient, abundant. There was no colonial power to fold the tent when the campaign was done, and the Afrikaners were not about to become "when-we's" in some other place as whites in Kenya or Rhodesia had done, earning the sobriquet with self-pitying reminiscences that began "When we were in Kenya . . ." or "When we were in Rhodesia . . ." The Afrikaners had nowhere else to go. And part of the distinction lay in the perceptions of who exactly was oppressing—or was likely to oppress—whom.

From the outside looking in, South Africa was a cartoonist's image: white jackboot on black neck. In essence, that was the reality. But for the Afrikaners, looking out at the great wave of majority rule pressing down from the north, the view was different, drawing on an older mythology.

Deon du Plessis, a massively built Afrikaner journalist of Huguenot stock, given to pumping iron, drinking vast quantities of beer, and depicting his tribe in terms he thought foreigners ought to understand, described what he said was the scenario that haunted his people: they would be sitting, encamped, around the fire, the wagons drawn up, when all about was dark. Then in the gloom, like fireflies, the enemy eyes would begin to glint, and, using their codewords, the Afrikaners would begin to signal their defenses. "The eyes, the eyes," he said lugubriously, as if that specter of being crept up on in the dark was what most troubled his people. Afrikaner history was punctuated by those eyes—and the lessons learned in the wars with those who peered from them.

The Voortrekker Monument—the huge granite temple of Afrikanerdom just outside Pretoria—depicts, in a vast wall-frieze hewn of stone, the progression of the Great Trek of 1838 from the oppression of British liberalism in the Cape to the treachery of Dingane, the Zulu leader, shortly before the Battle of Blood River in the Transvaal.

In February 1838, Dingane lured Piet Retief and many of his followers to his kraal, and ordered his warriors to fall upon them. "*Bambani abaThakathi!*" he told them—"Kill the Wizards!" Then he sent his impis—warrior battalions—to massacre the women and children in their covered wagons in the foothills of the Drakensberg Mountains. In response, the following December, a commando of 464 Afrikaners under Andries Pretorius moved into Dingane's territory with 64 wagons and 3 cannon. As they advanced, they offered a covenant to God: if he would "deliver the enemy into our hands," then Afrikanerdom would keep the day of the battle a holy day forever. On December 15, 1838, the commando drew the wagons into a laager on the banks of the Ncome River.

The Zulus, numbering 10,000, struck on December 16. In six hours, they lost 3,000 men and the Ncome River turned red with their blood to give it its new name. Pretorius's trekkers sustained only three injuries. With God—and guns—on their side, the Afrikaners had won, and December 16 remains holy, even though the official history omits to mention that black cattle hands and mixed-race grooms for the horses were inside the laager at the time—evidence, perhaps, of a racial symbiosis some Afrikaners would rather ignore. The Battle of Blood River is woven into the Afrikaner myth, as is Dingane, the symbol of the adversary, reincarnated since those days in Godless communism and the ANC. The mythology made talk of change all the more difficult for many Afrikaners to accept. Blood River was not the only battle as the Afrikaners fought to carve out—and sustain— their own Boer republics, the Transvaal and the Orange Free State.

From 1899 to 1902, they waged and lost a war for freedom and self-determination against the British—just as many other African tribes and peoples were to do—and they suffered. Their women and children were incarcerated in concentration camps, and thousands died. The Afrikaner farmers—the Boers—fought their adversaries as mobile commandoes on horseback, raiding and harassing, when the setpiece battles were lost. The war bred the "bitter-enders"—a tradition of Afrikaner extremist prepared for no compromise.

They saw themselves as the oppressed, or likely to be, if they did not guarantee their own future against the depradations of the British and the Zulus. That was the view cultivated by the National Party as it built its base in the 1930s, when the Afrikaners had yet to move in large numbers to the cities and the messianic imagery of the oxwagon, the Bible and the land, the Great Trek and the Anglo-Boer War, found its echo among the rural white poor struggling with depression and hard times. The National Party thrived, driven by believers, like the youthful P. W. Botha, who achieved a reputation for disrupting his adversaries' political meetings, and strengthened by Afrikaner urbanization that spread the power base into the cities. There a new kind of Afrikaner seemed to emerge.

The oxcart endured in pageant and mythology. Yet there was nothing particularly heroic or messianic about its contemporary image of large men in over-powered pickup trucks packing .357 magnums in the glove compartment in the manner of some parts of rural America. Indeed, modern Afrikaners seemed to draw a new self-image from the United States. Texans were a popular brand of toasted, unfiltered cigarette. Once, checking into a small rural hotel in the eastern Transvaal, I asked the owner—an Afrikaner—if I could have some sandwiches. "You'll have to wait," he said ponderously and with a secret smile, "because the ladies is watching *Dallas*." It was raining heavily that night, and when the owner assigned a black retainer to show me to the rondavel in which I'd be sleeping, he did so with the injunction to me: "Don't let him in the car." So, to my shame, the man ran ahead of me, in the headlights and the rain, and I did nothing to stop him.

For all the trappings of modernity—the urban life, the V-8 engines, and the heavy pistols—when the eyes began peering through the gloom, the old images and reflexes revived. This time, in the early 1980s, there was a critical difference. The unity of purpose the Afrikaners had displayed at the Battle of Blood River—and for over a century afterwards—had begun to fray. Since 1948, the National Party had been Afrikanerdom's great political monolith, solid as the Voortrekker Monument itself. Now, talk of reform fissured its very foundations.

While President Botha encouraged a new, white constituency of predominantly urban Afrikaners and English speakers who believed they had to change a little to maintain control, those who dissented staked out the conservative ground to the right (such labels, of course, were relative). In 1982, Dr. Andries P. Treurnicht led his supporters in forming the breakaway Conservative Party, committed to reviving those same canons of traditional apartheid as Botha seemed to deny. The result was a seismic shift in the line-up of white politics. During the long years of unquestioned National Party unity, parliamentary opposition had come from a small group of relative liberals grouped in the Progressive Federal Party and committed to modest reform. Now, the center of gravity shifted, and the Conservative Party became the official opposition in Parliament. White opposition thus no longer meant liberalism, but revolt from within the most conservative clans of the Afrikaner tribe. In Afrikaans, they called it a *broedertwis*—a feud between brothers, all the more bitter for sundering the family. The distinctions became apparent in the referendum Mr. Botha held in November 1983 on his reform package—a white ballot on the future of non-whites which specifically excluded the people the reform was supposed to benefit; only whites were entitled to cast a ballot. Botha secured 66 percent of the vote and called it a mandate. "It is a decisive majority in favor of the attempt to secure security, peace, stability and prosperity for South Africa," he said. "The Government now feels strengthened to go ahead with proper and evolutionary reform for South Africa." But that was only one way of reading the bones. The turnout represented only three quarters of the eligible white voters, so that meant that fully one half of the white electorate was either unconvinced or indifferent or against.

"As far as we are concerned, the nearly 700,000 'no' votes are a very firm base on which the freedom of the whites will be won again." Dr. Treurnicht declared.

But that begged questions. What was "the freedom of the whites"? When had they lost it? Was it solely a freedom to dominate? It came back to the same issue of the entire era for black and white alike: choosing between confrontation and acquiescence to secure a niche in a future that offered no one any certainties. When the eyes began to glisten, two people whose names sounded similar but who were not at all similar offered me some insight into the choices they had made. Their stories showed just how much P. W. Botha had asked of his people.

Ora Terblanche was an amply proportioned widow in her sixties who ran the Highlands Guest Farm near the small village of Hobhouse in the Orange Free State. Eugene Terre Blanche, a bearded, blue-eyed man in his early forties, led the Afrikaner Resistance movement, an extremist organization that owed a lot in its style to Nazism. In French, *Terre Blanche* means "White Earth." Conversations with these two people in different places left me feeling that both of them saw their very nomenclature under challenge.

When she voted in the 1983 referendum, Ora Terblanche told me, she voted yes, in favor of Mr. Botha's reform program. "It was not because my heart told me so; it told me quite the opposite," she said. "It was because my head told me to. Things have changed; we have to go forward, not backward."

She was sixty-six years old when I spoke with her in August 1984, as the country readied itself for elections among Indians and mixed-race people supposed to breathe life into the "new dispensation." (Instead, these elections would largely be boycotted, stripping the reforms of legitimacy.)

Mrs. Terblanche was the descendant of Afrikaners who had trekked for ninety-eight days from the Cape to the Orange Free State—a province so profoundly conservative in racial attitudes that people of Indian descent were officially barred from even spending the night there. That did not hold out much hope for black advance on those great estates of corn and wheat that led the eye to distant horizons and the mountains of Lesotho. But Mrs. Terblanche had concluded that whites had to be more generous with power. "We have to," she said. "We are outnumbered."

She was not easy with the whole business. It was something she would rather not face. Her life had been built around Afrikanerdom's basic mythology. She believed blacks still needed to be fundamentally civilized—the messianic role that Afrikaners had ascribed to themselves in Africa. She had decorated a wall with a framed montage of her tribe's heroes and statesmen—Paul Kruger and Hendrik Verwoerd and D. F. Malan. She gave her black workers gifts of practical things—sets of cups and saucers, pots and pans—but she had not increased their cash earnings for years so as not to "spoil" them. When she sat down to dinner, she said grace in the prayers of the Dutch Reformed Church that offered apartheid a spiritual counterpoint by segregating church services and clerics themselves according to race—white, "Colored," and black in separate branches of the church. Echoing words I had heard before in Africa, she said she understood "these people"— the blacks—because she had grown up with them and spoke their language. She summoned one maid by bell, spoke to her in a Sotho dialect, and required her to wear white gloves to pour the tea. (Even her pet parrot was trilingual in English, Afrikaans, and South Sotho.) Yet, she also required her maids to take turns sleeping in a cot at the foot of her bed in case she needed help rising in the night. And, in a way, she was inseparable from them: I could not imagine Ora anywhere else, or any way different.

When the maids' husbands got drunk and nasty, she said, she'd take her late husband's old revolver and wave it at them to make them go away. And, though she had voted for it, she was not sure about even the most cautious change. She believed in "these people" as individuals in an assigned role, in the fixed relationship that she had inherited from her forebears. She had no faith in their collective goodwill or their collective readiness to remodel the old relationship in a way that did not threaten her. "My people here on the farm would not murder me in the night," she told me. "They might go to the next farm and murder my neighbor. And my neighbor's lot might murder me." She paused a little over the tea and cakes, then said: "There's a kind of loyalty in that."

Eugene Terre Blanche had no such doubts and was not looking for black loyalty, either. Terre Blanche was a former policeman and cattle farmer. He liked to ride horses and dress in the kneebreeches his forebears wore as they launched their sorties against the British and the blacks. His overt following was limited, but his strident bullhorn of a voice found secret echoes among many. At his office in Pretoria, unusually in South Africa, a white acolyte brought the visitor's tea or coffee; there would be no sullying of the vision—or physical threat— from black retainers. And no black would work there, either. That was the only point of agreement between Terre Blanche and the black majority.

"There is only one Volk in South Africa and that is the Afrikaner Boer," he told me, his bright blue eyes lighting with visionary fire. What he was saying was that in white South Africa, only one group of people—the Afrikaners—had the cohesive identity that imparted true nationhood. "With the Afrikaner Boer, I can stand along with any other nation and ask for myself the same as other nations demand for themselves."

Under the "new dispensation," he insisted, Mr. Botha was leading the Afrikaners on the road to surrender, and that was something Terre

Blanche's movement would never accept as it fought for an independent Afrikaner state.

"We will be there when this government capitulates, that you can be sure of. We will take back our land and we will immediately give our people a people's state. If this government hands over its power to enforce law-and-order, and law-and-order perishes, we will not run like the people of Angola or Mozambique did, or like in the rest of Africa," he said. "I will never let the ANC, which is Communist-inspired, murdering gangs, take over my country. I will fight until the end. And I believe we are in for the worst bloodshed Africa has ever known."

In a way, with all its mumbo-jumbo and Masonic signs, the AWB was faintly ridiculous. The Afrikaans name *Afrikaner Weerstandsbeweging* meant "Afrikaner Resistance Movement," and it fought with several thousand followers to establish an exclusively white state within South Africa. The name evoked old notions of perceived heroism. Its adversaries were not exclusively blacks; whites seen as seeking appeasement were also the foe. It took as its emblem a swastikalike jagged star, made up, I was told, of the three sevens—an allusion to the seven angels, seven stars, and seven seals of the Revelation of St. John the Divine that were the antithesis of the three sixes, the mark of the devil. The emblem was topped by a silver eagle that looked as if it had been designed in Nuremberg in about 1936. Terre Blanche's supporters chanted the Afrikaans initials of the organization—*Aaah-Veeya-Beeya*—as if they were chanting "*Sieg Heil.*" Terre Blanche adopted the brusque open-palm salute of the Fuehrer himself as he inspected his paramilitary platoons with their sand-colored uniforms and gave them names like "Storm Falcons" and "Fire Watch." In his youth, his associates told me, he had been engrossed with the history of Nazism. He went out of his way to say he was neither racist nor anti-Semitic, but the fact that he raised the subjects without even being asked seemed to undermine his gratuitous denials. Now this small, bearded man was playing out his adolescent fantasies to a crazy audience on the far-right fringes of white uncertainty and fear. And he filled the persona with a rhetorical style acknowledged even by his adversaries.

On a stage in Durban one night in late 1986, hectoring and roaring in a silvery suit, the eagle and the emblem caught cobalt blue in the spotlights, he conjured an oratorical force that was almost tangible, evoking a vision of the *Boerestaat*, an independent Afrikaner state like those of the nineteenth century, in which the farmer-warrior would, Terre Blanche claimed, redeem the dream of freedom and self-determination.

The following day, as he snoozed in Coach on the flight back to Johannesburg, he seemed crumpled and exhausted and small, as if, without the lights, the microphones, and the stage props, he had no reality and was a hollow thing inflated only by rhetoric. Indeed, a couple of years later Terre Blanche was diminished even further when it came to light that he had formed a friendship with a white, English-speaking newspaper columnist with whom, one night, he had driven his car through the fence at an Afrikaner monument. Such liaisons and irresponsibility did not measure up to the Calvinistic standards of Afrikaner faith and purity that he so often evoked, especially not extra-tribal liaisons with a *rooinek* or redneck, as Afrikaners called whites of English descent because of their propensity for sunburn. The Fuehrer was supposed to know better.

Yet there was an incident in Terre Blanche's past that summed up the real danger he presented. In November 1983, he and two aides were given suspended jail terms for illegal possession of weapons, including Soviet-made AK-47 assault rifles—the weapon of choice among black insurgents. As reform gathered pace in the 1990s, more-over, it was AWB supporters who translated the rhetoric into action with assassination plots and the murders of blacks. What Terre Blanche really represented was not the vision of order in an Afrikaner state, but the specter of vengeful, racial bloodshed in whatever land emerged from the promises of change. And he existed only because he offered one, extreme answer to the same question that challenged the entire country: Where do we go from here?

Terre Blanche talked in terms of apocalypse and survival, but for the black majority, the realities were much more immediate. The exclusion of blacks from the reforms of 1983 led directly to resistance and protest. As President Botha scheduled his referendum that fall, his adversaries marshaled their forces for the fight to come by creating the United Democratic Front (UDF), an umbrella of myriad anti-apartheid movements that drew inspiration from the still-outlawed

African National Congress. And when protest took root in September 1984, it began a cycle of killings and burials and more killings that set the land on course for upheaval, emergency rule, and even deeper international isolation. The bloodshed spread far and wide, consuming the land. To try to grasp how it had come about, it was sometimes easier to look at the smaller places, the crucibles of revolt.

9

State of Emergency:

Living by the Sword

in South Africa

"There can be no turning back."

—P. W. BOTHA to a National Party rally in Durban, July
1985

I had come to cover a funeral in a place called Cradock. It was
a time of many funerals—political funerals—in South Africa,
but this one was different.

In the violent, emotional years after nationwide black revolt began
in September 1984, mass funerals had become the shifting focus of
what both blacks and whites depicted as a revolution. Sometimes,
these sad, intense occasions were no more than amorphous outpourings
of rage and grief at the death of young people elevated from obscurity
only because they had died in the daily confrontation between the
authorities and the foot soldiers of the revolt. But at other times, they
were a barometer of protest, a way of gauging the strength of the
challenge against apartheid. Apart from funerals and sporting events,
blacks had no other lawful means of gathering in large numbers, so
what was said by political leaders on these occasions—and the way
the messages of protest and insurrection were received by their audiences—assumed an overwhelming importance.

In July 1985, in Cradock, there was another factor which I tried to
ignore at the time: I had known, liked, and respected the dead, and
could not easily watch the burial of Matthew Goniwe, Fort Calata,
and the two others with the dispassion reporters are somehow supposed
to display on such occasions.

Only a few months earlier, I had come to know Goniwe in particular
as a deceptively mild-looking schoolteacher leading a revolt in his

small and fiery township on the Fish River in the distant reaches of the Eastern Cape. More than many other activists, he had helped me try to understand how this revolution tried to work. When he and his three colleagues were murdered in mysterious circumstances in late June, I felt a personal loss.

Far more important, though, his funeral was different because its message of dissent—borne by 35,000 mourners and representing the central challenge to President P. W. Botha's program of reform—was delivered at a point of no return.

On the very same day as the burial, after nine months of violent protest scouring the land, the authorities finally acknowledged their inability to deal with the revolt through anything but force. At midnight, they issued the first of a series of emergency decrees that were intended to strangle protest. Tacitly, the decree acknowledged a great political failure, shaping the future in ways Botha could not bring himself to imagine. His limited offer of change, his "new dispensation" had been destroyed by those same people it rejected—the black majority; the velvet glove, anyhow threadbare, fell away altogether.

What the emergency decree said was this: in thirty-six magisterial districts around Johannesburg and Port Elizabeth, including Cradock, all security forces would henceforth wield limitless rights of arrest without charge, detention without trial, and search without warrant. The usual paperwork that accompanied South Africa's draconian security laws, predating the emergency, fell away. The officers who enforced the decree could not be prosecuted for crimes committed in the process; curfews and press censorship could be imposed; reporters, or anybody else for that matter, could be ordered out of any area; and those detained had no access to lawyers, friends, help. Within five days, nine hundred people—all but a handful black—had been arrested in massive police sweeps, pre-dawn raids, the full repertoire of oppression whose rhythm is set by the 3:00 A.M. beating on the door, the dogs, the guns. Within ten days, mass funerals had been outlawed under the terms of the decree, itself declared under the Public Security Act of 1954—a legal veneer that reflected the authorities' overweening desire to be seen as custodians of law, Christian values, and constitutional power, playing by the rules of the Western community of nations to which they so urgently wanted to belong and from which they so rapidly excluded themselves. For their adversaries, however, the state of emergency was not so much a legislative decree as the acknowledgment of a state of mind: it was the bully's stick, the false strut of the fearful in enemy terrain.

On Saturday, July 20, 1985, as the funeral approached, no one except the authorities knew of the momentous change that was coming, or that the announcement would catch so many activists in such an out-of-the-way spot; as a town, Cradock was far more a symbol of protest than a place in which you would choose to spend a weekend.

In earlier times, it had grown as one of those small and obscure outcrops of humanity that seemed to signal an immutable order established when the National Party of Malan and Verwoerd took power in 1948 and embarked on the Grand Design of separation, rooted in the notion of ethnic difference and distinction, of a land composed of many "nations" that should be kept apart from one another to develop in their own way, at their own pace, under the tutelage of a white "nation" that, implicitly, would always remain supreme. The white part of town was neat, tended, orderly. The segregated black township, where the funeral was to take place, bespoke all the injustices that underlay its very existence in Africa's richest land: minute homes cramped together without electric power or running water; cracked, unpaved streets scarred and seamed by rivers of rain; and ragged children born to a system created to deny them a hope of escape.

Yet, months before the nationwide protest, boycotts, and confrontation that began to spread in September 1984, this small place had simply gone ahead and shaken the racial grid that apartheid sought to glue in place against the forces of economic and demographic change. Hundreds of miles from the glamour of Cape Town and Johannesburg and the big-name players who made the headlines, Cradock had proceeded with its own revolution and, in microcosm, had foreshadowed everything that was to happen across South Africa in the decisive and bloody years that readied the land for change. While Mr. Botha's policies beyond his borders—in Mozambique and Angola and Zimbabwe—spread a lesson of subservience to the Afrikaner will, Matthew Goniwe had taught his young black "comrades" different notions, shedding fatalism for activism, believing that, somehow or other, they could translate their dreams into a new reality. "The people," Goniwe once told me, "have come to realize that they can defy the government." Leading them to that realization had been his principal achievement.

Goniwe, a spare, bespectacled headmaster in his late thirties, had been ordered to Cradock from the Transkei black "homeland" as a punishment because of his reputation as a political activist—worse yet, a Communist. The move did not subdue him. He had molded Cradock the black township into a place that established its own alternative authority to Cradock the small white town nearby whose neat villas and lace curtains offered the familiar emblems of white conservatism. Goniwe's message was that, through organization and forethought, the township's blacks could free themselves of the paternalism implicit in apartheid's distinctions and, thereby, achieve a kind of autonomy that challenged the sense of inferiority apartheid was supposed to nurture. Cradock township formed its own organization, Cradora, to run its affairs: on the day of the week when the state pensions were paid out—an excitable moment prone to argument and obstreperousness—the white plainclothes officer with the pistol on his hip bowed to the authority of Matthew Goniwe to settle any disputes that might arise. When Goniwe's pupils started boycotting classes to protest his suspension as headmaster in February 1984, the white authorities were powerless to stop them. Indeed, his message survived him. The school boycott endured long after he and his three colleagues were murdered in mid-1985; some students stayed out of class for three years, simply to defy the official edict ordering them to return.

Several months before the funeral, Mark Peters, the photographer, and I had visited Cradock to find out why the people there thought the tiny ramshackle township with its unpaved streets and matchbox homes had achieved such a reputation.

Lingelihle—as the segregated black township was officially known—was not just a township but a kind of revolutionary connoisseur's township, small and compact, a laboratory of protest. Even its name was politically charged: rather than accept the official distinction between "white" Cradock and "black" Lingelihle, Goniwe and his followers insisted that their segregated township was called Cradock, too. But they could not change apartheid's geography.

The township was invisible from most of the white town, literally over the hill. A highway and scrubland, moreover, separated the black township from the adjacent "Colored" township. Between the two creations of apartheid, children sold windmills made of wire, driven by a solid, stiff breeze that picked up garbage and deposited it on the scrub so that the notional line between black and brown lives resembled an untended cemetery. Driving north or south, you could miss Lingelihle simply by looking the other way for a couple of seconds—as the burghers of the white town had done over a much longer span of time. That was the intention of apartheid's planners. Cradock was not an anomaly.

Just about everywhere we traveled in South Africa, on those long, smooth roads where distances were measured in hours rather than miles, the vista of an approaching town would be the same: on one side, the church steeple and the grain silos designated whiteness; on the other side of the tracks, a smudge of smoke hanging over small homes demarcated the township for the black people. When working hours began, the black women would trudge across the tracks to the white homes—maid to madam—and the black men would be picked up by truck to work at menial jobs on the farms. Then, at evening, like a video cassette on rewind, the process would be reversed and the blacks would return to the township. In the wealthier places, the servants lived in small homes in white yards, to be on hand whenever required. But, out there, on the lands where the Afrikaners had first built their identity and power, another school of thought held that it was better for the blacks to go to their own, separate places after work, in the dark hours most suited to the perception of their inherent skulduggery. (Even in the wealthy suburb of Johannesburg where I lived, there was, technically, a 9:00 P.M. curfew after which blacks should not be seen on our leafy thoroughfares. The notion was known as "white by night"—an acknowledgment of a need for black labor, but a rejection of any further racial intimacy and, implicitly, a perception of hazard.)

Cradock was a stubborn callus of resistance that infuriated the white Security Police, because it routinely refused to bow to their will, and thus showed the limits of their power. When Mark and I first entered the place clandestinely but fairly ostentatiously—we were driving a hired BMW painted metallic silver—the Security Police came after us to question us, searching the streets where they had last observed our presence. Technically, at that time, whites needed a permit to enter a black township (permits and passes, as any good bureaucrat knows, produce a supplicant state of mind that makes physical barriers redundant). We did not have a permit and therefore, in the terms of the various regulations governing intercourse between the races, had committed a misdemeanor. The catch, of course, was that if we had applied for a permit, it might have been refused, and our presence would be advertised, our mission frustrated. So we had gone, as most reporters usually did, without our small piece of legitimizing paper. And we had disappeared. The policemen cruising the cracked streets in their blue Toyota sedan did not find us—or the BMW—and no one would think a township as small as that could keep many secrets that obvious for that long. Indeed, it seemed to baffle these armed plainclothes men with their 9mm pistols and shorts and cropped hair that two whites could simply disappear willingly into the thin air of a black township—to them, it must have seemed almost a perversion of the racial order.

Goniwe had sheltered us and hidden the car in a yard so that we could talk about what was going to happen throughout South Africa: the small grievance—in Cradock's case, Goniwe's suspension as head-master—unleashed the rage and galvanized organized resistance until the point of departure was forgotten in the overriding imperative of the campaign against apartheid. And Botha's reforms themselves mag-nified every grievance, providing a context for small hurts to take their place in the nation's catalogue of disparity. The crudely painted slogans on the low walls surrounding Cradock township's soccer field did not even refer to the local issue of Goniwe's suspension. Long before people dared to be so open elsewhere, they proclaimed: *"Viva Umkhonto we Sizwe*—Long live the Spear of the Nation," the ANC's military wing. And long before the ANC issued its called for black protesters to make the townships "ungovernable," Cradock had set itself apart from white governance: that was the lesson of the pensions line and the class boycotts. Professor Tom Lodge, a political scientist at the University of the Witwatersrand in Johannesburg, once told me that while "local events" might initiate protest, "very quickly political movements come in and play a leading role" by providing what he called "a kind of purpose and a long-term agenda." For all Goniwe's tongue-in-cheek insistence that his organization was little more than a young people's social club, that is what Cradora had done in Cradock. Black numerical superiority alone could not beat what Goniwe and his followers called "the system"; the key lay in organization, "structures" that marshaled the numbers behind the overriding priority—ending apartheid. But there had been a price.

In places with unfamiliar names—Graaff Reinet, Tarkastad, Steytlerville, Cradock itself—a version of war had been under way in the Eastern Cape for months before Goniwe's funeral, and its course, far from most people's gaze or scrutiny, had been marked by all manner of nastiness. The testimonies of the victims were studded with accounts of beating, torture, shootings as the authorities went about their business of breaking resistance, bludgeoning those they saw as leaders, displaying might and will, and, as important as anything else, keeping trouble where it belonged—in the townships, over the hill, beyond the purview of white settlement.

On February 3, 1985, on the first anniversary of Cradock's school boycott, the white policemen came to the township just as the soldiers came to the village in the other Africa far to the north.

"We ran away very fast" when the police arrived, said one young man, Mabhutiso Mboniswa, in an affidavit sworn to the white liberal activist Molly Blackburn, who spent much time in the remote settlements of the Eastern Cape, listening to and documenting stories of great hardship and tribulation. But running fast was not enough for Mboniswa's companion, Thozi Skweyiya.

"Thozi ran toward the toilet. I saw him try to jump over the fence. But because the fencing was high and loose he was not able to get over. The next thing I saw was Thozi falling down. I heard the report of a rifle." Thozi stood up, but there was a second shot, the account said, concluding: "I know that my friend Thozi has died. I have nothing more to say."

The daily confrontation produced its own habits of behavior. In Cradock, even the township's toddlers waved clenched fists and picked up rocks to throw when the police, or other whites, ventured into the area; from early 1984 onward, boys and girls in their early teens called one another "comrade," stayed away from school, and sacrificed their youth to a cause they oversimplified in their slogans. The brutality of oppression found its echo in the intuitive rage of the oppressed. One fourteen-year-old, Lucas, who became my guide on several expeditions into his hard, coercive, and unforgiving world, said his ambitions were to kill policemen, flee South Africa for training as a guerrilla fighter, and return with a bazooka to kill more policemen. "When I am eighteen," he said, "I will go to become a cadre in Lusaka. Then, instead of stones, I will have a bazooka." He gestured toward a police armored vehicle parked on the outskirts. "When I see that thing, I just want to get the bazooka and kill. Yes, I will be a cadre."

There were no broader horizons. He and his friends no longer greeted each other with such mundanities as "Good morning." Rather, in the shorthand of their revolution, they said, "Viva, com"—a new language as limited as its oversimplification of the issues. "Viva," borrowed from the Portuguese-speaking Mozambicans and Angolans, was a catchall exhortation for the long life of any number of persons and institutions—the African National Congress; *Umkhonto we Sizwe*; Nelson Mandela, to whose release their protest contributed many years later.

By 1984, revolt in Cradock had become daily routine, the old people bowing to the young who, clustered around Goniwe, had discovered the truth that they could, and would, simply say no. Apartheid was based on a notion of social engineering that took for granted—or enforced—the compliance of those it oppressed. The idea of blacks saying no was not factored into the arithmetic that, over the years, had forced 3.5 million blacks to live in tribal "homelands" that were deemed, for the purposes of the exercise, to be some kind of ancestral home. Nor was it included in the assumption that blacks would simply live happily in segregated townships as long as they were needed. When, in the mid-1980s, they said no, as they had done in Soweto in 1976, they did so through open revolt that cost many lives.

Now, in July 1985, as we drove north from Port Elizabeth along a route that had become studded with memories of earlier forays, Goniwe and his comrades had become the newest, grisly martyrs to the uprising.

Their four bodies had been found mutilated and burned in the dunes, just back from the Indian Ocean on the coast road from Port Elizabeth, before the turnoff into the hills that led to Cradock. They had been attending a political meeting of the United Democratic Front—the umbrella organization that marshaled six hundred local groups like Cradock's into a recognizable front of resistance (and an equally obvious front, in another sense, for the exiled African National

Congress). Then, as we pieced together the accounts later, they had left their friends in Port Elizabeth, assuring them that, in these dark and dangerous days, they would stop for no one on the way home. That was the last their friends saw of them, until several days later an army patrol found the burned debris of their car, and the viciously carved and incinerated bodies. No one ever said publicly who killed them, but the families came to believe that policemen stopped them at a roadblock, handed them over to black opponents in Port Elizabeth's depressed black townships, and left them to an excruciatingly painful destiny.

Port Elizabeth was where the police beat Steve Biko to the brink of death in 1977, then dumped him on the steel floor of a Land Rover for the long overnight drive to Pretoria, to die on the way, unattended, ignored, without so much as a blanket for cover or human contact for solace. Port Elizabeth had its rules, and they seemed no different from the bush rules further north, except that here they were applied in the name of Christian values, of maintaining those same standards as Ian Smith had promoted in Rhodesia. Port Elizabeth's policemen were virtual caricatures of South African internal security agents—clad in pastel blue safari suits, sporting pencil mustaches and slicked back hair along with the other accoutrements, holstered pistols and dark glasses. But no one underestimated their cruelty or their skill in manipulating the rivalries that seared many black townships.

As elsewhere in South Africa as the revolt unfolded, the white authorities in the Eastern Cape spoke of "black-on-black violence," as if it were some form of anthropological phenomenon, but they did not mention their own techniques of division—favoring one group over another through exemptions from prosecution, the limited supply of handguns to blacks prepared to cooperate with the authorities, the fine-tuning of division by promoting one personality, one group over another. Around Port Elizabeth, maneuvers translated into clandestine support for groups who dissented from the increasingly widespread political orthodoxy of the ANC and the UDF. And it was to dissidents such as those that Goniwe and his three colleagues had apparently been handed over. South Africa's tragedy lay not only in the killings but also in the ease with which the townships fell prey to the manipulation behind the bloodshed.

In the Vaal Triangle, south of Johannesburg, revolt started as a protest against rents in September 1984—most notably in Sharpeville, the same Sharpeville that had witnessed a bloody massacre of blacks by policemen in 1960. Twenty-four years later, the killing was more complex. Whites killed blacks, but blacks also slaughtered their fellow blacks who had acquired the taint of collaboration by working within the structures the authorities had established, supposedly to devolve some small powers to black councillors and mayors in selected townships. In reality, these black politicians faced impossible situations as nominal officebearers without funds to address the needs of constituents who had, often as not, abstained when they were voted to a kind of power.

Labeled stooges, they could no more redeem promises than escape the awesome responsibilities the authorities placed on them for gathering rents to finance the continued misery of the townships. In the killings, some died horrible, savage deaths, hacked and burned, their bodies left to smolder on the seedy, rock-strewn streets lined with gimcrack homes—easy targets, black emblems of apartheid, live people reduced to burned garbage.

The explosion in September 1984 set the markers: white power sought black acquiescence through division and coercion; blacks perceived to have collaborated with that power paid literally with their lives; and by setting people against one another, the authorities found many to do their dirty work for them.

On the eve of the Cradock funerals in the dark of another African night, the big issues entwined with personal loss. As in La Cité in Kinshasa eight years earlier, the one- and two-roomed homes were small and mean, and lives seemed just as programmed for defeat. There was an intimation of menace, too: lights flickered in unlit places, then were gone; shadows betrayed movement where there should have been no one.

We visited Matthew's widow. Mark played with the son, Nyaniso, to distract him, while the widow sat among the old women swathed in checkered blankets, women with faces gnarled as walnuts who would break into keening ululation or dirge, harmonies that seemed to swell from great depths of resignation and loss, not anger. "They were all young men," Nyameka Goniwe said. "And now there are four young

widows." The children, the women said, were their big worry. Some
did not understand why all this was happening, why the vegetable
soup in great vats for the mourners was simmering in small kitchens,
why the women huddled and clustered beside the bodies and wept and
swayed. And some would ask, with the piteousness of their years, when
Father would return. He was dead, yes, they said, but they did not
grasp death's finality: so when was he coming back? Should the children
be sheltered or not? Should they attend the next day's burial and maybe
then come to terms with their loss? When she attended Biko's funeral
in 1977, Nyameka told me, she had been particularly saddened by the
wailing of children there. So would her own children now confront
that same trauma? And what about the other crazy decisions that had
to be made: supposedly, the township was boycotting the white stores
in Cradock, so where would they buy the food for the mourners?
Where, for heaven's sake, would they locate sanitary facilities for
35,000 people the following day?

The night was filled with anonymous emissaries along broken
streets, mourners moving from house to house, "comrades" on their
secret patrols, guarding the organizers of the funeral who burned with
a bitter rage and who feared, always, the peremptory knock at the door
that preceded detention. On Cradock's outskirts, silhouetted like primeval creatures, the armored police trucks known as Caspirs offered
their bulk and menace as the symbols of the oppression beyond the
wailing and the grief.

As Mark and I moved through Cradock that night, we were offered
soup and, incongruously enough, the thanks of the bereaved for our
visit. Only later did I realize that we were made welcome because our
visit was interpreted not as a necessity of journalism but as evidence
that we had made the choice to show, that night, where we stood.
Our whiteness took on a completely different meaning than the authorities' whiteness because we had crossed a line to get where we
were, and so our choice was all the more obvious.

As foreigners, the gesture was easy. For us, crossing a line did not
evoke the notions of collective and personal survival woven into South
Africa's racial perceptions. For South Africans, black and white, by
contrast, crossing the same line held far more sinister perils. Blacks
who joined the white police force, ultimately, were hounded out of

Cradock—as they were from many other townships—their homes razed along with the other emblems of direct or indirect white control: the beerhall, whose revenues perpetuated subjugation, the administrative offices where a white officer handed out passes and permits from a desk decorated with color photographs of his pet bulldogs. And the whites who came to visit, like the activist Molly Blackburn, drew a special fondness from black people and a particular opprobrium from the white authorities.

When Molly died in an automobile accident in December 1985, her funeral in a white suburb of Port Elizabeth was attended by 10,000 blacks. There were stirring speeches and Christian hymns and marches by the comarades from the Port Elizabeth townships of Kwazakele and New Brighton and Zwide, where Molly had often been one of the very few whites to attend black political funerals. But the memory that endures is of one chance encounter outside a telephone booth that showed just how little blacks expected of many whites. A middle-aged black woman—plump and sobbing—told me Molly was different simply because she did not close the door in a black person's face. That was all—no grand vision, no soaring ideology. But closing the door in people's faces was precisely what apartheid—and P. W. Botha's attempt to refashion it—had done to the majority of the people. And at Matthew Goniwe's funeral, we saw the results.

Robed priests and revolutionaries, black and white, gathered below their banners—the red flag of the South African Communist Party; the hammer and sickle; the black, green, and gold of the African National Congress, all of them illegal. The dust rose in the township's crude stadium. Everything about the funeral seemed a denial of South Africa's concept of law and order, and, therefore, all the more exhilarating as a celebration of revolt for the thousands who gathered at the graveside under the gaze of the police in their armored trucks. The four bodies were lowered into graves themselves decorated with the ANC colors. Back from the crowd, for one brief moment, Lucas, my youthful guide, allowed a little humanity to show through the carapace of a fourteen-year-old self-appointed revolutionary, as he wept for Goniwe. By his own definitions, Lucas had been a valiant comrade. He had confronted the foe. He had told me he rejected the Christian God of his parents, and tried to locate himself in the world of fire and revolution. And now he had lost his mentor, at the very moment South Africa reached a turning point that would set the coordinates for change.

Somehow, in the turmoil, the chaos, the anger, the grief, word began to leak of a momentous event. At midnight that night, the strengthening rumor had it, the authorities would declare a state of emergency, a decree limited predominantly to the Eastern Cape and the fissile metropolis of Soweto, but a state of emergency nonetheless, a license for greater repression, a signal that battle had truly been joined, an implicit acknowledgment by the authorities that President Botha's reform program had foundered. The emergency decree had already been made known, under a midnight embargo, to the newspapers and new agencies in Johannesburg. They, in turn, had contacted their correspondents in Cradock. And they, in turn, demanded responses from the politicians and priests at the funeral—a tactic that would enable them to break the embargo without doing so directly. So the details began to seep out—of enhanced police powers, press curbs, the erosion of the few rights left to those who confronted South Africa's labyrinthine security legislation.

By the standards of subsequent decrees, the emergency was limited. But its thrust was nonetheless clear: this was the declaration of war. On the hill, overlooking the funeral, the policemen must have known it, must have known that from midnight onward they would wield unlimited powers of arrest without trial and that, in the terms of the decree, they would not face legal proceedings for the killing and torture that came with such powers. As journalists, we would confront an ever more complex tangle of restrictions on what we could legally report. And, most of all, for the protesters it would mean detention without access to lawyers or family visits, without even the right of families to know where their sons and daughters were being held and, in many cases, beaten and tortured. With hindsight, what few of us grasped was that the authorities had set in motion a chain of events that was to bring such vilification to their name that American banks would call in their debts, sanctions would spread, and South Africa's financial and psychological isolation would deepen beyond all levels of tolerance, forcing the authorities to accept the very demands for political change that the emergency was supposed to suppress.

From that viewpoint, the declaration of the emergency—the first since the Sharpeville massacre of 1960—illuminated the quintessential paradox of the underdog: defeat becomes victory when enough outsiders decide that the beating has gone on long enough; but to reach that point, you have to be beaten beyond endurance. And, as with most other aspects of South African life, the declaration of a state of emergency held diametrically different meanings and messages, depending on prespective, and skin color.

Since Sharpeville's explosion in September 1984, more than five hundred people, mostly black, had been killed, mostly by the police. Similar fatalities were recorded after the Soweto uprising of 1976, and that had been quelled, without an emergency decree, within a year. This time, though, it was different. The Soweto violence had "happened in a virtual political vacuum," Professor Lodge told me, but "this unrest happened after seven or eight years of political development, mobilization, the development of political organizations, and the expansion of the role of the ANC in the townships." The authorities spoke of a "revolutionary climate" in the land that defied control. The location of the next protest was unpredictable and therefore all the more difficult to second-guess or eradicate; the flames spread faster than they could be extinguished. The rioters were supported by a notion of organization they called "structures"—street committees, zone committees providing the base of a pyramid at whose apex stood the grand vision of freedom, personified in the still-incarcerated Nelson Mandela, who had devised this form of township cell organization—the M-plan—in the 1960s as a tool of guerrilla warfare.

The authorities, too, seemed hoist on their own petard. After the Soweto unrest bared the Achilles heel of massive black numbers and equally threatening black urbanization, the nation's white leaders had sought to co-opt an organized black political force by offering the black labor movement some legal status. But the move rebounded on the authorities when the unions themselves flexed political muscle. Where the rocks failed to dent white consciousness because they were thrown in the segregated and isolated black townships, labor strikes brought the message of discontent across the line. On those days when the workers stayed away from the factories, when no maid came to madam and the dishes piled high in the sunlit kitchen, whites came to know that there was trouble indeed in the locations. White managers were forced to run the supermarket checkout. The grass grew tall and the pool went green without its daily fix of chlorine because the gardener had not arrived.

What the emergency did was to give the authorities their own structures to counter the structures of organized protest.

At Goniwe's funeral, as Lucas wept and the dust rose and the young men danced the war dances and sang their refrains that called for the blood of the Boers, the revolt still seemed trapped in a kind of innocence: the momentum was gathering, victory was over the next hill, the enemy line had wavered, one more battle, comrades, and the campaign would be done. It was a false conclusion, but one that had to be instilled by the organizers of revolt if the insurgency was to continue and build in scope and support.

Since 1976, the authorities had prepared the ground for a further conflagration. Informers honeycombed the big townships like Soweto, and the armored trucks that had been developed in the earlier protests needed only fuel and policemen to set out to meet the challenge. South Africa's black townships are anyhow designed, where geographically possible, on geometric grids, easy to patrol and seal off, and the authorities took full advantage of that tactical advantage. But when the revolt started, the government's elaborate preparations and security regulations met daily challenge that built like the bruised skies of southern Africa's summer, when the clouds darken and fill and finally explode with the huge release of the rains. The young people went out onto the streets and burned tires and threw rocks, scorning parental caution. The police responded with tear gas, baton charges, whips, shotgun blasts, live ammunition from automatic rifles. The dead, then, were feted at mass funerals, like Goniwe's, and the funerals became the theaters of new confrontation, where the fire of the speeches and the refrains of hymns and battle songs reaffirmed the belief that, somehow, this time, it was possible: one more push and the gates would fall. This, the insurgents thought, was the final act of the war that had started when the Portuguese Empire collapsed, when the stockade began to crumble.

And so it went, gathering strength and martyrs, a protest that swept up its followers under the banners of the UDF, the ANC, the South African Communist Party, the Council of Churches. It swirled from area to area. Sharpeville might be still, but then the fire reignited in Port Elizabeth's townships—Kwazakele, Zwide, New Brighton. And if they were quiet, what about the East Rand—Duduza, KwaThema? Everywhere the imagery was bloody and violent: the burning of purported collaborators, "sentenced" by kangaroo courts of young zealots, cowardly acts, offsetting and undermining the greater passion of the massive rejection of apartheid. The ANC in Lusaka was caught unawares, unable to muster trained fighters to galvanize the fight to higher levels for both sides—possibly mercifully—and hidebound by the very secretive cell structures that supposedly protected it from government penetration, yet made its command lines slow and cumbersome. "When the ANC calls for making the townships ungovernable," Professor Lodge said in Johannesburg, "they are not leading the way. They are trying to associate themselves with what is happening." It had been happening in Cradock for months.

From the point of view of the comrades, the paradox of the emergency decree was that while it promised even harsher oppression, it was an acknowledgment of the threat they now presented to the authorities. That was a victory of sorts. But as the state of emergency was declared, President Botha offered his own followers—and the outside world—a different explanation. There *was* trouble in the locations; but not in the way the protesters depicted it.

For months, state-run television had broadcast no footage of the violent protest, deepening the white illusion that, most of the time, whatever was happening in the black townships need not concern them. "We don't know what happens over there," a large white man in Uitenhage once told me, gesturing to the black township of Kwanobuhle as he grilled fat sausage over charcoal. "They go their way and we go ours." ("Over there" a funeral was then under way for eight dead.) But when the television news broke its silence and showed Goniwe's funeral—the red flag, the unlawful pennants, Godless communism abroad in the land—it manipulated its coverage of events in a significant way. Without a break to explain that the venue had shifted, a horrific image flickered across the screen, of a young mother called Maki Skosana in Duduza township, far to the north on the East Rand, being incinerated as a collaborator—a charge that by many accounts turned out to be false. An enterprising TV crewman, his camera held low so no one would see that he was filming, had captured the terrible moment in terrible intimacy—the screams, the pouring of gasoline, the flames, the kicking of the body as it burned, the woman's desperate effort to pull off the blazing clothes. This, President Botha maintained, was the justification for the emergency—not the suppression of a legitimate revolt, but an effort to restore order to the mayhem of the black townships, where the savagery implicit in blackness was running amok, and where the specter of the Communist Total Onslaught had risen. By linking two unconnected moments from Duduza and Cradock, hundreds of miles apart, the authorities created their subliminal message: black politics meant chaos, so the demand for black power had to be dismissed.

"Can anyone realistically expect the Government to stand back and observe the breakdown of stability?" the pro-government Afrikaans newspaper, *Beeld*, asked its readers. "Without emergency measures, the massacre will only escalate and anyone who is familiar with the element of black anarchy should realize that there is nothing 'irreproachable' about it."

The decree lasted until the following March, when it was briefly suspended. Then, in June 1986—shortly before the tenth anniversary of the Soweto uprising—it was reimposed, this time across the nation, ever more refined and all-embracing: a total response that endured into the 1990s, a statement of Afrikaner will, expressing the whole style of government embraced by President Botha—uncompromising, finger-wagging, tough-talking, take-it-or-leave-it.

On the night of Goniwe's funeral, the crowds dispersed peacefully—as the organizers had insisted—and the dust settled. Cradock was left to its grief, embedded in the four new graves. But the preparations for implementing the decree were already in place. As we drove back fast and late to Port Elizabeth, the headlights picked out the new road-blocks: blue-uniformed policemen with shotguns and dogs at roadsides, waiting for the witching hour that would grant them unprecedented powers.

If the government's supporters were meant to be reassured by the display of force, then their adversaries were meant to be terrified by it.

The old African proverb had said that to kill a snake, you must first crush the head, then the children. That was part of the function of the thousands of detentions over the years of emergency rule—to sever the protest from its leaders, its ideologues, its symbols and organizers, from those who could articulate the dreams and visions that sustained its momentum. In the first wave of detentions, virtually every small-town politician known to the authorities was either swept up or on the run. And over the years, the scope widened. Churchmen, political activists, and labor leaders all found themselves on the wanted list or detained. Their stories showed how their choices had been refined. It was no longer whose side are you on? but, rather, what sacrifice are you ready to make?

One night in 1986, I arranged an illicit meeting with a fugitive labor leader from the Congress of South African Trade Unions—on the run from the authorities but desperate to show that all had not been lost. I had met Jay Naidoo before, all wild hair and Zapata mustache, jeans and defiance. Now, as he entered the room, I barely recognized the neat, shorn, clean-shaven figure in slacks and tweed sports coat who sat down to tell me that the struggle was not over, that though they had fallen back on subterfuge and disguises and a life of clandestinity, the effort to wield the weapon of organized labor was continuing. "The perception that an attack on us will go unchallenged is quite fallacious," he said. The understated talk seemed curiously appropriate to a disguise that suggested a mild-mannered college student or a clerk rather than a revolutionary firebrand.

In Alexandra township, I had met a woman whose family experience was as tough as they came. Victoria Gasela's husband was a policeman, and so the comrades had sought to burn the house down. But her twenty-six-year-old daughter, Mathilda, was herself a comrade, so the police had come for her. "When your child is arrested," the mother said, "it is like death." But when your husband is a policeman, "you just live like birds—you cannot sleep." In July 1985, Mathilda had become detainee number 701 after the emergency decree allowed her to be seized near her home in Alexandra. It was winter in South Africa when she was taken, and summer when she returned 101 days later. During that period, she told me, she had been questioned only once, for thirty minutes; so her incarceration, like those of many others, seemed designed simply to keep her out of the way, to chastise her and demonstrate who wielded real power over her life. Others had different experiences—of torture and interrogation about the where-abouts of other insurgents, of police efforts to "turn" them and send them back to their townships as paid informers. Some of those detained were barely more than children, and the chronicles of ill-treatment were too numerous to ignore. The overwhelming intention was to deprive the revolt of momentum. But as another activist, Mkuseli Jack, told me in a bizarre interview during his detention, the very organizational style of the protest was designed to keep the impetus going despite the detentions and to sustain the belief that, some day, the protests on the street would yield political gain.

Jack was a leading UDF organizer in Port Elizabeth and spent much time behind bars. His influence, however, was acknowledged even by white businessmen who were suffering badly from a boycott of white-owned stores that he had orchestrated and who sought him out as a negotiating partner, much to the annoyance of the authorities. When he was transferred from his cell to a hospital for some minor treatment, a mutual friend helped me slip through the wards to his room. Under the terms of the emergency decree, that was pretty irregular for both of us. Jack's attitude, however, was pretty much: well what else can they do?

I had come to know him, as I had first known Jay Naidoo, as an energetic rebel, punching the air with clenched-fist salutes, exhorting his young legions to greater resistance. Now, in pajamas and robe, sitting on a hospital bed sipping tea, he seemed more subdued, but just as convinced of his cause. "The government should seize the opportunity now because, ultimately, they'll be forced to come to the table," he said, prophetically, as it turned out. At the time, I thought his optimism misplaced, because, like many others, I allowed myself to be deceived by President Botha's greatest illusion: that he embodied the immutable will and voice of Afrikanerdom that would never countenance the more conciliatory policies associated with his successor, F. W. de Klerk. So I asked Jack how he and others could physically maintain revolt against such formidable and unyielding power. Firstly, he said, detention itself had become a breeding ground for political organization. During exercise time in the prison yard, political seminars were held to spread the line among those who would one day be released to propagate it. Visitors smuggled out messages and instructions to those still at liberty, he said. And, on the streets, the organizational network of alternative leaders provided for substitutes to step in when the main figures were seized: in place of a snake, that is, they offered a hydra. What the authorities confronted, commented

Robert Schrire, a political scientist in Cape Town, was "a degree of mass discontent that is unique" and a "political decentralization."

"There is no political head that you can just nip off," Schrire added. The authorities tried nonetheless. During the first emergency, almost 8,000 people were detained for various periods. And during the second, the figure reached a staggering 22,000 by early 1987.

The arrangements on the streets, Jack knew, were imperfect, for the substitutes did not have the authority of the known leaders and rebellion often slipped out of control, into the hands of a thuggish lumpenproletariat that spread terror among blacks without denting white power. But the skeleton of organization remained, and that was what the authorities sought to dismantle, as they confronted not only revolt but the reporting that spread word of it around the globe.

The emergency decrees affecting journalists became so restrictive that reporters were supposed to absent themselves from scenes of protest, were not to report most black political statements, and could not even allude to the movements of any security forces without the government's consent, which was rarely given. Television cameras were held in roughly the same opprobrium as the ANC colors, indeed, were seen by the authorities as little more than the public relations wing of the rebellion. The government seemed to have reached its own conclusion about the philosopher's conundrum: if the tree fell in the forest, and no one saw or heard it, then, indeed, it had not fallen at all. Within the country, the regulations meant that a silence fell on reporting of much of the protest, so that no one was supposed to know what we all knew to be happening. To extend the metaphor, the theory was that if a rock was thrown in a township, and no one recorded the fact, then the rock had not been thrown at all, and so no one else would be encouraged to emulate the rock thrower who, by this argument, did not exist. It was even illegal for a newspaper to print a blank page to show it had been censored. T-shirts bearing slogans were pronounced subversive and outlawed. By denying reality, the authorities were trying to will it away, and, ultimately, on the streets, their will prevailed. But it was a Pyrrhic victory, as events beyond the government's control and far from South Africa's shores were to show.

The emergency sought, in part, to shelter whites from the crisis in their own land, and, as important, to prevent the imagery of the protest from spreading to those distant lands in the West, notably the United States, whose backing Pretoria had long courted in return for its self-assumed role as a bulwark against Soviet encroachment. How, the authorities would say, could the West not support those who, in its name, defended from communism's onslaught the sea routes around the Cape, the mines that provided half the free world's gold, the diamonds, the uranium? The arguments drew their legitimacy from the Cold War and, doubtless, Cold Warriors in the West responded to them with the same deliberate myopia toward internal developments that had blurred Western attitudes in Zaire. In one way, though, *South Africa* was different. Its urge to repression collided with its profound desire for association with the First World, the West, the assembly of civilized, Christian communities that it perceived as its natural kin.

The first emergency in 1985, thus, was limited and produced ambiguous results—it damaged Pretoria's international standing, without excising the protest or its images. But by the time the authorities got round to throwing caution to the winds with full-blown repression, it was too late: the revolt had crept around the barriers of the emergency, and was hurting white business and fiscal management; it had conjured demands in the West for economic punishment and pressure; and it was forcing choices and decisions not only on politicians but also on those who stood to gain or lose most from Africa's most robust economy—white business and the emergent black labor unions.

News coverage, thus, fed into an explosive issue: sanctions. For American Democrats in the Reagan era, the question was easy, oversimplified, and inviting. For South Africa's white leaders, it showed just how far they had drifted from that same Western world whose benevolence they most craved.

10.

Crossing the Rubicon:

Black Protest,

White Money

"If we really want to lose everything, then we must hang on to everything now. If we want to keep something, we must share now."

—DONALD MASSON, FORMER PRESIDENT OF THE AFRIKANER INSTITUTE OF COMMERCE, to the author, in June 1986

✳ When Senator Edward M. Kennedy came to visit South Africa in early 1985, I had been appalled at the showmanship and manipulation: here, the television crews were invited to film the senator in conversation with the poorest man his aides could locate in the grimiest single men's hostel at Soweto; here, the staged long-focus shot of him stricken with grief in a cemetery for black children in an appalling squatter-camp called Onverwacht. Others, more savvy than I, saw beyond the gross media circus—and its use of impoverished blacks as unbidden extras—to the impact it was designed to have in the United States, where the pro-sanctions lobby was gathering force as a power for change in South Africa itself.

The attitude of Congress and large slices of the American public infuriated many white South Africans, far more than they felt comforted by the Reagan administration's implicit offer of protection in the policy called "constructive engagement"—which held that it was far more productive to coax President Botha than confront him.

In July 1986, a month after the latest emergency decree introduced reporters to the harshest restrictions they had yet known, I went to see David Steward, the head of the newly formed Bureau for Information, the government agency responsible for managing the media regulations. Pretoria's one-time representative at the United Nations, Steward had lived in New York for four and a half years; in his well-cut pinstripes and Ralph Lauren shirts, he seemed a departure from the more familiar images of South African authority—raw-boned policemen and dour bureaucrats.

What he said about Americans, however, did not seem all that different.

"Americans like to feel righteously indignant about distant problems which remind them of their own days in the sixties, when they had causes for which to fight. They like to feel that such-and-such is a baddie and such-and-such is a goodie. It gives them a warm feeling in their breasts when they commute into New York from Connecticut. It gives them direction in life. It's very pleasant." White South Africa, he seemed to be saying, had become America's tar baby.

He was not very kind to my work, either, and if he had been, the benediction would have been about as ambivalent as his evaluation of the way American newspapers were handling the story. "The overwhelming impressions are created by the one-minute forty-second TV clips," he said, "not by the closely reasoned articles in *The New York Times* and *The Washington Post*, which often are equally far from the mark but much more articulate."

We would never agree on most other things, but if Senator Kennedy's media blitz was anything to go by, I could understand white cynicism about the intertwining of South Africa's revolt and American politics. The most striking impression from the encounter, however, was that his comments made no attempt at damage control and, indeed, seemed calculated to further alienate those Americans now in open cry for the defeat of David Steward and all he stood for.

That, possibly, reflected the calculation that the damage had already been done.

The U.S. Congress finally imposed sanctions in October 1986. They remained in force for five years and included bans on American imports of South African steel, iron, coal, uranium, textiles, and agricultural produce, along with the withdrawal of landing rights for South African Airways, the state carrier, at American airports. But long before that, a different set of events had produced a seismic shift in South Africa's financial relationship with the rest of the world that would have tested the outer limits of any economic Richter scale.

Shortly after the declaration of the first emergency in July 1985, President Botha scheduled an address to the Natal Provincial Congress of the National Party and let it be known that he planned an announcement. In advance of the speech on August 15 in Durban, various senior South African officials leaked word to selected journalists and diplomats that Mr. Botha planned to proclaim major concessions that would lead South Africa across a racial Rubicon and even bring about the freedom of Nelson Mandela. Mr. Botha, however, did not deliver the speech everyone expected, and his failure to do so stunned some of his own followers as much as it bewildered those who had so eagerly forecast a sea-change.

Much later, a South African diplomat told me one version of what had happened. Initially, the South African leader had indeed been inclined to improve his offer to the black majority. He had shown his iron fist with the emergency decree, and now, as was his political style, he would make an offer from a position of strength. But the leaks to journalists and diplomats built up a wave of expectation, fed by newspaper and magazine articles. When, at a cabinet meeting shortly before the speech, an aide presented President Botha with a sheaf of clippings telling him what the world was expecting of him, he exploded in one of his celebrated paroxysms of rage. He would not, he said, accept this diktat by outsiders. And so he did lead South Africa across a Rubicon, although not the one that had been so enthusiastically forecast in the United States and Western Europe.

Wagging his finger, stern and belligerent, President Botha stood before an audience that went far beyond the 1,800 whites present in Durban's ornate City Hall with its Victorian British architecture implanted into the palms of the Indian Ocean coastline. Just about everybody in South Africa, and many people in the West, were waiting for a signal of change. But Mr. Botha showed them that, whatever else, he was his own man, who would set his own terms, at his own pace. His mood as he spoke showed, as much as his words, that the forecasts of change had been misplaced.

"I am not prepared to lead white South Africans and other minority groups on a road to abdication and suicide," he intoned.

"Listen, my friends, listen. Destroy white South Africa and our influence in this subcontinent of southern Africa, and this country will drift into factions, strife, chaos and poverty.

"We have never given in to outside demands and we are not going to do so. South Africa's problems will be solved by South Africans and not by foreigners. We are not going to be deterred from what we think best, nor will we be forced into a position of doing what we don't want to do." That was the message.

President Botha did, indeed, restate earlier terms for the conditional release of Nelson Mandela with the provision that he renounce violence. And he put forward the idea of some vaguely worded changes in the status of urbanized blacks, offering them a role in the "participation of all the South African communities on matters of common concern." He spoke of "structures to reach this goal of co-responsibility." What he wanted, effectively, was black capitulation, some kind of tame discussion, and above all, time to discover if there was some way of finessing the chaos. But his basic policies—the focus of the nation's division—remained intact.

Most South Africans, he said, clearly speaking of whites only, "will not accept the principle of one-man, one-vote in a unitary system. Such an arrangement would lead to domination of one over the other and it would lead to chaos. Consequently, I reject it as a solution." In his code language, "domination" really meant the end of white domination over the nation.

"I believe that we are today crossing the Rubicon in South Africa," he went on. "There can be no turning back. We now have a manifesto for our country, and we must embark on a program of positive action in the months and years that lie ahead."

His words were ominously prophetic—there was no turning back.

Within days, a panicky flight from the South African currency, the rand, brought its value down to 35 U.S. cents, about half what it had been and its lowest-ever level against the dollar; trading in stocks and foreign exchange was suspended; worst of all, American banks led by Chase Manhattan refused to extend credit lines and called for repayment of a short-term debt estimated at $4 billion. At a hastily called news conference in Pretoria on September 1, 1985, Finance Minister Barend du Plessis announced a four-month freeze on the repayments of overall foreign debt principal totaling $14 billion.

From a high-flying player in the Western economy, South Africa had been transformed into a Third World debtor. It had coped well enough in the past with embargoes on weapons and oil supplies. But now it had lost the capital-importing edge it garnered from its mineral and agricultural exports—gold and corn and diamonds and platinum and steel—and had become a net exporter of the very capital it needed not only to finance economic growth but to finance its own policies.

Over the next four years, the Central Bank estimated that more than $15 billion flowed out of the country to meet debt obligations. By some estimates, sanctions hindered economic growth by as much as one third over the next five years—with all that implied for a restive and growing black labor force. On U.S. college campuses, students called for divestment—the shedding of South African stocks and shares in their college's investment portfolios. With smaller investments than West European countries, particularly Britain, U.S. multinationals had a total of roughly $2.3 billion tied up in South Africa—1 percent of their total assets, which provided an equally small percentage of total profit. But these investments required a disproportionate amount of executive time to respond to the political web that anti-apartheid campaigners had spun around the whole question of doing business in South Africa. Eventually, many, including some of the most prominent—Ford, General Motors, and IBM—pulled out, (selling their companies and licensing arrangements to their own locally hired executives as they went, so all was not lost). The action of the American banks in August 1985 set the parameters for the economic pressures that were to build and to shatter the South African assumption that, whatever happened politically, no one would let that interfere with the economics of profit.

The rocks might have been contained in the black townships, but the impact of Western banks hit white pocketbooks and white self-perceptions. Shortly after the collapse of the rand, I spoke with a South African banker and his wife at a black-tie dinner in a swanky white suburb of Johannesburg, and the talk turned to their recent experience during a trip to Zurich. In South Africa, the banker was a member of the wealthy elite, with a big house and a big car and the money to live very well indeed. But in Zurich, when they had computed the small number of Swiss francs their devalued rands would now purchase, the South African couple had come to realize that the only dinner they could afford was burger and fries at one of the fast food chain restaurants.

Back in South Africa, aglow with good wine, encased in cummerbund and tuxedo, his wife in an elegant evening dress, under a tent where the caterers' black staff had laid out the candlelit tables and the delicacies, the banker told the story with some bemusement. There was frustration in his voice, too: he had been brought low by people whose power lay solely in their refusal to do what apartheid demanded of them. And the crisis showed no sign of abating.

In the weeks after Botha's Rubicon speech, protest—orchestrated, provocative, confrontational—spread to Cape Town, and 29 more people died as riots flowed from township to university campus to squatter camp. The death toll in a year stood at 650. Moreover, the rebellion, a year after Sharpeville's rent revolt in September 1984, had enshrined South Africa's ambiguous new warriors, the "comrades," as a kind of vanguard, setting a pace that neither their parents nor the labor leaders nor anti-apartheid church dignitaries like Archbishop Desmond Tutu could match. With an unschooled life of violence, retribution, and, they maintained, revolution, they had collectively said no to P. W. Botha's closure of the door. In the collision of negatives, their message to him was simply this: We will destroy our present to deny you a future.

That was not a message South African bankers and businessmen wanted to hear, for as sanctions unfolded and credit dried up, they came to realize that not only would there be no more free lunches from a world that had turned against their land, but there would be no lunch at all if they did not begin to share their place at the table.

For many years wealthy South Africans like the banker at the dinner party had made easy riches. Central Johannesburg was freckled with eateries that filled with white diners intent on midday shrimp and steaks and chilled white wine. Come early Friday afternoon, the freeways leading out of the city filled with homebound executives piloting sleek sedans after a short week of business borne along by the nation's combination of immense natural resources and immense pools of cheap labor. But now the executives, like everyone else, faced choices.

The combination of international punishment and increasingly politicized sentiment among their own black employees threatened profits. No longer could they rely on the authorities to shelter them. And so they had to decide what political concessions they could promote to placate both Western opinion and their own unionized labor forces. Yet, when they came to make their offers, they found that the protest on the streets had outstripped not only their calculations but those same government reforms that divided white opinion.

During my time in South Africa, President Botha repealed the laws forbidding interracial sex and marriage (though not the laws governing where people of each race were allowed to live or go to school, so the blissful miscegenous couple might have problems finding a home or educating their children). He legalized multi-racial political parties (though not all races had the vote and the principal black resistance movement, the ANC, remained outlawed). He announced an end to the policies of forcibly removing blacks from one area to another. (The authorities had already removed 3.5 million.)

But of all the changes he did make, none illustrated the momentous shift that had overtaken black and white thinking as much as his decision to scrap the thirty-four separate items of legislation that made up the pass laws—long viewed as the most hurtful of apartheid laws.

It should have been a triumph for black activism and the spirit of reform. For many years, after all, the repeal of the legislation—designed to limit black access to the townships on the peripheries of white South Africa—had been the central demand of black activism. The peaceful protests of the 1950s had clamored for it. The sixty-nine people shot dead at Sharpeville in 1960 had died in an orchestrated effort to hand in their passes and be free of them. The laws had been a crushing burden on a black majority that had lived for decades with the humiliation of pass raids on their homes in white backyards and arbitrary inspections on the streets of white-run cities. "Where is your pass, kaffir?"—those words, using the most pejorative of white terms for black people, roughly equivalent to "nigger," represented the quintessential image of the relationship between the races. And they reflected the ultimate refinement of control by bureaucracy: people reduced to the status of a piece of paper.

Only blacks—not Indians, or "Coloreds," or whites— were obliged to carry passes, and they had to carry them at all times, setting out where they were allowed to be in South Africa, if, indeed, they were allowed to exist at all in South Africa. People carried their passes—if they had one—like hidden gold, wrapped in plastic against rain and wear, secreted in clothing. The smart black executive in the smart BMW was supposed to carry his pass, even if he kept it in a Gucci wallet. Only blacks appeared at the myriad courthouses where pass-law offenders were processed with robotlike efficiency. "Ten rands fine or five days in prison," the magistrate would intone after brief consideration of each small case that showed, as much as the callousness of the system, the gargantuan proportions of the task the authorities had set themselves in trying to keep white South Africa white.

Since 1916, 18 million blacks had been arrested in the effort to stem black urbanization; in 1985, Helen Suzman, the feisty veteran white opposition legislator, told me, there had been 500,000 pass-law arrests in the two years since President Botha unveiled his reforms. Simple arithmetic showed there was a pass-law arrest somewhere in South Africa every two minutes six seconds. Still, the system could not beat the inexorable urge to leave the miseries of the homelands for the flawed promise of the townships. And so, bowing to the pressure, President Botha repealed the laws in July 1986. But the event went almost unnoticed, as if people were saying: so what? Blacks still could not vote for the government, still had to live in the townships, still sent their children to the segregated schools.

The passes gave way to identity documents, the same as whites and "Coloreds" and Indians had, and the system called "influx control" gave way to something called "orderly urbanization."

It was an ambiguous reform, because it excluded the homelands and thus did not apply to everyone within South Africa's traditional frontiers. And while it did formally acknowledge 14 million blacks as South African citizens—the antithesis of apartheid's intention—it brought no peace. President Botha stood accused by one side of capitulating and by the other of being more obdurate than ever because he would not give more.

Caught between an increasingly unionized and radical black work force and international opprobrium, the businessmen began to look for their own answers, but found few.

In September 1985, only a few days after the American banks withdrew their benediction from the South African economy and the currency collapsed, Gavin Relly, the chief executive of Anglo-American Corporation, led a delegation of businessmen and newspaper editors to Zambia to meet with the ANC leadership. President Botha was incensed, because the trip seemed to give the ANC unprecedented legitimacy in the white establishment. Harry Oppenheimer, the eminence grise of Anglo-American, whose father Ernest had founded the corporation almost seventy-five years earlier, also rebuked Mr. Relly for undertaking the trip. The ANC, he told the American Chamber of Commerce in Johannesburg, sought "an economic system that would destroy everything we in this room stand for" and should not be given "moral support or material support."

Neither did Mr. Relly seem to register too many gains from his safari. "There is little community of interest between us," he said, after the meeting with ANC figures, including Oliver Tambo, its exiled leader during Nelson Mandela's incarceration. "Our positions are very far apart.

"I put in a great cri de coeur, or rather, tried to point out the difference between exploitative capital and free enterprise," Mr. Relly added. "I talked about the necessity for people to have something to reach for." Fine, Mr. Tambo said, but he still wanted to nationalize the mines.

That was not surprising since the ANC's manifesto, the Freedom Charter of 1954, called implicitly for the nationalization of those very same mines that formed the basis of Anglo's massive wealth. But the pilgrimage to President Kaunda's game lodge in Zambia's Luangwa Valley underlined the extent to which the protests on the streets had come to force self-examination on the wealthy elite.

For years, South Africa's businessmen, the "randlords," had maintained that free enterprise—the capitalist system—would eventually prevail over apartheid; the need for skills, mobility, markets would break down the artificial barriers. Even in mid-1986, when the South African subsidiaries of American corporations urged accelerated change, they referred back to the same belief. Apartheid laws, they stated in a newspaper advertisement, were "totally contrary to the ideal of free enterprise." That was true in a way, possibly in a more ironic sense than had been intended.

The apartheid regime functioned in part as an Afrikaner welfare state, shielding the white tribe, and the conglomerates, from the notions of competition so central to the market ethic. Fully one third of all adult Afrikaners worked in safe jobs on the government payroll. At that time, key industries—iron and steel, armaments, the railways, electricity, and the expensive plants that produced oil from coal to circumvent the porous international oil embargo—were state-controlled. Like governments in many parts of Africa, the authorities held a monopoly on the purchase of the farmers' corn, and set the prices without permitting market forces to do the job for them. Even after the labor reforms of 1979, the senior underground jobs in the mines were still reserved for whites, while the law stated that 97 percent of all black mineworkers had to be migrants, meaning that their families back home in disadvantaged homelands became totally dependent on whatever sporadic remittances the men chose to send home.

It made for big profits, but not for a free market that would set the price of labor. (And it did little for social cohesion. The migrant labor system in general often meant that many men had two wives. "After a while in the town, the man will have two wives—one there and one in the village," Felix Nzama, a wise man of courtesy and substance, told me when I visited his well-stocked general dealer's store at Jameson's Drift on the slow sweep of the Tugela River in what had once been known as Zululand. "In the end, the one in town gets the diamonds," he added ruefully, ruminating on the weakness that flesh is heir to, and offering one more reason for the poverty of the homelands.)

The argument that private enterprise would somehow dissolve apartheid might have held true if private enterprise had really offered the equal opportunities it was supposed to. But it patently did not: it was shielded from doing so by those very apartheid structures it was supposed to be eroding; and the educational system prevented most blacks from even competing. The belief had been easier to nurture while apartheid and the Afrikaners held the stockade and business flourished within. When the stockade seemed to weaken, things began to look different, and taking a stand on political reform suddenly seemed not only palatable but shot through with urgency created by divestment, disinvestment, and sanctions.

South Africa's captains of private enterprise were not so much looking to dismantle apartheid as to ensure their own survival in a favorable and profitable political climate. Businessmen took to calling it "enlightened self-interest." If that meant the creation of a new political system, so be it, but the association of capital and apartheid had already taken root.

"South African business today faces a serious dilemma," Clive Menell, deputy chairman of the Anglovaal mining house, told an audience in New York in early 1986. Without the increasing involvement of blacks as wage earners, consumers, skilled workers, and managers, he said, business could not prosper. But, he continued, "The vast majority of black South Africans regard business, the Government, apartheid, the status quo and, if you like, the devil, as one."

If there was to be a cushion against such perceptions, many businessmen felt, it had to be provided by material prosperity and the creation of a bigger stake in a capitalist system for the black majority. The dilemma confronting South African business leaders was how to distance themselves and their economic system from the political system that had enabled them to flourish for so many years.

It was a messy problem that brought only messy, partial solutions.

Companies placed newspaper advertisements urging the government to accelerate change. But the protests on the street were rapidly producing demands far beyond those that business had factored into its calculations.

"The goalposts keep on moving," Tony Bloom, the chief executive of Premier Milling, once told me in an office the size of a couple of squash courts that, like his metallic green Maserati, seemed to contrast oddly with the role he had assumed as a champion of black advance.

"The question is now political power sharing," he went on. "And I don't think anything is a vehicle for political power sharing as long as Nelson Mandela is in jail." On the street, however, they were not talking about sharing power, but taking power in the name of the ANC and its ally, the South African Communist Party. Mandela's release was a symbol, an augury, not an end in itself. The goalposts had moved again.

"The sooner we start negotiating," said Raymond Ackerman, chairman of Pick'n'Pay, South African's most prosperous grocery chain, "the greater chance we have of not letting the forces of the left take over." Those arguments did not sway President Botha in the way they swayed his successor, F. W. de Klerk, but they were gaining currency among some Afrikaners.

"We accept that these people have to have political rights, that they are economically indivisible and therefore, we must support these people's rights. But we believe that we also have rights," Donald Masson, former president of the Afrikaner Institute of Commerce, told me, using the same longhand for blacks as Ora Terblanche had done.

"I'm saying: if we want to lose everything, then we must hang on to everything now. If we want to keep something, we must share now."

What everyone knew, however, was that the issue was not so simple because the question hovering beyond it was this: Who would wield final control over any kind of political sharing? After his release in February 1990, Nelson Mandela spoke for a lot of blacks when he urged the creation of a democratic South Africa under majority rule. Big business did not want to go that far. In 1985, Gavin Relly projected views that, I believe, a lot of whites will hold for a long time to come. "I'm not in favor of one-man, one-vote in South Africa," he told me. "It would simply be a formula for unadulterated chaos at this point in time in our history." Despite or perhaps because of the visit with the ANC, the conclusion and the language were not far removed from President Botha's comments in Durban, and it must have given Mr. Botha ironic comfort to sense an implicit coalition with those same English-speaking businessmen who had once projected the Afrikaners as dullards and bumpkins.

Anglo's mistrust of majority rule had historical roots. Over lunch in Johannesburg at 44 Main Street, Harry Oppenheimer once told me of an incident that, I suspected, had been woven into the corporate fabric as firmly as the warp and weft of the hunting tapestries on the wall of the Chairman's Dining Room.

In 1964, on the eve of independence in Zambia, where Anglo-American had substantial holdings in the copper mines, Oppenheimer said, he had been at dinner with Kenneth Kaunda, who was to take power the next day. "KK said there was no question of nationalizing the mines," Oppenheimer recalled with a flinty smile. "Then, at the independence celebrations the next day, he announced that he was taking over a 51 percent stake in them." Anglo got the management contract in Zambia and 49 percent, but it seemed Oppenheimer, a deft practitioner of corporate manipulation and control, had drawn his own conclusions from the alchemy of black politics and economic practices. He ended his story with a look that seemed to say: what can you expect?

Ultimately, politics is about choices—the choices people make, and the choices other people force upon them. Ora Terblanche and Eugene Terre Blanche had made their choices in white society, and the comrades had made and dictated theirs on the other side of the fence. South African business leaders, too, faced choices fringed with issues of profit and survival. And, when they sought to remold their relationship with the blacks who made up their work forces, they found that choices had been made there, too.

During our secretive and clandestine meeting in June 1986, when the emergency decree blanketed the land, the labor unionist Jay Naidoo hinted at some of the quandaries confronting labor organizations that now claimed to represent well over half a million black workers—the biggest lawful assemblage of blacks in the country.

"There has been a long struggle to win union rights and there is a strong commitment to protect those union rights," he said. "But that does not imply a subservient union movement."

Since its legalization in 1979, the labor movement had worked assiduously at building its shop-floor strength as a vehicle for the material advancement of its members. Political activism, as its leaders well knew, could lead to detention and repression that would leave labor unions as little more than shells, with no power or credibility. Yet the emergency decrees brought labor leaders up short against the same dilemma as confronted churchmen like Desmond Tutu: the violence of the townships scoured through the lives of their followers, and if they did not take a political stand on it, they risked losing all influence within their constituencies. If that happened, there would be even less restraint on the comrades, and more bloodshed on both sides. Yet, once they formally entered the realm of politics, the rules changed: union activism for economic goals had legal status; political activism confronted the ranged forces of the emergency.

I sometimes got the impression that it rankled with the labor unionists to be pushed so far and so quickly by the comrades who set the pace on the streets without any of the labor movement's notions of organization and democracy. Cyril Ramaphosa was the secretary general of the most influential of the unions, the National Union of Mineworkers, representing the blacks who sped below ground each day in steel cages to mine the nation's gold and coal. He wore short leather jackets and smoked incessantly from a pack of filter cigarettes. He was a lawyer by training, but that did not imply privilege: his childhood memories, he told me, included being shoved into a ditch by a white policeman; his memories of adulthood included a rerun of the same event in a different form—detention for political activism during the 1976 uprising.

When I first met Ramaphosa in 1985, the union was struggling to make ends meet and he answered his own phone at the rundown offices in Lekton House on Wanderers Street, Johannesburg, that offered such a fitting contrast to the opulence of 44 Main Street— Anglo's headquarters less than a mile away across town. For all its dealings with the powerhouse of industry, the union itself—like all black unions in South Africa—faced big problems: strike funds were virtually unknown, and the procedure for calling a legal strike was so cumbersome as to make rapid action impossible. For every six men working in the gold and coal mines, four more waited in the homelands or neighboring countries to take their place if they got the sack. Employers, thus, could pick and choose from a pool of 400,000 unemployed, and the law allowed them to dismiss strikers en masse. The migrant labor system itself discouraged activism because distant home villages depended for their survival on the miners' paychecks. And most homeland authorities simply refused to let the unions recruit there. "The homelands," Nicholas Haysom, a white laywer, had told me, "feel politically and economically threatened by trade unions. Homelands have one thing to offer—cheap labor."

But the protests on the township streets touched the labor movement as much as anybody else and demanded a political response. "No union can afford now to remain aloof from politics," Steve Friedman, a white labor specialist, said in 1985. "The issue is no longer whether unions should be politically active, but how they should be so."

That was something Cyril Ramaphosa thought about a lot.

"We pride ourselves on being an organized workers' movement," he told me as he chain-smoked Marlboros. "We pride ourselves on democratic organization. We have structures that ensure that things should be done in an orderly fashion." These were qualities, he noted diplomatically, "which unfortunately many other organizations do not have."

But those other organizations—the militant comrades—pressed the unions to bolster the struggle. In late 1985, when a new labor federation called the Congress of South African Trade Unions (COSATU), was formed, grouping Mr. Ramaphosa's organization and 35 others, and claiming a total membership of 500,000 black workers, its new chairman, Elijah Barayi, took high ground. "COSATU is going to govern this country," he declared, in a speech that went far beyond what other unionists were prepared to say in public. "COSATU is going to nationalize the mines under the government. And even some of the big industries will be taken by the government of COSATU." He also said the passes should be burned and Botha should stand aside for "the rightful people" to rule— "people like Nelson Mandela."

"This is the last warning to P. W. Botha that he should get rid of the passes," the sixty-year-old former mineworker proclaimed before 10,000 supporters gathered in a rugby stadium near Durban. "And he should get rid of the troops in the township before the house burns down." COSATU, he asserted, was fully supportive of disinvestment by Western companies. "We are no more going to be passive," he declared.

The new federation shied from formal association with the broad anti-apartheid movement of the United Democratic Front, but its fundamental leanings were clear. Mr. Ramaphosa had led his union away from the Council of Unions of South Africa (CUSA) that reflected black consciousness ideologies and into a federation whose very title implied an alliance with the African National Congress. Indeed, within months of its formation, COSATU's leaders went to Lusaka to talk with the ANC and the exiled South African Congress of Trade Unions, its historical forerunner. Much later, it transpired that several of COSATU's top men had for years been clandestine members of the South African Communist Party. Yet, in the mid-1980s, their power remained a topic of debate.

When, on May 1, 1986, COSATU called for a one-day strike to support demands for a public holiday, 1.5 million workers stayed away from their jobs—the biggest stoppage of its kind in South African history. But could that kind of pressure be sustained?

Bobby Godsell, the chief labor specialist at Anglo-American, told me that "a general strike could bring the country to its knees in a couple of weeks." The question, however, was whether the unions and their members could withstand the economic loss—and the certain government repercussions of such action.

"The trade union movement is still a fragile movement in South

Africa," Piroshaw Camay, the head of the rival confederation, CUSA, told me, "And to give it a role that is at the vanguard of the struggle is erroneous."

Political involvement, moreover, exacted its price, and labor leaders, included Mr. Camay, were detained. That, in turn, alarmed employers who had come to recognize one of the most curious twists of the mid-1980s: organized labor offered the bosses the only chance they had of preventing the chaos of the townships from spilling onto the shop floor; the erstwhile adversary had become a tacit, unbidden, and uncertain ally. And that in turn produced a phenomenon that showed just how much things had changed: white corporate executives took to interceding with the authorities for the release of black labor leaders detained under the emergency regulations.

The fault line had shifted again. If corporate South Africa had come to acknowledge and crave black economic organization, how could black political organization be denied? And, seeing that, how could black leaders avoid the intimation that they had touched the heart of white vulnerability?

President Botha was right. South Africa had crossed the Rubicon, and he must surely have known that his land would never be either the one he wished to create or the one to which he had been born. But he had not surrendered, for, physically, on the streets where his army and police force contained the revolt in the townships, he had not lost, and no one has ever just given power away for free. The detentions themselves showed that the physical power, the raw muscle remained with the authorities. What their adversaries offered was an increasing commitment to a violent response.

After the Sharpeville massacre of March 21, 1960, when the police killed sixty-nine blacks, Nelson Mandela had justified the ANC's turn to guerrilla warfare and violent resistance with the simple argument that nothing else worked. "There comes a time, as it came in my life, when a man is denied the right to live a normal life, when he can only live the life of an outlaw because the Government has so decreed to use the law to impose a state of outlawry upon him. I was driven to this situation, and I do not regret taking the decisions I did," he said in 1963 in his final address to the treason trial that was to jail him for twenty-seven years, until his release in February 1990.

Earlier, a pamphlet in his name had stated the case for violent resistance more bluntly. "The choice is not ours," it said. "It has been made by the Nationalist Government which has rejected every peaceable demand by the people for rights and freedom."

The question of the whole era was how that freedom should be achieved. The independence of Mozambique and Angola in 1975, however flawed by war and misery, reinforced the same conclusion that Mandela and others had reached in the 1960s—that violent revolt, guerrilla warfare, and sabotage were the only option.

Physically, "armed struggle" offered the prospect of an uneven fight, but it proved that violence worked. It became the very symbol of black advance toward political self-determination. How, then, would any one expect South Africa's gritty black townships, with their smog and potholes and craziness, to be immune from the patterns of an entire era?

"The unrest," Tom Lodge said after a year of revolt in 1985, "has seen the expression of very violent feelings and these feelings being accorded a degree of popular legitimacy." The same conclusion had been drawn, in bloodier language, on the streets; sometimes conversations with its practitioners left a chilling sense that it would not easily be reversed.

11.

Time of the Necklaces:

Black Choices

"They must feel our pain."

—RESIDENT OF KWATHEMA TOWNSHIP, explaining why black
collaborators had to be executed by fire.

✴ Vusi wore a white shirt and gray slacks. We met, by prear-
rangement, at a school in Soweto where the classrooms were
empty of pupils and the windows were all broken. As often was the
case, the school was being boycotted by its students to protest inferior,
segregated education. The teachers who turned up out of a sense of
duty had long resigned themselves to being ignored and insulted by
students who frightened them.

When Vusi and a sidekick arrived for the interview, the men in the
teaching staff smiled with gratuitous ingratiation or looked away, and
the women offered tea, deferential as maid to madam. Vusi swaggered
a little, not quite at ease with the role reversal with his elders, but not
about to change it. Vusi was a comrade.

He held no particular title or eminence, no status in the myriad
political organizations that permeated the township. He was simply
another nineteen-year-old black South African, lean, tall, and angular,
who lived in the great black conurbation outside of Johannesburg, did
not go to school, hung out on street corners, and raged against the
system he had been born into but could not accept.

He and his peers called one another "comrade," privates in the
army of revolt. And it was people like Vusi—apartheid's spindrift—
who forced the choices across the land. Because of Vusi and Lucas
and all the others, the churches, the black labor movement, big business, and the state itself were forced to define where they stood in
terms of their own future. The rocks they threw—and the news coverage of them—had brought the state repression that inspired sanc-

192

tions. Vusi and his comrades forced the choices because they did not shy from violence against an equally violent notion of how a minority should govern a majority.

In the process, they raised one central question of the era: If violence and confrontation were indeed the only means available to black majorities to effect self-determination, what were the limits of its legitimacy? Who set the rules of engagement when the whole purpose of the campaign was to defy the rules?

In South Africa, the question held a seminal significance: the comrades called violence a legitimate part of the struggle against repression; the authorities called it lawlessness and mayhem that justified more repression. Somewhere between the two lay a whole generation of teenagers to whom violence—against black or white—had become second nature. But if it had some political justification, who would decide when and where it should end?

Vusi's humdrum status was the reason I sought out his views, for I had a particular issue to raise with him. I wanted to ask him about the practice of the "necklace" execution of purported collaborators that, by mid-1986, had become so widespread that it was beginning to raise a lot of worrisome questions in South Africa and in the United States.

In American boardrooms and on the streets and college campuses of many American cities, the battle had been joined to pursue sanctions and divestment as a means of hastening the demise of apartheid. Back there in America, I often had the impression, the issues must have seemed simple and lofty. But on the streets of South Africa's townships, the tactics of intolerance and coercion pursued by those who led the revolt seemed far more troublesome to define and accept. The necklace was a particularly gruesome and painful form of execution: a tire was place around the victim's neck, gasoline was poured into it and then ignited. Was this, South African officials asked me sardonically, the kind of new society Americans wanted to promote?

Comrade Vusi, I thought, might help me see how it looked closer to home, from someone who had, by his own account, administered the punishment, in effect committed premeditated murder. Often, I had heard the big-name players of the revolt offer anguished justifications for the practice, evoking the immense frustration, anger, and rage of the townships. Some even seemed to endorse it in their less guarded moments, and others accepted it as a cruel inevitability. But how did it seem from the streets? And did the comrades even care, as they pursued a flawed and crude justice, that they offered the authorities a way back from reform by redefining the revolt as a morass of what Pretoria came more and more to describe as "black-on-black violence"?

From the beginnning, fire and retribution had run through the months of protest. At the very first spasm in Sharpeville in September 1984—ominously on the same day that Mr. Botha's new constitution officially came into effect, with its gestures toward the Indians and "Coloreds" and its rejection of the blacks—Sam Dlamini, Sharpeville's deputy mayor, had been hacked to death on his own doorstep as a supposed collaborator. Then, in March 1985, volleys of police fire killed twenty-one demonstrators near Uitenhage in the Eastern Cape and drew a correspondingly horrendous response: the comrades of Kwanobuhle township incinerated seven blacks in revenge. Their fury had turned on those near to them who were vulnerable to the charge that they had "collaborated." The men in the armored trucks, the police and army with their shotguns and rifles, were not such easy targets.

The most prominent of the dead in Kwanobuhle was T. B. Kinikini, a black councillor, depicted by his adversaries as part of the system of repression because he had accepted a role within it. For a while he gave his name to the whole practice of death by incineration. "Another Kinikini," people would say, as someone burned and the spiral of black smoke rose from the inert body—a gruesome epitaph for the councillor who, shortly before his death by fire, shot his own son to save him from the same agony. By August 1985, incineration had acquired yet another title—"Kentucky," after the fried chicken franchises that did brisk trade in fast food. "There should be more Kentuckies," one man told me in August 1985, after I had watched—in horror—as a crowd in the nominally independent black homeland called the Ciskei ran down a black Ciskeian police officer and, before the eyes of many foreign reporters, knocked him senseless with a large rock and set him alight. No one even asked his name, let alone assigned him a sin. His uniform bore its own judgment: he was part of "the system," the enemy. Someone kicked his slack lower body as the torso burned and was still.

Gasoline was easily available, and there were plenty of used automobile tires and empty bottles about. Guns were not so easy to come by. Death by incineration produced a central discussion about the image and audiences of the protest: if the overriding issue was to solidify black support for the rebellion in the townships, then the necklace had a cruel logic; but if the revolt was to build a wider constituency, both within South Africa and internationally, among people who cherished peace, then it did not.

In July 1985, at Duduza township on the East Rand, Desmond Tutu, then bishop of Johannesburg, wrestled bodily with members of a crowd who wanted to burn a purported spy in their midst.

"This undermines the struggle," the bishop cried as he sheltered the man the crowd wished to burn.

"No, it encourages the struggle," another man shouted back as Bishop Tutu and Suffragan Bishop Simeon Nkoane struggled to prevent an execution on the pyre of the man's automobile, which had already been overturned and set alight in readiness. Duduza was closely associated with death by fire: it was there that the young Maki Skosana was incinerated in front of a television camera to provide the footage aired on the night of Matthew Goniwe's funeral and the purported reason for the emergency rule imposed in July 1985.

On another occasion in nearby KwaThema township, Bishop Tutu had appealed for an end to the burnings, but the crowd before him did not respond. "They must feel our pain," one man in the crowd told me, to explain what the necklace was supposed to do to people presumed to be collaborators or informers. By informing on political activists, the man explained, informers condemned their own people to certain detention, probably torture, possible death. So the punishment had to fit the crime. There were a lot of suppositions about the necklace, primarily the supposition of guilt.

I sat down with Vusi and his friend in a backroom at the school to talk about this. Yes, he said, he was a comrade, and had no problem with the necklace, indeed, had taken part in an execution or two himself. He offered the information with some pride, as if it established revolutionary credentials.

Why, I asked, were executions necessary in the first place. "We cannot allow an individual to delay our struggle," came the reply, seemingly well rehearsed or heard from others, and based on the fundamental, revolutionary premise that the common weal (as interpreted by the group of individuals with the upper hand) outweighed individual choice. But how did the comrades know whom to burn? He smiled and said: "We know." He would not elaborate on how they knew, but I had heard of the revolutionary courts that handed down rough justice. Some executions were even more impromptu.

Was there not some other way of punishing informers or spies or collaborators—short of killing them, I asked. No, came the reply. Why not?

"Say we take someone and tell them they must not inform on us. Then we let them go. They go straight to the system and identify us, and then we are all detained.

"So it is better"—he paused to allow his friend to complete the sentence—"'Just to get rid of them. Finished." The two young men smiled comfortably at one another.

Well, I continued, beginning to sound a bit too insistent, even to myself, was there not a more humane way of doing things. Why choose such gruesome tactics?

"Then the others will know better than to inform," Vusi said patiently. "They will know not to delay the struggle."

The argument had come full circle. The imperative was the struggle—not the nature of the society it was supposed to build.

We talked for a while about other things—the school's history curriculum, for instance, that started with Dutch settlement of the Cape in 1652 and did not even mention the ANC or Nelson Mandela. That, Vusi told me, was one reason the school was empty; no one wanted to go to classes that taught such filtered history. What they wanted was people's history, political enlightenment, and debate, not a syllabus that saw their land through the eyes of the conqueror. Possibly, too, they did not want school when the street was a much easier and exciting option.

So nobody went to class, and black educational levels slid even further. Examinations were still held, but they were boycotted or attended by teenagers who had hardly been in class. The statistics they produced showed even lower percentages of blacks securing the academic qualifications that were their only hope of advance, however limited the opportunities were. I wondered what Vusi and his friends would be doing ten years on, and wondered, too, how well this diet of dogma and refusal would nourish them in manhood. Then I left and we parted ways—he to gimcrack home, me to white South Africa, the pool, the tennis court, safety.

He had not answered all my questions. The one question that would never be answered satisfactorily was: How many of these useless, charred bodies dumped in the vacant lots of ugly townships bore any guilt at all?

After Maki Skosana's death in Duduza, I asked a black policeman who had been hounded out of the place, Sergeant Joel Msibi, if she had really been on the authorities' payroll. Sergeant Msibi was lean, hard-eyed, and thirty-one years old, the kind of cop Clint Eastwood plays, an enforcer, the Dirty Harry of the townships. He still carried his heavy pistol in the waistband of his trousers, even though, like all the other black policemen living in Duduza, he had been evacuated to a makeshift camp on the grounds of the precinct in the nearby white town of Dunnottar.

Three times arsonists had attacked his home, he said, and on the third try, they burned the place down, so he had abandoned the uneven fight and the comrades had scored a victory. Ridding townships like Duduza of cops like Sergeant Msibi—and all the other 18,000 blacks in the 45,000-member police force—was a prime tactical goal. The aim was, simply, to shift the townships beyond the range of official formal control, to make them ungovernable by conventional methods, and to replace state power with a revolutionary administration they called "people's power." That had happened to an extent in Duduza: the authorities entered only under protection of arms which they did not hesitate to use.

Ungovernability represented a perilous state of being. To raise their own banner, the police fired guns. To raise theirs, the comrades hurled rocks. In Duduza, white cops on the beds of pickup trucks would cruise the township, firing rubber bullets, shotguns, and tear gas, simply to show that state power would not be so easily beaten, and they did it as casually as if they were on a duck shoot: they knew no one would fire back. (Some of the police on the trucks would shout the blacks' own slogan—*Amandla,* meaning "Power"—as they opened fire, in an ironic statement of where power lay.) If the police represented one pole of existence, the comrades' insistence on a new order represented the other. If you were black, you could not ignore either of them. And people's power brought with it some pretty arbitrary justice.

Sergeant Msibi, for instance, insisted that Maki Skosana had not been an informer—an assertion that even some activists supported—but acknowledged that she may have drawn suspicion. Sergeant Msibi said he had been the investigating officer who had been looking for Skosana's brother—"a naughty guy"—in connection with a theft. That was his way of explaining why he had been to her house on several occasions—enough to establish the link between the authorities and Ms. Skosana. "She had not been in trouble," Msibi said. "She was not an informer." Subsequently, her murderers were identified from the videotape of the killing and stood trial: testimony established that one reason for township suspicion about her was that she had taken a black police sergeant as a lover. (It was never made clear if the lover was Joel Msibi. But the liaison explained, in part, his exoneration of her and her execution on the flimsiest of evidence.) In any event, she was dead and her child was orphaned. She had died because of the beliefs of people like Comrade Vusi that the struggle should not be delayed, even if accelerating the struggle seemed, to an outsider, to mean a descent into hell.

The overwhelming impression from my conversations with Vusi and others like him was their total self-confidence. There was no shiftiness, no nervous giggling, no shame. They knew they were right. They knew how things had to be done. And they knew they were the custodians of this struggle that must not be delayed by their parents, by informers, by anybody.

In a cramped, packed church building during a political funeral in Soweto, a young woman had leaped forward to tell her story like this:

"When I came here, my mother asked me: 'Where are you going?' I told her: 'You have no right to know. It is we who have the right to say what will be done. You have done nothing, so now it is our struggle.' "

The belief in the abject failure of their parents' generation drove South Africa's comrades to fury, and once the protest was launched, they came to another realization: they could do it; they could shake the same white self-confidence that had wrought their parents' capitulation. They could burn and rampage and say no, and many times get away with it.

Over 2,000 people died between September 1984 and early 1987. More than 30,000 were detained without charge or trial for varying periods under the two emergency decrees. But the black majority in those days numbered 23 million and, as activists like to say in their bravura, the authorities could not detain the entire country, much as they seemed to try, and they could not detain a state of mind. They could only try to break it.

The power exercised by the comrades was the power of the underdog. The very existence of the struggle was a victory because it denied the official definition of the relationship between black and white, slave and master. The authorities responded with the detentions under the emergency regulations, because the protesters—like the conspirators and the whole population in Kinshasa much earlier during my time in Africa—had to be taught that they could not get away with it. But, in South Africa in the mid-1980s, the strategy failed because it could not halt the process that had, years before, shifted many black attitudes across an important divide. In Cradock, Matthew Goniwe had taught young people that they had options beyond inertia, and the message was repeated with every hurled rock, every sloganeering evocation of the still-outlawed ANC. Even in the far, conservative reaches of the northern Transvaal, at a little crossroads town called Alldays, where the old Afrikaners in their shorts still chuckled about the day an Indian came into the bar and was chased out of town, the old definitions had been loosened.

For no easily discerned reason one day in late 1986, Frankie, the stunted white bartender at the Alldays Hotel, confronted a black laborer sitting in the back of a pickup in the small car park while the boss had a beer inside the pub—a familiar arrangement in a land where blacks had, generically, been relegated beyond the back seat to the flatbed.

"You are a kaffir," Frankie told him in Afrikaans. It was a shocking word, a crude gauntlet, flung down with coarse malevolence. Everything stopped, silent in the heat. Other black laborers bridled, waited.

"No," the man replied softly, also in Afrikaans. "I am a black man."

Frankie screamed, "Kaffir!"

The stand-off turned yet nastier, with both men repeating the same irreconcilable basic perceptions—a kaffir was an object, a subhuman, something that could be dealt with, like a dog; but a black man was something altogether more threatening, a being with the ability to translate will into action. Then the boss came from the bar and drove away, but the moment left a smear across the sunlit day. Frankie had tried to restate the racial order and, when he failed, he was frightened: a kaffir was too docile to exact vengeance, a black man was not.

That night, after the raw confrontation, Frankie slept on the floor at the foot of Mark Peters's bed inside the hotel—himself the dog now—rather than face the loneliness and hazards of the small rondavel in the hotel grounds that was part of his reward for the job.

On a far wider scale, the comrades too redefined their relationship with white authority and with the black generation that had given up the fight. Their reply was the same as the laborer's in Alldays—they were not kaffirs, and they would no longer accept the labels and practices of the past.

"They are in the kamikaze mood now," a black schoolteacher in his fifties told me in a township near Port Elizabeth at about the same period in 1985 as my conversation with Joel Msibi. "They would rather commit suicide than swallow what's being offered to them."

The youth, older people used to say, had taken over, and their elders had no choice but to support them. "The oppression is far worse than in my day," said Elizabeth Sibanda, a robust sixty-four-year-old widow in Cradock, who traced her political activism to marching against the pass laws in the 1950s, "so the youth know more about politics. We are prepared to be with our children. We should be much closer rather than let them fight alone."

"If the youth are prepared to fight for their education," an older man from the black labor movement in an East Rand township told me, "then we must be prepared to fight for our rights."

To be sure, there were many, many black people in South Africa— people like Victoria Gasela in Alexandra—who would probably have preferred the quiet life. Indeed, a local headmaster told me in KwaThema, maybe apartheid was right, maybe blacks and whites could not live side by side, if only the whites would share the riches a little more evenly. But when the fires took root, the flames spared no one.

12.

Divide and Rule:

"Black-on-Black"

Violence

"Together, hand-in-hand, with our sticks and our matches, with our necklaces, we shall liberate this country."

—WINNIE MANDELA, addressing a rally at Kagiso township, April 13, 1986

If there were two local issues that fueled the wider protest, they were rents and education. "When we pay rents," an older man in Sharpeville told me, "we are paying to live where we don't want to. We are paying for apartheid."

A rent protest had ignited Sharpeville and the Vaal Triangle in September 1984, and the refusal to pay the township rents that financed residential segregation persisted: by August 1986, it was reckoned that 300,000 householders in 42 townships—including Soweto—were not paying their rent, at a cost to the authorities of $500,000 a day in lost revenues. In 1990, they were still boycotting the rents in Soweto and elsewhere.

But even before the rent protest in Sharpeville, students in places like Cradock and Atteridgeville near Pretoria had been boycotting classes to protest a form of schooling that apartheid's architects had labeled "Bantu education"—a notion that, like Frankie's insult in Alldays, implied a perception of the black majority as a sublevel of society that was going nowhere.

There was no point in offering blacks too advanced an education, apartheid's founders argued, because, as "temporary sojourners" in white South Africa, they would never be called upon to do more than the menial work and then depart. Why create an architect who would never be more than a hod carrier on the construction site? Why build

decent housing for these "temporary sojourners" who, by one of apartheid's most curious twists, were somehow supposed to vanish into the
thin air of the homelands even as their presence around the cities
become more and more evident. As it usually did, apartheid collided
with commonsense.

The schools were where the young people most intimately embroiled
in the revolt came into their most intimate contact with the system to
which they felt their parents had surrendered. The schools had been
the cradle of protest in 1976, and now they played the same role again.
It was hardly surprising. In the racial gradations from black to white,
the education budget told its familiar tale of inequity. In 1984, the
state spent seven or eight times more on the education of a white child
than on the education of a black child. Between the two extremes,
the 2.8 million so-called "Coloreds" got more than the blacks, and
the 800,000 Indians got more than the Coloreds. But the 4.5 million
whites got most of all. There were at the very least forty black pupils—
and as many as sixty in some schools—for every black teacher, and
nineteen white pupils for every white teacher. White teachers were
qualified. Black teachers, often as not, were the products of the same
Bantu education that had denied black abilities to learn, so many had
nothing to offer their pupils anyhow and merely perpetuated the cycle
of inferiority.

In the townships, "the school is associated with everything they
hate," said Peter Nixon, headmaster of a private, fee-paying multi-
racial school called Woodmead, located in a white area just north of
Johannesburg. Since it did not face the same racial rules as government
schools, Woodmead was picking up pretty good business, not only
from white parents who did not wish to send their children to segregated
schools, but also from parents of the embryonic black middle class
who wanted their kids out of the townships and educated.

Woodmead lay on the wooded banks of the Jukskei River. Birds
sang. The grass was green. Some children boarded; others were day
scholars. It had libraries, laboratories, space and staff, and, most of
all, peace.

Back in the townships, by contrast, Mr. Nixon said, school was "a
symbol of inferiority, state control. It's a symbol of incompetent and
lazy teachers. It is a symbol of everything that makes their teenage
years of very little value, so it's a natural target for them."

But school was only one part of the dismal education of the townships. When white children went home, in most cases, they had a quiet room for homework, electric lighting, desks, pencils, books, warmth, food. Most black children went home to the matchbox houses where life squeezed its way between a big old stove in a small kitchen full of pots, a living room—if there was one—filled with elders, bedrooms filled with siblings, talk filled with indignities. For the growing white generation, there would be no midnight summons to the streets to join the comrades, no 3:00 A.M. rap on the door as the police came by to seize brother, sister, or self. White children, for the most part, lived with a simple, basic assumption: school would be there for them tomorrow, whether they liked it or not, and teachers with authority would lead them in prayer and learning. Whether black children liked it or not, school was a fickle thing, a label of inferiority that might function or not, a place with no authority to guide them or legitimacy to lead them in anything. Education provided another example of apartheid's achievement: one land, two realities.

In the mid-1980s, hundreds of thousands of blacks boycotted their classes, spilling onto the streets to confront the authorities. When protest spread to the mixed-race youth of the Cape, hundreds of "Colored" schools were closed down by the very same "Colored" authorities installed under P. W. Botha's reforms, discrediting them from the start.

The militants' slogan—"Liberation before education"—rattled white authority, but replaced a formal eduation for many blacks with education on the streets in the ways of confrontation and coercion. Colliding with the liberal ethic that attached so much importance to individual will and responsibility, the self-appointed leaders of the revolt enforced their own laws in the name of the struggle—rent strikes, schools boycotts, consumer boycotts—with the same sense of rectitude as they enforced the necklace.

"We did not want to be thrown out," Maurice Matemba, a twenty-nine-year-old man, told me after the authorities evicted him and his family from their small, red-brick home in Sharpeville for not paying the rent. "But the comrades say they'll burn your house down with everything in it if you pay the rent." In Port Elizabeth, black housewives who defied a boycott of white-owned stores saw their new purchases tipped onto the garbage heap, or, worse still, were made to drink detergents or cooking oil bought in white stores while gleeful teenagers danced about them chanting "Viva Omo"—the name of the detergent. Whites faced choices, too, but not like this.

When a school boycott started near Cape Town, a nineteen-year-old who termed himself a leader told me: "Those who are not for it will suffer." In the psychology of the struggle, in the quest for the routing of state power, the collision of competing wills produced hard rules. "It is difficult now to convince young people that what they are doing is barbaric," a political activist in his thirties told me in 1986 as he hid from the authorities and the discussion turned to the necklace. "They see it as being on a par with killings by the other side."

As an outsider who had grown up on notions of the sanctity of individual belief, my overriding impression was that people's power gave people about as much personal freedom as apartheid did. But those who led the revolt kept on telling me that this was the transition phase to a collective freedom, and individualism was a luxury that could not be afforded. I'd heard talk like that in Angola in the 1970s. They probably said much the same in Russia in 1917, too. It took an act of faith to believe that South Africa's revolutionaries meant things to turn out differently.

In Soweto, one reason that the huge place did not just explode when the rest of the country did in September 1984 was that, within its embrace, there were people who had things to protect: jobs, homes, children, pension rights, savings. Soweto had been the focus of the efforts of white businessmen to create the embryo of a middle class—black men in suits and BMWs.

When Warren Hoge, then foreign editor of *The New York Times*, came to visit Johannesburg in 1985, we espied a very smart black man driving a very smart car in the center of town. What fascinated Hoge was not so much the trappings of a wealth not usually associated with South Africa's blacks, but the fact that, for all his obvious riches and success, this man, like most other blacks working in the city, still had to go back to Soweto when work was done. Individual wealth or status did not buy a ticket out of the system. And the system brought far fewer rewards to most: rebellion was easy for people who had nothing much to lose.

In Zwide township outside Port Elizabeth, I stopped to give a ride to a man called James Vumile Mpunthe, a thirty-nine-year-old laid-off auto worker and father of five. I wanted to talk politics. He wanted to talk shoes.

"Look at them," he said, gesturing to his well-polished but expiring footwear. "They are worn down. Why are they worn down? Because every day I am walking to town to look for work. But I find no work and have to walk home again." In 1984, he had been laid off by Ford, at that time the biggest American employer in South Africa. "Ford was my mother and my father," he said. He showed me a 1982 paycheck that he hauled from a drawer of mementos and old bills in the living room of the cinderblock, two-room home whose rent— when it was paid at all—was financed by his wife's earnings as a maid in a white home. In 1982, the paycheck showed, his take-home pay for a 32-hour week before overtime was the equivalent of $45.

"If you had a job at Ford, you were a big man around here," he said. But the recession cut the numbers of the big men with jobs, so plenty of little men without jobs joined in the protest.

"Some white people haven't woken up yet," Tony Gilson, director of the Port Elizabeth Chamber of Commerce—a white business association—told me on the same day in February 1985. "Some of them haven't felt the chilly breeze that's blowing through Port Elizabeth at the moment."

The recession had hit hardest in Port Elizabeth and its hinterland, and that was one reason that it became such a focus of protest.

When people considered why the Eastern Cape became so steeped in revolt, they evoked many issues: its close tribal and political association with the leaders of the ANC, its long traditions of resistance and war from the nineteenth century onward. But if they wanted one more reason, all they had to do was to ask Mr. Mpunthe about his shoes. And if they wanted to see the battlefield to which his children had been drawn, all they had to do was to look at where they lived.

South Africa's comrades were fighting a different style of war from that of the bush guerrillas of Mozambique and Zimbabwe. To the north, they had guns. Here, they had rocks and gasoline and slogans and placards and great numbers, but no guns.

Up there, in Zimbabwe and Mozambique, there had been space— a rural war fought with the imagery of Vietnam: land-mined tracks and helicopters pouring fire, infiltration trails and rear bases and villages that offered the insurgents some respite.

Here, in South Africa, there were only the townships: liberation began and ended at two-room homes like Mr. Mpunthe's; there was nowhere else to retire to when the orgasm of conflict had ebbed. Where the guerrillas to the north claimed whole slabs of territory as "liberated zones," the comrades in the south were contained within the perimeter of the townships as both apartheid and the emergency decrees intended: all they could liberate was their own backyard, and they could only liberate that by making it "ungovernable." And what kept them in their backyard was not a settler regime with an escape route, but a government with roots that fed on the resources of Africa's richest, most powerful, and most industrialized nation.

Yet one similarity with the comrade to the north offered government propagandists a weapon: fifth columnists, spies, dissenters were eliminated whether by the bullet or the necklace. That raised the fraught and complex notion of what government propagandists took delight in labeling "black-on-black violence," as if it excused their own violence.

From September 1984 to April 1986, President Botha told Parliament in 1986, "508 people, mostly moderate blacks, were brutally murdered by radical blacks." His tally continued: "No less than 1,417 black-owned businesses, 4,435 private homes—including 814 homes of black policemen—28 churches, 54 community centers, several hundred schools and a number of clinics, all serving the black community, were either totally destroyed or badly damaged by petrol bombs or other forms of arson."

Vusi and Lucas and all the others had been active indeed, with ambivalent results.

Only the merest handful of their direct adversaries—the white-led security forces—had met the same fate as the "black moderates" whom President Botha tried and failed to conjure from the conflict as a black constituency to vindicate his reforms. If the brutal murders in the townships had achieved one goal it was that no one came forward to Mr. Botha to say yes. But the murders also fed the attempts of the white authorities to tell the world that what Pretoria confronted was not legitimate revolt but an inherent black instablity that would, if left unchecked, reduce the land to anarchy.

South Africa's rulers used the term" black-on-black violence" to imply that all African violence welled from some dark, Satanic source that spewed from the Congo and stained the red earth of many parts of Africa—from Chad to Uganda, to Mozambique and Angola and Zimbabwe. And, in suggesting inherent black savagery, the authorities sent their own message to their adversaries and critics: How can you expect us to deal any differently with "these people"? With every necklace, the comrades obligingly deepened the propaganda trap they had set for themselves, obliterating their cause in the dense smoke of the execution, too convinced of their own rectitude to pause and wonder whether this really promoted the struggle. And when the protest in the townships of the mid-1980s gave way to bloodletting in Natal Province from 1987 onward—killing in one year more than Beirut did in the same period—it seemed arguable that Africa was doomed to fall prey to some schizophrenic violence that denied the very gentleness and decency of so many of its people.

But, as always, it was not so simple or so monochromatic, and it was not new, either.

What President Botha did not mention when he gave his statistical survey was that 1,500 blacks—three times as many as were murdered by fellow blacks—were killed by the police between September 1984 and July 1986. Nor did he allude to the history of division that brought together black distinctions and white maneuvers in such bloody symbiosis.

When they explained why things had to be the way they were, South Africa's white rulers maintained that their land was not a "homogenous society," and that was true. They had made it true.

Apartheid did not just mean dividing black from white, but, in its own lexicon, offering each "nation" a place of its own, whether it wanted it or not. South Africa, the National Party ideologues insisted, was a nation of minorities—Zulus, Xhosas, whites, and many others. No single minority should dominate the others, they said, meaning the opposite.

But apartheid did not invent tribalism. It used it, as my forebears had done, to splinter black nationalism. The map of Central and southern Africa in the nineteenth century was latticed with the trails of tribal empires and fiefdoms, expanding and contracting according to the dictates of military and economic power. That was true as much in Zambia, Zimbabwe, or Malawi as it was in South Africa, where the campaigns of Shaka Zulu redrew the demography of the entire region.

Apartheid sought to fix the lines while the modern economy pushed against them. The magnetic wealth of South Africa's cities drew men of different tribes and different countries to the same places around the mines, and the tribal divisions back home came with them and were perpetuated by the attitudes they found when they arrived.

The single-sex hostels provided by most mines offered different dormitories to men of different ethnic backgrounds. The reason, the mine managers assured me in what I took for sincerity, was to reduce internecine feuding. Among whites, black separation was virtually an article of faith. Cutting through the surf off Durban to inspect the shark nets that guarded white (not black) beaches, I asked the white skipper of the 21-foot speedboat how he chose his black crew. "They're all Pondos," he said. "You can't mix them with the Zulus. They'd only kill each other."

The fashionable view was that places like Soweto were the melting pot of tribalism, so big and urban that the old distinctions did not apply, and that their influence was eroding the tribal divisions elsewhere in South Africa. I was not so sure. Outside Port Elizabeth in the scrublands adjacent to the black townships, it was common enough to see the small, crude shelters that young Xhosa men had erected for the initiation rites into the manhood of their tribe. In Lebowa homeland, the Pedi people still clung to their tribal belief that a benevolent wizard could see the face of a malevolent witch reflected in a smooth, polished stone from the river; and once identified in this way, the supposed witch would be burned at the stake.

Tribalism dovetailed with the notions of "group rights" by which some Afrikaners sought to remodel apartheid and juggle the figures to offset demographic reality. And it nourished one of the great gulfs in black politics that set the Inkatha movement of the Zulu chief Mangosuthu Gatsha Buthelezi against other movements, notably the ANC and the UDF, the leading anti-apartheid movement inside South Africa. But black division also drew white interference to widen it.

Inkatha had built a claimed membership in excess of 1 million. Its identity was exclusively Zulu, and it reinforced its tribal profile with the assertion that the leadership of the ANC was overwhelmingly Xhosa.

In August 1985, South Africa's violence spread to Durban and almost seventy people were killed. The casualties, symbolically enough, included the former home of Mahatma Gandhi, burned and looted by a mindless mob that wrenched the zinc sheeting and the wooden planks from this shrine to peaceful resistance.

In the cruel conflict, blacks fought one another and blacks fought Indians, tearing at the frail peace between them, and recalling for many Indians an ambivalent status betwen black and white that had not been changed by the embrace of Mr. Botha's reforms. The mob, jealous of Indian wealth, offered only hostility. And the police, indifferent to their color, offered no protection.

"We've got the whites on one side and the blacks on the other," a young Indian man called Anwar Rumharak—a nineteen-year-old invoice clerk—told me as we stood together on a ridge watching young Zulus on the next ridge massing and chanting. "We're like the sausage in the hot dog." He meant it as a joke, but no one laughed. Some of his friends had pistols and fired them when the Zulus ran toward them. But the Zulus kept on coming until the Indians fell back.

The self-confidence of the Zulus drew partly on a martial tradition that demanded courage. But it relied too on a tacit alliance with the authorities that contributed not only to Natal's bloodletting between 1987 and 1990—when 4,000 people died in what amounted to a civil war—but also to the killing that stained the Transvaal after Nelson Mandela's release in 1990.

In 1985, Chief Buthelezi deployed his impis—battalions of men in tribal dress with cow-hide shields and stabbing spears honed to a gleam—just as Dingane and Shaka had done in the nineteenth century. What was significant was that the authorities allowed the impis to take to the streets, just as they allowed Chief Buthelezi to hold political rallies when others were forbidden to do so. An armed crowd marching in support of the UDF would have drawn strong official reprisals. Inkatha's impis did not. The authorities wished to build Inkatha as a bulwark against the ANC and the UDF, to encourage black division and to reward Inkatha for its policies: its opposition to sanctions, its supposed commitment to non-violence (meaning non-violence toward the white authorities) and Chief Buthelezi's tacit acceptance of the creation—although not the independence—of KwaZulu, the most populous of all the homelands.

But what events also displayed was the raw power of the tribe, harnessed to a goal that ultimately benefited neither Zulu nor Xhosa. The official statements about "black-on-black violence" omitted one critical factor: frequently, the authorities took sides.

Nicholas Haysom, the white human rights lawyer in Johannesburg, for instance, traced official connivance in the activities of black vigilante groups in several black townships, where, to defend the established order, shadowy groups with names like "The A-Team" and "The Green Berets" took to the streets to challenge the comrades on their own turf.

If street power was to determine the outcome of the struggle for the townships, the authorities seemed to be saying, then the rules of street warfare, gang warfare, would prevail. Somehow, the vigilantes gained access to guns. Somehow, they were never prosecuted. Toward the end of my time in South Africa, civil rights activists told me of a new, black municipal police force that had been introduced into the townships near Port Elizabeth to combat protest in the area, often in brutal ways. That, indeed, was "black-on-black violence" of a different kind than the authorities implied.

But of all the conflicts of that period to be labeled in this way, none rewrote so many people's lives so quickly as the vicious confrontation in May 1986 between the comrades and their adversaries at Crossroads, a squatter camp near Cape Town. Never until then, for that matter, had the comrades suffered such a humiliating and total defeat, losing ground not only figuratively but literally: when the battle was over, great swathes of the Crossroads camp had been burned to the ground and as many as 30,000 people were homeless.

Their plight highlighted a curious demographic twist: of all of South Africa's regions, the Western Cape was the only one where blacks were in an absolute minority compared to the total number of whites and mixed-race people who had grown as a result of miscegenation, a reminder to the Afrikaners of their guiltiest secrets, the skeletons in the racial cupboard.

("You should talk to Coloreds about Afrikaners," the Reverend Allan Boesak, a high-profile activist who was himself of mixed race, once told me, "because they created us.")

To some whites, the Cape offered the tantalizing prospect of a last bastion against black numbers, ringed and protected by its spectacular mountains, speckled with vineyards, united by the Afrikaans language common to white and "Coloreds," a linguistic alliance at least. Whites and "Coloreds" prayed to the same God in the Dutch Reformed Church, although apartheid insisted they worship in completely separate branches. The Cape had been declared a "colored labor preferential area," meaning that employers were obliged to hire a person of mixed race ahead of a black. The unspoken white agenda was to thwart black settlement.

Yet, since 1975, Crossroads had grown as possibly the most celebrated squatter camp in South Africa. Its fame, I sometimes thought, might have some bearing on its proximity to the fine hotels and restaurants of Cape Town, where reporters and other concerned foreigners enjoyed tarrying a while. Filled with fugitives from the black homeland of the Transkei who broke all of South Africa's laws about where blacks were supposed to settle in order to seek work in Cape Town, Crossroads made a visitor wonder what awful miseries there must be in the Transkei if this place with its shacks and mud was better. But the figures and history spoke for themselves: in the Transkei, as in other so-called "homelands," upward of 100,000 black children were receiving supplementary food from charities like Operation Hunger. Crossroads drew people by default.

Frequently, in Crossroads, the white men from the West Cape Administration Board—an Orwellian term for the enforcers of apartheid legislation—would come with sledgehammers and crowbars and shotguns to knock down whole chunks of the place while residents were either present to bemoan the fact or away at work. Off came the outer layers of zinc sheeting and plastic, the inner walls of newspaper, until finally the core was revealed, someone's wretched belongings: bed, paraffin stove, pots, cupboard. The men from the West Cape Administration Board went at it with a vigor that was matched only by the resilience of the residents.

Working hours at the West Cape Administration Board were fairly strict. Thus, at 4:00 P.M. the men with their sledgehammers and crowbars and shotguns went home. They, too, had wives, families, a beer to drink with their buddies, a life to lead. At around 4:01 P.M., the cycle would begin again, the zinc and newspaper and plastic reassembled and the shacks rebuilt until the next time. Some at Crossroads sought to preempt the process and tore down plastic shelters before dawn to rebuild them late in the afternoon, when the men from the West Cape Administration Board had gone home.

To talk to Crossroads' residents at the beginning of the cycle, you went to Crossroads before the first sun chased the harsh nocturnal chills of a rain-swept Cape winter. The only coordinate in the quest to find them was the coughing of small children in the dark.

As it grew, Crossroads bred its own underworld rules, its own distinctions and fiefdoms and territorial barons demanding rents and loyalties. There were people there who would have thrived in Dickensian London—*skollies*, the Afrikaans term for scoundrels.

Initially, in the early 1980s, the official plan was to transfer all the black people from Cape Town's townships and squatter camps to a totally new place called Khayelitsha, set in the dunes of the Cape flats, miles from anywhere. When the sand was being leveled to make way for it, the area seemed so vast and lunar that the bulldozers doing the leveling looked like small yellow toys. Over the years, however, the authorities relented a little and said some of Cape Town's blacks— those who lived in officially recognized townships like Langa, Nyanga, and Guguletu—would not be moved and neither would some of the residents of Crossroads. But Crossroads itself, they said, would have to be gentrified, and not so many people would be able to live there. That, in turn, heightened the competition between the pro-ANC militants and others, known as "vigilantes," who were prepared to cooperate with the authorities in return for a promise of tenure in Crossroads.

Over the space of one week in May 1986, vigilantes identifying one another by the strips of white cloth they wore to earn their Afrikaans sobriquet, *witdoeke*, moved in force on the areas of Crossroads where the comrades had spread their influence. As the *witdoeke* beat back their adversaries, they torched the homes. When they were winning, the army and police stood by. When the *witdoeke* looked like losing, the security forces intervened to push back their adversaries. Shots were fired. People were hacked to death by the *witdoeke*. Great gouts of black smoke blocked the Cape sun. A friend of mine, George De'Ath, a cameraman, was brutally murdered by the *witdoeke* when his sound man mistook them for the other side and called them "comrades." For the comrades themselves, it was a rout. And for one third of Crossroads' 100,000 people, it meant there was no home to go to any more and they had lost most of the few possessions they had assembled over the years. The charred mess of the battlefield was bulldozed flat and the army threw a cordon of razor wire around it to prevent rebuilding. There was, intially, some rage. "They are going to have to kill us before we move," Maggie Mbamobo, a fifty-six-year-old activist, said. But the anger eventually fizzled. And the most telling words came from Chris Heunis, a senior minister in President Botha's government. "There is no possibility," he said, "that the people can go back to Crossroads." All of Crossroads people had come from the same Xhosa background. But they had been turned against one another by a white design that played on their most basic need for a home.

That was "black-on-black violence," too.

The rifts that made black choices so laden with risk ran through society. For decades South African black politics had swung between two poles. On one side was a school of thought that embraced all races in the struggle against apartheid. On the other was the belief that only blacks—or at least non-whites—could throw off the oppressors. The cleavage had become evident in 1959 with the break between the ANC, which supported the multi-racial approach, and the Pan Africanist Congress (PAC), a splinter movement that excluded whites from the effort to end apartheid, believing blacks alone should liberate themselves.

The distinctions invited interference, not only from the Security Police. When the Soviet Union channeled its support to six particular movements—the ANC, SWAPO, ZAPU, the PAIGC, FRELIMO, and the MPLA—it deepened the divisions, forcing other movements to seek help from China. In South Africa, Moscow's choice was not surprising since the ANC was in open alliance with the South African Communist Party. Soviet backing for the ANC left the Pan Africanist Congress out in the cold, just as Robert Mugabe's ZANU had been excluded from Moscow's embrace by the Soviet decision to back Joshua Nkomo's ZAPU. The PAC set up its external headquarters in Tanzania, where the Chinese had some influence, while the ANC established its base in Zambia, the nerve center of Soviet diplomatic operations in southern Africa under Moscow's ambassador, Vladimir Solodovnikov. Then the CIA joined in, trying to discredit and divide ZAPU.

Such was the tangle of the times—and the perceived solidarity of the so-called "authentic six" liberation movements supported by Moscow—that ANC cadres were said by ANC dissidents to have fought alongside Joshua Nkomo's ZAPU cadres, not simply to overthrow minority rule in South Africa or Rhodesia but also to challenge Robert Mugabe's ZANU in Zimbabwe. If the Cold War produced craziness, Africa magnified it. And in South Africa, the pendulum had swung both ways.

In the 1950s, the ANC's defiance campaigns attracted many to mass protest. But in the 1960s, it was the PAC—led by Robert Sobukwe— that took responsiblity for the Sharpeville protest against the pass laws that plunged the nation into its bloodletting. In Soweto in the 1970s, it was generally acknowledged that the Black Consciousness movement and its leader, Steve Biko, had become the custodian of black aspirations, pursuing the same purist goals as the PAC. By the time I arrived in 1983, the ANC—and its internal affiliate, the UDF—held the high ground, but the division persisted over the central notion of how freedom should come.

The UDF had its followers, grouped in six hundred organizations that sought either to marshall individual township protest, as Cradora had done in Cradock, or to cast a broader net with organizations that appealed to wider constituencies—black students, white liberals. The PAC's newest derivative was the Azanian People's Organization (AZAPO), which consistently espoused more radical and ideologized positions, its followers—many of them students and intellectuals— drawn to the talk of black exclusivism, anti-imperialism, and class warfare.

The black labor movement was divided by rival confederacies that owed their allegiance to one side or the other. AZAPO might not have had the numbers, but it had a voice. When, early in 1985, Senator Edward M. Kennedy scheduled an address to the congregation at Regina Mundi in Soweto, it was the threat of disruption by AZAPO that obliged him to cancel.

My colleague Mono Badela confronted the divisions in a more intimate way.

Mono was a small, round, effervescent man who worked in Port Elizabeth for *City Press*—a newspaper that appeared twice a week for a readership made up primarily of blacks, diplomats, and journalists who read it to get a sense of where things were going. He also worked, in an informal way, for me and other foreign reporters as a fixer, arranging appointments, helping as a translator, assisting with access to places whites did not generally go. Mono was courteous, cheerful, and courageous.

As his name implied, Mono was single-minded in his approach to the politics of the cause and was an unswerving supporter of the UDF and the ANC. Mono knew everybody. And, conversely, everyone knew Mono. That did not always help. One night, the AZAPO people in New Brighton black township where he lived took him away to kill him. He escaped only after someone—supposedly fighting against the same enemy as he was—slashed him around the head with a knife and left him in the back of a pickup while a debate continued among his captors about whether he should be necklaced or not. My UDF friends in Port Elizabeth threw up their hands in outrage and shock, and blamed "the system" for permitting AZAPO to function even as the police sought to obliterate the UDF. I did not doubt that the authorities were trying to choreograph black division, as they had always done. But sometimes, "black-on-black" violence made me wonder why people made it so easy for them.

It was a violence that blurred the protest, dispersed its energies, and raised the levels of hazard. At times of protest, the townships were dangerous enough. Confrontation brought perils for everybody, reporters included. Internecine strife only added to the risks. When friends asked, doesn't it frighten you, the answer was yes.

13.

"Rock-and-Roll":

Covering the Townships

"This is an illegal gathering.
You have three minutes to
disintegrate."

—UNIDENTIFIED WHITE POLICEMAN,
mispronouncing a pro forma warning
to black protesters in Cape Town's
Guguletu township, 1985

Jammed in a line of traffic at the entrance to Alexandra township late one evening, at a time of high tension and much shooting, my hired car came under tremendous attack. The rear window shattered; the side windows blew in under the impact of rocks; the windshield exploded in splinters; a sharp, triangular rock flew past my head and weighed in later on the kitchen scales at a little over seven pounds. I thought the stoning was an end in itself. Then I saw the real purpose of the onslaught. A tall, slim young man detached himself from the crowd and in his hand I glimpsed a homemade gasoline bomb, the wick aflicker.

The stoning had been intended to clear the way into the car interior for the Molotov cocktail.

The ambush was well organized. I could no more get out of the car to remonstrate or beg mercy than I could move forward. Everything was happening in the bright, familiar freeze-frame that adrenaline produces when the mind demands responses faster than the body can give them. The seconds compressed into a maddening slow motion. Then, ahead of me, I saw salvation in the black taxi driver whose car blocked my forward advance. He was surveying the situation in his rear-view mirror. He looked straight at me and our eyes met for long enough for some kind of message to pass between us. At that point he made a choice that could have cost him his life.

216

His car inched forward, just enough to permit my escape, not enough to be noticed in the fury of my attackers. I sped out of the ambush. The petrol bomb landed in a billow of flame exactly where I had been trapped. It took some fairly crazy stunt driving to get out of Alexandra once more after I had lurched forward into it, and the rocks came again as I sought a safe exit. I recount the story only to say that it was the taxi driver who provided an enduring symbol of hope, for his action seemed to overwhelm the rage of the comrades seeking vengeance for their dead wherever they could find it.

When, in a white home shortly after the incident, I recalled the events to a group of white South Africans, they told me I had gotten it all wrong: what my encounter in Alexandra showed was black savagery that had to be opposed at all costs. The cab driver was the exception, not the rule, they said. I prayed they were wrong, but did not really want to argue the point: not all the comrades, as I well knew, were simply disaffected scholars. The protest drew to it a disconsolate band of drop-outs and unemployed, the rejects of a recessionary and imbalanced economy and of a system that devalued their very existence. Revolutionary theory has it that their violence would cleanse them of the emotional trauma of subjugation by an alien settler. At the point of contact, though, the violence of the man with the Molotov cocktail seemed as reflexive as my urge to escape: both of us saw the hostility of an implacable adversary and reacted accordingly.

The stoning in Alexandra was not the end of the episode. When I turned in the battered car, the hire company reported the damage to the police as part of the procedure required for an insurance claim on a new automobile. The police contacted me and asked if I would— or could—identify the rock throwers from a rogue's gallery of mug shots in the precinct near the township—a substantial album of people who, I guess, were the usual suspects to be rounded up whenever trouble overflowed. When I said I simply could not recall the faces because it had all happened so quickly, the interviewing officer suggested that, perhaps, I was procrastinating, that I was reluctant to cooperate with his inquiries because of my political views.

The reality was that conscience would not permit me to identify my assailants any more than I would finger a policeman to the comrades: like most of my colleagues, I cherished a notion of neutrality in a situation that did not readily admit it. The effort to avoid taking sides was denied by both the authorities and the comrades because both sides saw foreign reporters as players in their game, embraced by some, abhorred by others.

For those comrades who paused long enough to think about it, news coverage—particularly television coverage—of their uneven battle, their funerals and defiance, was part of the strategy to marshal important Western constituencies behind their demands for sanctions and other pressures on the authorities. And by the same logic for the police and the government, foreign reporters were no more than fifth columnists, subverting the crusade against communist agitation.

That was one reason why the emergency decrees of 1985 and 1986 laid such increasing stress on inhibiting news coverage. What's more, it seemed to the government, the TV cameras encouraged violent protest: when the cameras started rolling, officials maintained, the rocks started flying, conjured by the wizardry of electronic news gathering. TV reporters were even accused of paying blacks to throw rocks at the police to provide exciting footage. I never saw that happen, and do not believe that it did; but in the bravura of the times, unrest became known to reporters as "rock-and-roll," the rock of the comrades, the roll of the cameras.

Just by doing their jobs, thus, journalists became part of the events they were supposed to chronicle. News reports and television footage molded foreign opinion, and foreign opinion assumed a huge importance for both sides, though for different and somtimes ambiguous reasons.

Perceiving themselves as an isolated outpost of Western values, Christianity, and civilization, white South Africans seemed to crave some distant endorsement from those same people they so quickly alienated with their policies. South Africa, they insisted, was holding the line, restraining chaos, maintaining "standards." The outsiders did not understand, but if only they could, they would see the fundamental justice that underlay the repression that drew such easy foreign condemnation.

By their own lights, Afrikaners, like the Rhodesians before them, were fighting a misunderstood and wilfully misportrayed war for the same values that were supposed to be inherent in the West. The people who were primarily responsible for misrepresenting their campaigns were the foreign reporters, and that perception bred hostility, blocked visas, and led to confrontation between government and press. It also meant an obsessive interest in what the world's newspapers—particularly those they wanted to silence—were saying about them. Even my own humble expulsion merited a street-corner billboard on the newspaper stands: "Evicted U.S. newsman regarded as hostile," it declared.

The preoccupation with what the press was saying also led South Africans into a quandary. Despite an array of restrictive press laws predating the emergency, South Africa's newspapers were always far more vigorous, accurate, robust, and free than any other in Africa. The authorities liked the distinction because it supported their claim to the status of a First World society laboring among the calamities of the Third World. When they finally clamped down on their own newspapers, they widened still further the gap between themselves and the West, and between the reality and their own image of themselves. Survival dictated the same denial of public accountability as they had so long ascribed to their African adversaries to the north.

If foreign reporters touched an emotive nerve with the authorities, however, they were seen in more calculating, strategic terms by the comrades, or, at least, by their leaders and strategists.

That was partly why the incident in Alexandra was an exception. Most times, reporters traveling to black townships would effectively be offered the protection of anti-apartheid groups, the shelter of small homes, and guidance through the back streets to get to where they wanted to go. Many townships residents, too, felt lost and alone in the fight. They wanted friends and allies, and sought the sense of outside support from foreign reporters, just as Jonas Savimbi had done in Jamba. And that seeming complicity deepened the distrust and hostility of the police toward the press.

According to the rules of engagement, police officers were supposed to give warning of their intention to use force in the townships, and they generally preferred to evict reporters from troubled areas before they set about quelling revolt. But often, journalists, by their own design, would get caught up in the confrontation: rock-and-roll, after all, was what they had come to chronicle.

"This is an illegal gathering," the commanding officer would call through a bullhorn. "You have three minutes to disperse." That was the starting gun, the signal—not always given—to crowds of protesters that they had options: to run or be attacked.

The notion of precise timing seemed elastic and there were many occasions when barely three seconds elapsed before the warning was followed by volleys of tear gas, rubber bullets, birdshot and worse.

The same options—to run or to take risks—applied to reporters, with slight variants. Few journalists, for instance, favored standing behind the police lines because that, in the eyes of the comrades, might suggest complicity with the authorities, undermining the journalists' credibility for the next visit. Thus, reporters stood where the police were firing and got shot, too. Their presence at moments of conflict helped embed the authorities' belief that some kind of solidarity existed between them and the comrades.

The perceived alliance was frail, vulnerable not only to mishaps but also to the more remote machinations of those who wished to steer South Africa's anguish to their own political ends in the United States.

News coverage fueled a political battle in the Reagan era that used South Africa as a device, a yardstick of morality. The only source of information to feed the furies on both sides came from reporters on the ground, far from the easy distinctions of polemicists in Washington and New York. So reporters themselves came under personal attack: it was easier to assail the messenger than the message. And that, in turn, entwined newspaper and television coverage all the more intimately with political judgments that had nothing to do with the basic process of gathering and transmitting the news.

For all the apparent welcome reporters received from anti-apartheid groups in South Africa's townships, apartheid's deeper reflex provided a strong and sometimes dangerous undercurrent to the coincidence of interest between journalists who wanted to see what was happening and protesters who wanted their defiance to be seen. Ultimately, white reporters worked the townships on sufferance, relying on activists to shield them from a history that had made their skin color synonymous with enmity.

The ANC ideology said race was an irrelevance—a view most reporters devoutly wished to share. And, considering South Africa's racial divisions, it seemed miraculous that we were so often treated with courtesies and forebearance that on few occasions gave way to hatred. But only the hypocritical would suggest that crossing the line was free of the thrill of danger that makes most reporters' hearts beat a little faster, and sometimes quite a lot faster.

South Africa was a violent country and had been for a long time. Even before emergency rule and conflict with the authorities, Soweto managed to notch up twenty or thirty murders every weekend in brawls and stabbings and gang fights. In a convoluted sort of way, the Monday morning police tally—a staple paragraph in most newspapers—was comforting to many whites because it reinforced their belief in black unsuitability for greater advancement. And anyway, it was happening over there, over the hill where they never went.

A reporter's job by contrast, meant many trips to Soweto, and it left different impressions. On one occasion in particular, when I visited the place at night with Lucky Michaels, a speakeasy operator and underworld baron, I was struck not so much by Soweto's callous peculiarities as by the uncanny resemblance the evening bore to some of the evenings I had spent as a teenager in the rougher parts of Manchester, heart of the depressed industrial northwest of England, where the barons had once grown rich on the cotton of the colonies.

Many years before, I had been in a barnlike, bustling, rambunctious pub in Manchester, where a rock singer was failing to impersonate Eddie Cochran. The doors swung open and the whole place fell silent, as if a Mancunian-version Al Capone had just walked in, which it had. I looked up at the hatchet-faced man in the tight-brimmed leather trilby and leather coat who had caused even the band to fall mercifully still, but someone sitting next to me whispered: "Look at your boots." I said: "What?" He hissed: "Look at your boots." I looked down at my boots, turned to the man next to me, and said: "Why?" And the man said: "Because you don't want him to catch you looking at him." So I said, again: "Why?" And the man said: "Because he'd slit your throat from ear to ear and grin at you while he did it."

Soweto had the familiar feel of a place where you looked at your boots on a Saturday night if you didn't want to end up a statistic by Monday morning.

Lucky Michaels was an anomaly—a Soweto millionaire. His real name was Cecil Anthony Michaels and he owned speakeasies, known to blacks as shebeens, and a nightclub, the Pelican. Lucky was heading for Soweto with my colleague, Robert Rosenthal of the *Philadelphia Inquirer*, on August 17, 1985, and I went along for the ride. He picked us up at a glitzy city center hotel—just to show that a man of color could hit downtown in a $50,000, plum-colored BMW 745i—then took us on his tour, which made for an interesting comparison with the way officialdom presented apartheid.

A few weeks earlier, I had been on a government-approved Soweto bus excursion that started from the same hotel and treated the sprawled, cramped, bursting settlement as an object of anthropological interest. Amazingly, the tour continued right up until the first state of emergency made it a less alluring item on the itinerary of foreign visitors.

"I have found they are usually very neat in their own homes," the guide, Mike Pretorius, a small, crisp Afrikaner, told us as we rolled in a white mini-bus through some dump of a place where the houses were so small that odd bits of cast-off furniture or appliances had to be piled outside the doors. "But, sometimes, they are a little neglectful of the outside." From his tone and fond little chuckles, Mr. Pretorius might have been talking about the mountain gorillas of Rwanda.

Mike Pretorius's unhurried spiel—honed over twenty years, delivered in precise, calm, accented English—never once suggested that Soweto had grown up as anything but a rather curious natural phenomenon, certainly not as a result of official policies of segregation. When we drove by Mayor Edward Kunene's home, he explained: "The black marks on the wall are from the latest petrol bomb." He did not say why a petrol bomb might have been thrown. When we confronted a wall-slogan reading "Let every creed and race find an equal place," he said over his little microphone: "Well. I'm sure I don't know what that means."

Lucky's tour was different. Because of the emergency regulations proclaimed one month earlier, Soweto was under night-time curfew from 10:00 p.m. to 4:00 a.m., but, in his fancy leather jacket, a snub-nosed .38 revolver strapped to his ankle, Lucky didn't seem to care. He must have bought official protection, because the only other vehicle we saw on the streets all night was a blazing Volkswagen mini-bus, the object of some vague conflict, a surreal pillar of flame in the middle of nowhere. He took us first to darkened places on Soweto's outskirts that, with apartheid's curiously hurtful cartography, had once been for blacks and were now set aside for "Coloreds." Then we drove on to other places, once black and now demarcated by law for whites—poor whites, Lucky said. And then we cruised on to a place where someone was building small homes that the law said could only be occupied by mixed-race people. They were so small you couldn't even get a decent-sized bed into the bedrooms, Lucky sneered. "This," he said, "is apartheid."

In Soweto, at that time, there was one movie house for possibly 2 million people, a smattering of discos, and at least 4,000 shebeens—back-room speakeasies where the point was oblivion. It reminded me of Manchester on a Saturday night—get drunk, go home, but most of all, get drunk.

In the back streets, which composed most of Soweto, you could buy Transkei gold or Durban poison—marijuana—by the fistful. People ordered liquor by the flask, not by the shot. Beer was sold by the liter bottle, not the more decorous small bottles offered in the white bars, known as "dumpies." There were few special ornaments to the rooms. The idea was to drink, dance, find company, but certainly not admire the view. The shebeens were mostly illegal, prone to police raids. But there was nowhere else to go, even for the wealthier residents of the more gentrified areas; most restaurants and night spots in Johannesburg, ten miles and a world away, were, if not directly segregated, patronized exclusively by whites. So people stayed and drank with their friends.

The weekend was release, but an imperfect release because it left people trapped in the same place that underlined their miseries all week. They didn't have pool parties and garden cook-outs here. White Johannesburg boasted 65,000 private swimming pools; Soweto had five municipal pools. Where I lived in Johannesburg's wealthy northern suburbs there were open spaces, and tennis courts. Here, there was dirt and unpaved streets and no verdancy. Ridiculously, there was a golf course near what was called the Soweto Country Club. It had yellow fairways and brown greens, and, according to Mr. Pretorius, the world's longest hole, the 9th—"594 yards and a par 5." Mr. Pretorius had a way of suggesting that the only real difference between the gracious fairways of Scotland's Gleneagles and the world's biggest ghetto was the length of the course.

Soweto bred knife fights and desperation, muggings and theft. In the single men's hostels, migrant workers—men without women—fired up feuds they had brought from the far lands beyond the Tugela River and fought them out on the streets. Everyone seemed to be getting drunk or stoned. It was easy to see how the Monday morning tally of statistics would build.

Lucky piloted the BMW past Regina Mundi—the church where people commemorated the June 16 Soweto anniversaries—gunning it up to 125 mph on a stretch of road not built for speed after I made some remark that he thought challenged the virility of the engine. We hit a few shebeens—Sophie's, Spoon's, Rowena's—the smartest, with plush sofas, armchairs, and even a ladies' room.

But you could never escape the issue. At Sophie's we ran into an ideological debate. A young man who said he worked for IBM vouchsafed that there should be disinvestment to force change. Lucky rounded on him. "Are you ready to be out of work for two years? For two years, sitting at home without a job? If you are not ready for that, don't talk about sanctions." The man fell silent, looked at his boots. At Spoon's, Benny, a black traffic cop issued with an 850cc Suzuki motorcycle, bemoaned the fact that white traffic cops with the same years service as him got to drive patrol cars. Apartheid again. At Rowena's Lucky derided the ANC. "Let them bring guns and fight the system," he said. "What have they done so far? My passbook is still in my pocket." It was not a fashionable thing to say. But Lucky had the snub-nosed .38 on his ankle and the BMW outside. People looked at their boots.

Then we clambered back into the car, heading for the Pelican, Lucky's flagship. It was dark, hot, loud, bigger than the pub in Manchester. The music was better, too. Everyone boogied and the rhythms pulsed. You shouted to be heard, craned your neck to listen. It was so late that the curfew was drawing to a close, but the energy of Saturday night was still building in the Pelican, fueled by booze and dope. One of Lucky's underlings took us in charge, telling us how great this was, how cool—blacks and whites, no bad feelings, all having a good time. Together. Right on. We could barely hear him over the music. Have a drink, he said. Have a woman. Look at these nice girls. You can dance with them. Anything you like.

Outside, there was a state of emergency. In under a year, over six hundred people had died, most of them black, most of them killed by white police officers, or blacks under the command of white police officers. But we did not want to seem hostile, so we danced. It was a mistake. We had reached the outer limits of the welcome. In Manchester, as intruders, we would never had made it to the dance floor.

Lucky's tour was a sideshow to South Africa's drama, but you could extend the metaphors. The emergency and the revolt meant no one could look at their boots any more. The situation demanded a response, a commitment, a hard look at the eyes. South Africans of any skin color were all out there on the floor and had decisions to make: not whether to boogy, but whom to boogy with. And it touched them all, from townships to remote white farmsteads, from the dingy offices where the black labor movement sought to build union power to the board rooms of South Africa's mining barons who sought to contain it. All had to make their own choices.

What they had to decide was this: should they seek accommodation or confrontation; should they pin their hopes to a future imperiled by South Africa's own history of violent division or turn away from change? And having made that choice, to whom should they turn to seek its realization?

White choices were the most simple because they were made in the luxury of homes far from a theater of conflict that demanded response and commitment. The decision to vote for reform or conservatism, liberalism or the revanchism of Eugene Terre Blanche was unlikely to cost lives. In the townships, with their daily battles on dirty, dangerous streets, the urgency was far greater, the penalties far more severe. If you were not part of the struggle with all its attendant risks of gunshot and detention by the authorities, then you were part of the system with all its hazards of punishment by someone like Comrade Vusi.

The message of the comrades, the necklace, the struggle itself was that you could not remain aloof.

Sometimes, being a foreigner, an outsider, was a benefit: it established a rare, noncombatant status when the immediate war turned South Africans against one another.

When Inkatha supporters took to the streets in Durban in 1985, they called themselves "impis," as Shaka's battalions had done, and the resonant chant as they marched—"*Usuthu, usuthu*"—was the same as the Zulus had chanted when they advanced on my kinsmen over a century before at their triumphant Battle of Isandhlwana on January 22, 1879.

In the mid-1980's, they were advancing on the comrades, not on the British. But I was not immediately sure of their intentions when events left me stranded on a roadside with a young Zulu guide called George.

An impi of about five hundred men jogged toward us. It was heading somewhere else, but we were in its path. The men had spears, knob-kerries, shields. The chanting resonated. "*Usuthu, usuthu.*" I had seen the movies—*Zulu Dawn* and *Zulu*—recounting the battles of Isandhlwana on one day and Rorke's Drift the next. My ancestors lost in one, held their own in the other. In both movies, however, the Zulus had chanted "*Usuthu*" as they advanced for the fray. The word often translated as "kill," but others said it was more an expression of self-praise. When people heard it, they knew the impis had been loosed.

My instinct was to run, but George advised against it, saying that would create suspicion and hostility and I would be hounded down for sure. Instead, he said, I should stand my ground and, in his words, "show no fear." I asked George how to say hello in Zulu. He answered: "Say, '*Sawubona*'. Over the next few minutes I said, "*Sawubona*," many times and learned the word well as the battalion flowed by on either side of us, intent on other quarry.

The battle was between the Inkatha warriors and the comrades whose loyalty lay with the UDF and the ANC. I was irrelevant to it. The impi stamped on toward its murderous tryst. George never told me whether I showed fear or not. I suspect that his reticence was intended as a courtesy.

Toward the end of my time in South Africa, Mark Peters and I decided to retrace our steps, to take a car from north to south, from the Limpopo to the Indian Ocean, touching the bases, revisiting places we had come to know in different times, two, three years earlier. It was a drive that mixed craziness and rumination, from the Alldays Hotel in the northern Transvaal, to Durban and Port Elizabeth on the coast, through Johannesburg and Bloemfontein and Cradock.

Everywhere, the signs seemed to be the same: something had shifted, but no one knew either a way back to what had been or a way forward to whatever might come. So everyone was relying on old and tiring reflexes.

It was as if the country was in a holding pattern, and protest had become a habit, slowly subsiding under the weight of repression. That is what the emergency ultimately achieved—not a dramatic excision of revolt, but attrition, a contest of wills in which the men with guns held the line against protesters with rocks even as the battle slipped beyond their grasp in the counterattrition of sanctions.

As the odyssey unfolded, we stopped to talk to people at the miserable squatter camp called Onverwacht, near Bloemfontein in the Orange Free State, and discovered it had doubled in size to 400,000 in the two years since we had first visited, as if some unseen hand had been at work, molding apartheid's designs, even as we had focused on the battles in the distant townships and listened to Mr. Botha's promises of change. In Alldays, the white men at the hotel still chuckled about the Indian they had hounded away, and the owner, known as Oum Piet, said there would never be blacks in his bar. Outside, the stoic laborers still sat on the open beds of the pickups.

The drive gave time to come to terms with other things. I was weary of—and frightened of—the frustrated anger of the people of townships who would never really trust me; and I was tired of the mindless, reflexive authority that seemed embodied in the Afrikaner traffic cop who could barely write out the speeding ticket he gave us in some dead village in the Orange Free State. I was tired of the hectoring speeches that said nothing new and the hypocrisy of activists who thought we should write about the sins of others, but not about their own errors and wrongdoings; and I was tired of the derision of government officials who would not even listen to what I was saying, could not even see beyond their embattlement to understand that I knew what they were saying. Both sides demanded loyalty, but their tactics precluded excesses of sympathy. There was no dignity to a struggle that left charred lumps of humanity smoldering on the sidewalk, no honor to security forces who acted as bullies, not as custodians of law. Once, near Cape Town, the authorities placed lines of armed soldiers between worried mixed-race parents outside a police station where they were detaining teenage protesters. The parents were generally hardworking, middle class, the very people Mr. Botha's reforms were supposed to lure and co-opt. But by preventing them from even speaking to their children, the authorities seemed bent on self-destructing their own policies.

I was weary too of the way people assumed they could assign me a part in it, and of the way I took the easy choice of falling in with them rather than taking a stand that in any case might have drawn me further into someone else's contorted arguments.

When the car broke down and we hitch-hiked, I became irritable with a man called Henry who picked us up and told us that—"hell, man"—blacks are "not cultural like you and me." What did he mean by "cultural," by "you and me"? That we were white? The presumption of genetic affinity, common standards, infuriated me as much as the blacks who threw rocks at the car. And yet, in Alldays, when the woman in the grocery store moved me to the front of a line of black people with words "Let the boss go first," I had gone to the head of the line, making some feeble excuse to myself about being pressed for time, but knowing the guilt would linger for a long time. I had done exactly what the system expected of me and, in the process, had denied my own attempts at aloofness.

We arrived in King William's Town, and Johnny Clegg, the white leader of a black band called Savuka, was playing at the little townhall. Part of the act, when he danced Zulu dances with the Zulu band, had earned him the nickname "the white Zulu." You could not even go to a rock concert, it seemed, without confronting racial oxymorons and the press of white guilt. I was tired of it, yet I had jumped the line in Alldays, and, in doing so, had offered no protest to a racial system I loathed. So I fell between South Africa's poles, as my job in a way obliged me to do, bereft of the certainties that inspired both sides with equal fire.

In Soweto, Comrade Vusi never wavered. In Alldays, Stoffel van der Walt, an Afrikaner farmer, told me: "God gave us the blacks to use properly. And God is never wrong." I found the propositon pre-posterous—but his belief was as unshakable as Vusi's belief in the necklace. And I resented them both, because they had faith and I had not, and I could not see how so many conflicting faiths could be contained in one land that did not seem to justify faith at all.

I knew the people on both sides of the divide in the sense that all of them had enriched me with their stories, and I had absorbed them and could sense their responses before they offered them. But I did not know them in the sense Ora Terblanche implied: I did not have a niche in their birthright, so I would always be an outsider, asking questions that would draw mutually exclusive replies.

And yet I did not want to go. After three years, South Africa had me riveted to its stage: half-player, half-audience; a white who would never be a Zulu, and never be easy with the connotations of whiteness in South Africa, either. The final act was not in sight and I doubted it would bring faith.

We went on, then, across the emptiness of the Eastern Cape, passing small settlements without halting, until we espied the curl of the Fish River and came again to Cradock.

The flames had died since we had come for a funeral at a time of many funerals in South Africa.

No one had rebuilt the wreckage of all the official buildings—the policemen's houses, the administration block, the beerhall—so they stood there like reminders of some half-forgotten campaign. No one was paying rents, so there would not be much money for improvements; and no one was shopping in the white stores, if only in the hope that the campaigns would not be forgotten altogether. Lucas, the young and reckless activist, reckoned that if, as promised, the schools reopened as they were supposed to, he would have to catch up on two years and seven months education, because that was the length of time he had been boycotting classes. And he was not yet out of his teens. A friend of his did some small arithmetic and said he reckoned he'd be twenty five years old before he took a university entrance examination. Nyameka Goniwe still mourned her husband.

Our journey had showed that President Botha had lost one vison of a new South Africa, and had not found—or could not find—another to replace it. We knew that the campaign was not over, but the battle had ebbed; the citadel had shifted, but not fallen.

Matthew Goniwe's widow said: "We are beginning to realize that the struggle will take longer than we thought."

14.

Changes: Going Back to South Africa

"We want to have a new kind of South
Africa, where we all, black and white,
can walk together."

—ARCHBISHOP DESMOND TUTU, 1986

There had been chills in the night with a rumor of snow on the high ground. In the African winter, a shivery wind rolled off the tall, bald, brown hills of the Eastern Cape. The graves of Goniwe and his comrades lay much as they had been—low mounds held down by half-bricks, the headboards that called them sons of Africa beginning to look weary.

An editor had said: go back to Africa. So I had gone, at a leisurely pace, from Cairo, where I now lived, via Zimbabwe, and on to South Africa. It was July 1990.

Mandela was free. Botha had gone, brought down not by black rage but by his own party, sensing that his time had passed. And Lucas— the one-time schoolboy bent on guerrilla warfare and bloodshed—was still around to recount what had happened in the time I had been elsewhere, what was happening now.

He was older—not only in years—and the brightness, the innocence was gone. His body had thickened slightly into manhood, and the infectious grin, the mischief, had been replaced by a somberness born of a life that had denied him most things except "the struggle."

When I first met him, in 1985, he had been boycotting classes for over a year, protesting Goniwe's suspension. He had never gone back to school. Then there had been been two years in detention under the emergency decree, a time, paradoxically, he called the best in his life because, in the prison in Port Elizabeth, he had met the veterans, the big names, and they had taught him the language of politics that offered an ideological frame to his yearnings. He told me that on the night of his arrest, the flickering torchlight outside his shack in some- one's yard had betrayed the presence of intruders at 3:00 a.m. Then, he said, they had burst in to arrest him, disturbing him with a girlfriend. There was no charge, trial, or recourse. No one read him rights, because he did not have any. No one offered him a last telephone call because he was not entitled to it. "I've been looking for you." That was all the plainclothes security policeman had said as they took him away, and even that was more than he needed to say. It was a familiar enough pattern, one repeated thousands of times as the emergency hit home in 1986 and 1987. The only surprising thing was that it had not happened to Lucas earlier.

"The struggle," he said, was all he knew, but he knew it well and made his boast with some pride. These days, too, he held high office in the South African Youth Congress—a particularly radical organi- zation allied to the ANC. Oddly, though, he was no longer fiery. Detention had tutored him out of high expectations. He had discov- ered, as all South Africans had discovered, that, as he put it, "there are no easy answers." And, since Mandela's release in February 1990, he had encountered a curious phenomenon.

Already the schoolboys in their mid-teens were making the same demands of him as he had made of his elders when I first met him: give us guns. And, just as Goniwe had counseled him five years earlier, he was now counseling others: be patient, build your organizations on the ground so that they are resilient enough to withstand repression. He had not gone to Lusaka, had not received military training in those distant camps in Angola, Tanzania, and Zambia where many young hopes fizzled in malaria, malnutrition or even torture for being sus- pected a spy. Instead, he had become a party man, a commissar of the townships, hailed in distant Johannesburg as a man with all the credentials—Cradock itself, detention, the struggle. With ironic ref- erence to the military conscription to which all whites—but not blacks—were subjected, he described his two years behind bars as his "national service."

Together we toured the township, noting how streets had been paved, new houses built for teachers and state employees, other than policemen (the black policemen, hounded out of the place, had never returned). He was concerned, these days, about a new plan the authorities had to extend the township southward because it foresaw offering blacks squatting rights, communal faucets and roads, but no houses. There was controversy, too, about a planned increase in the service charges levied on black residents—a paltry sum, two or three dollars a month, but simply too much to bear in a place where unemployment had hit 60 percent. From the big issue of apartheid, the worries had reverted to the small, grinding details of getting by. He was troubled by the street kids, pre-teens who headed for white Cradock each day to beg or steal enough to buy a loaf of bread or a cup of soup. We met them together, and, as I had been taught by James Vumile Mpunthe in Port Elizabeth, I examined their footwear for clues to their destiny: a nine-year-old in discarded workmen's boots many sizes too large; an eight-year-old boy with a cast-off girl's school pump on one foot and a torn sneaker on the other, all split heels, and no laces and no socks either. If these children ever looked at their boots, all they would see was misery. But far more worrisome to Lucas was the sense that while detention had offered a structured life, things had somehow started to unravel in the months since Mandela had walked, first uncertainly, then with gathering confidence, from the gates of the Victor Verster prison farm in the Cape into the freedom of a bright summer's day on February 2, 1990.

Mandela was free, as the slogan had always demanded, and the ANC—the repository of Lucas's ultimate loyalties—had again been legalized as President de Klerk sought interlocutors to deal with the country's crushing problems. But the organization had yet to transform itself from an amorphous symbol into a functioning, political party. There was no ANC office for miles, no guidance, no real consultation. Those who had returned from exile had not gotten used to the idea of a daily joust with the press, and a constituency far more diverse and demanding than the ideological coterie and in-fighting of Lusaka or Luanda. There, they had operated with minimal accountability. Now their own people and the reporters, some openly hostile or doubting, asked questions of them that they did not always like to answer. The organization was strapped for cash. Promises of money from Algeria and Libya had not come through. There were ANC offices in the big cities, but where on earth would they find the funds for cars, telephones, faxes, Xerox machines, desks in all the myriad places like Cradock that had carried the banner while the leaders were in exile and now wanted to see their leaders with them on the ground? One issue was of particular concern.

A few weeks before I met up with Lucas, Mandela had spent long hours in negotiation with de Klerk and had conceded the suspension of the "armed struggle"—the notional military effort to overturn apartheid that had become more an emblem of the ANC's resolve than any real threat to state power. He had done so without the explicit approval of the grass roots, or of many ANC old-timers still in exile who got the news that the war was over, one of them told me later, from listening to the BBC, not from any party directive.

That had given Lucas a problem. "These young guys keep coming to me and saying: 'Why did they suspend the armed struggle?' They say: 'We want guns to defend ourselves.' And I have to keep telling them: 'Be patient. When the time comes our leaders will come and explain it all to us.' But they don't like being patient." Patience, he acknowledged with a tight smile, had not been one of his strong suits, either.

In a way there was a kind of inevitability that the "new" South Africa should be born like this—in confusion, uncertainty and, as events were to show, in unprecedented bloodletting in those same black townships that had been the seedbeds of liberation. But still, going back, it seemed wondrous that this ungainly birth had happened at all.

The reasons for change were manifold. Paradoxically, they started with P.W. Botha, before a stroke to his body—and a sea-change in his party—ousted him from power.

Botha's policies had been designed to avert the same concessions as de Klerk now offered to the black majority. Yet it had been Botha who introduced the notion of reform into the Afrikaner lexicon, and who thereby winnowed the party ranks, weathering its division to create the white constituency, however unsure of itself, that de Klerk would inherit. It was Botha, too, who, through his fearsome splicing of diplomacy and raw military power had emasculated the ANC, forcing it out of its sanctuaries in Angola and Mozambique, ensuring that, when de Klerk came to legalize the organization, he need have no fear of being seen to bow to insurgent military pressure or of confronting a real military force. And, most of all, it was Botha who deployed emergency rule to make clear to anyone who thought differently that the sinews of state power remained intact, that the violent alternative on the street to negotiation and compromise led nowhere.

In that sense, de Klerk could make his offer from a position of strength, seizing a moment in history that demanded new ways. He had been profoundly influenced in his judgments by the demise of communism in the Soviet Union and Eastern Europe and by the shifting realities of a world where the rules had changed. For decades, communism had been elevated in Afrikaner demonology to the status of the anti-Christ. Years of propaganda had ascribed virtually every act of black defiance to a Communist conspiracy to undermine this wealthy, distant outpost of Western values that straddled the Cape sea routes. The notion of a Communist Total Onslaught against the South African regime provided the most basic justification for surpressing the inexorable march of change southward through Africa. But now the Marxist citadel had crumbled and the ideology had been exposed as a hollow shell, and with it went all justification for invoking its name to win whatever residual sympathy for South Africa's rulers still lingered in the hearts of Western conservatives. There was no mileage in raising the Communist threat when the menace itself had died on the streets of Berlin and Prague and Moscow. President de Klerk—and the security policemen who would find it much more difficult to recant—remained profoundly mistrustful of individual Communists, particularly Joe Slovo, the head of the South African Communist Party, and his secretive entourage. Yet the ending of Soviet domination in Eastern Europe contributed significantly to the self-confidence de Klerk displayed when, in early 1990, he removed the legal prohibitions on Slovo's party and even granted its leader immunity from prosecution to enable him to return to the country.

Those were the credits on the account as President de Klerk surveyed the future of a land that had lost its moorings in its own history yet had no coordinates for the future. The debit notes, though, were being called in too.

Harald Parkendorf, a respected Afrikaner commentator and former newspaper editor who had lost his job because of his liberalism, and who knew his people well, told me that, in some arguable ways Mr.

de Klerk was playing out what some of his tribe had percieved as an inevitability decades earlier.

Ultra-conservative Afrikaners had long argued that the Grand Design of apartheid contained a central and corrosive flaw. If the authorities acknowledged a black right to political self-determination when they created the so-called "homelands" in 1959, then it was inevitable that they would ultimately be obliged to concede the same rights within South Africa itself. The argument took other forms, beginning with the premise that any concession would lead incrementally to other concessions. Thus, if the authorities permitted non-white participation in, say, sporting events, then the crack in racial purity would inevitably widen: there would be other mixings—sexual first, then political. Ultimately, the very notion of Afrikaner identity, advanced and nurtured by total control of the environment that bred it, would be diluted, and the white tribe would be undermined and lost in Africa's inherent chaos. The conclusion drawn by the ultra-right white minority was easy: to avoid such conundrums, as Eugene Terre Blanche had told me, the answer was simply to create an all-white state. As on many occasions in South Africa, debate with the fringes left the impression that great spirals of thought could be constructed on the most frail of premises.

The central preoccupation from the very beginnings of power in 1948 was the preservation of the tribe in security: apartheid itself was the expression of that primeval urge, and security could only be bought with control and privilege. But, from the mid-1970s onward, black protest had pressed the authorities to seek new definitions of the relationship between black and white. In the process, as the conservatives of the 1960s had forecast, one retreat had led to another. First, the labor unions had been legalized. Then the pass laws had gone. Then Mandela had been freed and the ANC had been made legal. Now, in 1990, as President de Klerk made his accounting, he was even talking of the National Party's readiness to end the Group Areas Act and the Population Registration Act and of opening his party to all races—the sacking of the temple by the very hands that had built it. One year later, the conservative prophecy came true in the repeal of the very legislation that created apartheid.

Yet historical progression did not fully explain his actions and promises. What distinguished de Klerk's computations from those of his predecessors was that he could no longer set the pace, because it was being dictated by outside economic pressure for change. With the states of emergency, Botha had sought to slow time, to give himself space to proceed cautiously. In the process, he had brought international monetary and commercial sanctions on his nation, American companies had shed their stake in his land, the economy had slowed while the population, disaffected, half-educated, expectant of change, had burgeoned. Botha did not go gently into the good night of political oblivion. And when he did retire to his hometown of George, on the Cape coast—a reclusive, disgruntled figure who felt his work had not been completed—his reluctant bequest to de Klerk was corroded from within by sanctions.

South Africa was intimately familiar with international embargoes—and with their circumvention. Technically, sporting links with the outside world had long been severed—a punishment designed to bite deep into the self-confidence of a race whose Saturday rugby and mid-week squash and weekend cricket formed sturdy pillars of self-image. Musicians and artists risked ostracism in their own countries if they played South Africa's stage. No one was supposed to sell arms or oil to the pariah state. But all of those strictures could be skirted: Rod Stewart played Sun City, in the nominally independent homeland called Bophuthatswana; rogue cricket teams braved demonstrators to strut the greensward of the South African wicket; South African engineers built vast, expensive plants that turned coal into oil, and disused mines were used to store crude imported clandestinely from the Persian Gulf. The domestic arms giant Armscor, finished up not only substituting for lost imports of weapons but exporting its own products. With the bewildering promiscuity of the international arms bazaar, its customers reportedly included both Iraq and Iran, and its collaborators included Israel. Armscor produced an artillery piece—the G-5—that outgunned the best cannon available to the American Marines, and the CIA estimated that, probably with Israeli collusion, South Africa had built a nuclear capability.

But while South Africa might manufacture guns or oil, it could not manufacture American dollar bills or British pounds to pay its debts. The financial sanctions that began in 1985, when Chase Manhattan and other American banks called in their short-term loans, could not be circumvented. Governmental sanctions by the United States and Western European countries restricted South Africa's markets and trade routes. In his discussions with President de Klerk, Mandela found it relatively easy to suspend the armed struggle; but sanctions were the trump card, to be played only when the dismantling of apartheid had become irreversible.

By that time, though, billions of dollars had been lost in the re-payment of debt. Access to credit was severed. The gold, diamonds, platinum still came out of the ground, but their income no longer offered shelter from international opprobrium. South Africa's political leaders despertely needed an escape hatch, yet it could be opened only with real political change. And, as both sides acknowledged, the key would only be found in negotiations with the ANC.

But sanctions were an ambiguous weapon, and by the early 1990s it had become apparent that the government was not the only victim. In squeezing the economy, sanctions also robbed the land of the very wealth it needed to come to terms with the problem that apartheid had sought to deny: people.

When P.W. Botha lifted the tattered barriers of the pass laws in 1986, it was already too late to remold "influx control" as "orderly urbanization" because there was nothing orderly about what happened when the restrictions on black access to the cities were abolished. The effect was not a gradual easing of pressure, but an explosion. Millions streamed to urban areas that could not sustain their presence in any conventional manner. Neither could they eke an existence in the so-called "homelands," which, according to Francis Wilson, a noted South African academic at the University of Cape Town, had grown in population from 5 to 11 million between 1960 and 1980.

Burgeoning with high birth rates and black workers displaced from white farms by mechanization, the numbers grew while the land did not. "Influx control ended because it was becoming impossible to sustain the control," Professor Wilson said. "As time went on, it became impossible for these areas to sustain the people. So they would do anything to come to town."

Influx control might have offered a respite for the white authorities, but, in the long term, its result was the precise opposite of what it was supposed to achieve: the fringes of South Africa's white cities and townships had come to resemble the shacks and shanties I had known much earlier in Zaire.

Returning to South Africa in 1990, I was told by many of my friends that I would be shocked by the "Africanization" of downtown Johannesburg—the sidewalk vendors of grilled corn, the market mamas with their spreads of bananas and apples laid out before them, the mini-buses plying the routes to the townships, crammed with people. These mini-buses, unlike the old and lumbering Putco buses with their drivers' windows protected from rocks by iron grills, darted to and fro across the divide with speed and relative impunity. Therefore, they had earned the sobriquet "Zolas," after Zola Budd, the Afrikaner child athlete who had run the world's fastest 3,000 meters before fame and exposure to the endless decrying of her South African roots had burned her out in her late teens.

The transformation of downtown had been well under way when I left in 1987, partly because the central shopping areas had long been abandoned by whites who sought refuge in gigantic, glitzy suburban shopping malls like Sandton City, where, in 1990, the women in their metallic 3-series BMWs still felt obliged to manicure and bejewel themselves and dress for consumption in lamé and leather. But in central Johannesburg—around St. George's Catherdral, on Bree and Rissik and Wanderers Streets—it seemed the authorities, like the white shoppers, had simply written off the area, making no obvious attempt to restrict this growth of hawkers and vendors and the mafiosi of the mini-bus concessions.

What did surprise me was the disapproval of some black activists at this redefining of their status and style in the manner of a continent to the north whose empirical, economic lessons they wished at all costs to avoid as they strove for political freedom. The day was not far hence, a radical newspaper editor told me with resigned annoyance, when he would no longer be able to find parking for his car amid the mini-buses. That was a personal grievance. But perhaps, in an obtuse way, he sensed a new class struggle emerging that would pit the opportunists of the new order against those who had suffered and would continue to do so. The shops near his office seemed to bear him out.

With an exclusively black clientele, the shoe stores on Bree Street were selling American-made Florsheim brogues at $200 a pair. One importer of footwear made modest headlines when he began marketing Italian alligator-hide loafers at the equivalent of $500 a pair. He had no doubt they would sell—principally among the mini-bus drivers. Despite generally low wages compared to whites, the sheer numbers of the black majority ensured that they had become the nation's largest consumers. Many whites muttered darkly that this economic weight was no surprise—blacks paid no taxes and boycotted rental payments, and so had cash left over to spend on fancy shoes. That might have been true of some, but certainly not the majority. With James Vumile Mpunthe's pedestrian obsession in mind as a point of social reference, I wondered how soon South Africa's perennial contest between haves and have-nots would shed the purely racial overtones traditionally associated with it: there were far more split heels and hand-me-downs than Florsheims.

The true shock was not in central Johannesburg, however, but on the outskirts of Cape Town. With some difficulty I located the same rise of land as had offered me a view, just six years earlier, of empty, flattened sand dwarfing yellow bulldozers as if they were children's toys. That was when Khayelitsha was being readied as a black satellite city, a place that would offer small plots of land and what were called "core houses" that could be expanded by their black occupants and owners as they advanced toward a peaceful niche in the new bourgeoisie, out of sight of Cape Town's verdant white suburbs. "We make owning your own home easy," the builders' billboards announced. The irony was unintentional: as far as could be seen, the apartheid notion of Khayelitsha as an ordered settlement of blacks had been buried beneath endless shacks as if Crossroads had pollinated the area with some relentless seed that multiplied without restraint. Row upon row of them spread like a carpet, completely obliterating the vision and the vista of 1984. Homeowning was easy, it seemed, if its price was measured in corrugated iron and plastic sheeting.

In late 1986, the black squatter population at the Cape was estimated at 100,000, principally in Crossroads. Now the figure was anything from 500,000 upward. New shacks grew daily. The press of people had simply been too much for the authorities' original vision, and so all the white administrators could do was lay out roads, install communal faucets, and leave the rest to the ingenuity of the new arrivals. When whites decided to renovate the gentrified tin-roofed homes that had a certain cachet among the liberal elite of academics, artists, and journalists, the discarded roofing was quickly purchased by people who wanted the cast-offs for entire homes. The South African Institute of Race Relations estimated that a full 7 million blacks were living in "self-erected housing"—that is, squatter shacks—around Africa's richest nation. Nowhere seemed immune.

At Hout Bay, a white dormitory town on the Atlantic coast of the Cape Peninsula, the Princess Bush squatter camp had suddenly appeared in dunes only a couple of hundred yards from white homes designed with large picture windows to offer a breathtaking vista of sand and surf, not an intimate picture of deprivation. Deon du Plessis, the Afrikaner journalist, liked to recount the likely conversation, as he imagined it, between two whites—whom he named Reginald and Emily—and who, in this fictional account, had moved from the Congo to Kenya to Rhodesia, trying to keep ahead of the black tide before seeking their final refuge on the beaches of the Cape. "My god, Emily," says an alarmed and bewildered Reginald as he opens the drapes to find the squatters have arrived to blight his panoramic view, "here they are again!" The joke mocked white worries, yet in a way black and white destinies mirrored one another. If Reginald and Emily had nowhere else to go, neither did people like Mongezi Sonqwelo, a twenty-five-year-old man who lived in Princess Bush and who was able to make a living because, he said, he possessed "a knowledge of bricklaying." Money in the Transkei, where his family lived, was "too little," he said, maybe four dollars a day, while in the Cape, a bricklayer could earn twice as much. One problem was that, since Mandela's release, the white employers who cruised by Hout Bay's pickup point for casual labor—a place called Peter's Quick Stop Cafe—had taken to telling blacks: "Go to Mandela and ask him for a job."

But, Mr. Sonqwelo said, after some thought, "our biggest problem is that this land is somebody's land and this land is already sold to the man. So he wants to chase us away. But we cannot leave our property and stand there beside the road with our hands folded. We need somewhere else to go." In the wintry Cape, the winds are raw and insistent, southeasters that howl from oceans. Beyond Africa's southernmost outpost, there is literally nowhere else to go.

• • •

There was no suggestion, either, that these places—or "these people"—could simply be wished away. On the Cape flats, Khayelitsha had established its own subeconomy. Virtually every other shack with a roadside position offered fruit, or vegetables, or hairdressing (the equivalent of four dollars for braiding or a perm). One man who had a postbox address of his own allowed it to be used by many, and so people came to collect their mail from his modest supermarket and, generally, spent a little money. And, just as the soi-disant smart set of Johannesburg dressed to consume, so, too, the new arrivals in Khayelitsha set forth from tin shacks—permed or braided and snappily attired—to brave the new world they had come to from the homelands.

In Cradock, in the mid-1980s, there had been a smattering of squatter huts on the fringes of the township. Now the number of people living there in "self-erected housing" totaled 10,000—almost one third of the population—advancing quickly towards the white part of town across a scrawny, scrubby valley that had once demarcated apartheid's clear frontiers. Here were people who had lost farm jobs, or railway jobs. Here were the relatives of people living in Cradock's small homes who, as they grew older, needed a place of their own to raise families and built it from zinc and plastic. The shacks perched perilously on a sandstone cliff that plunged a vertical 100 feet to the Great Fish River. Two people had died falling from it. The area reeked of human faeces on the lip of the precipice where children played with broken toy bicycles made of wire.

Even in Alexandra township—the counterpoint to Sandton City near Johannesburg's northern suburbs—25,000 squatters had somehow sandwiched themselves between the 200,000 people who lived in what was no more than a slum in the first place. Durban had become, they reckoned, one of the world's fastest-growing cities as the shacks marched out onto the hills of Natal. And, since the pass laws had gone, there was no legal way to prevent the poor from meandering through the grand white suburbs, gazing in envy at resplendent white homes, open parklands, and broad avenues shaded by jacaranda trees. Even to me—who had once lived in a big house in the northern suburbs—the size of these mansions seemed all the more bewildering now that the point of reference for comparison had become shacks,

10 foot square, with roofs that flapped in the wind and leaked in the rain. It was no surprise that, at white dinner parties, the conversation turned often to the rising crime rate and the cost of security walls, razor wire, fences, alarm systems, dogs. For all its reputation as a police state, South Africa was underpoliced—by now perhaps 60,000 for a land of over 30 million, and most of them on duty in the townships, fighting people, not crime. Private companies offering "instant armed response" were doing a brisk trade in installing panic buttons that promised the arrival of men with shotguns within minutes of an intruder being detected on the premises; it was even possible to sign a form indemnifying them against the results of shooting intruders on sight. Some whites set up neighborhood watch committees, taking turns to patrol in their cars at night and alert their neighbors to any suspicious activity around their homes. The gun shops were overwhelmed with orders for bedside pistols.

All that was a side issue. What really mattered was that, since Mandela's release, the squatters and many other black people had harbored hopes of redemption filled with expectations of jobs and betterment. Like Lucas in Cradock, they wanted their leaders to produce magic from the hat. That put the ANC in a particular quandary: without the lifting of sanctions, there was no hope of the economic growth that might fulfill a little of the dream. But once sanctions were lifted, the ANC's leverage was diminished.

Julian Ogilvy-Thompson, who had succeeded Gavin Relly as chairman of Anglo-American Corporation, and who maintained the corporate mistrust of majority rule, reckoned the stalled economy needed to grow by 8 percent a year if it was to provide the jobs to keep pace with popular expectations—an impossibility without access to credit and markets, particularly at a time when parts of Eastern Europe suddenly seemed to offer more alluring prospects for foreign investors. In their private moments, even senior ANC officials acknowledged that sanctions could not go on forever. "The last thing we want," an ANC commissar told me, "is to inherit a ruin."

In the immediacy of the negotiations with the white authorities that unrolled in the colonnaded sandstone mass of the Union Building in Pretoria, the ANC also had a conflicting and more pressing interest at stake even though its own economic blueprint seemed barely sketched. Sanctions were the only means of keeping the white authorities on track, and, in the ANC's thinking, if they were lifted too soon, the Afrikaners would renege on their promises of change. Yet, while they persisted, there was no means of securing even the most basic improvements for its constituency or redeeming the promise inherent in the ANC's long struggle. When Nelson Mandela agreed to the suspension of armed conflict on August 7, 1990, the decision reflected the urgency of the ANC's need to advance the negotiations to a point where sanctions could be lifted and the economy revived before disenchantment overtook the hope and fervor that had surrounded his release six months earlier.

As he surveyed the land and its pell-mell black urbanization, its wild hopes and fears and fervor, President de Klerk must have arrived at another conclusion: apartheid's legacy promised such uncertainty, possibly chaos, that the Afrikaners would need others to share responsibility with them for the indistinct future, to shield them from the results of policies belatedly acknowledged as an awesome mistake; and the price of shared responsibility was shared power. The alternative, after all, could be nothing but further convulsions of bloodshed and even greater isolation.

The bloodshed came anyhow.

15

Killing the Wizards

"War is therefore an act of violence designed
to force the opponent to submit to our will."

—KARL VON CLAUSEWITZ, *On War* (1833)

✳ In the African winter of 1990, President de Klerk's strategy came
under severe physical and political assault, both from whites
who did not agree with it and from blacks who feared it would destroy
their political ambitions. In the space of a few weeks, during August
and September 1990, almost eight hundred people died in a spasm of
fighting that shook townships and squatter camps in the industrial
heartland of the Transvaal and continued with commensurate slaughter for much longer. The intensity of the violence was far greater than
anything reporters had seen during the anti-apartheid protests of the
mid-1980s, and, indeed, represented the most serious civil unrest
South Africa had witnessed in the entire twentieth century. Initially,
the authorities sought to depict the killing as tribal, but in the end
they had to acknowledge it was far more complex than that. A "hidden
hand," President de Klerk told Nelson Mandela, was at work.

Part of the problem lay with the squatters themselves, for, as they
flooded into townships and set up their makeshift settlements, offering
to work for less than unionized township residents or the single men
who filled the migrant workers' hostels, they upset a frail balance of
interests and resources that had often shown strains. In the past, most
migrants came from Zululand where, as Felix Nzama had told me at
his store on the Tugela, a spell in a township near the city was seen
as an initiation rite into manhood. The migrants might spend eleven
months without a break in the hostel, returning home at year's end
with tales of thrills and adventure. In reality, while in the township,
they remained apart, a source of competition for girls and jobs, country
bumpkins prone to drunkenness and violence, who had different ways
and were not easily absorbed. When the pass laws came to an end,
and more young men thronged to the relative glitter of the Transvaal,

the hostels themselves became more crowded, and the ethnic mix shifted to encompass other tribes, notably the Xhosa, the second largest tribe, who, by accident or design, provided most of the leadership of the ANC. In August 1990, the fabric was sundered.

August 12 was a Sunday, a day off for everybody. In one of the hostels at Thokoza township, hard by the mine dumps of the East Rand, on the gold-bearing reef near Johannesburg, one of the inmates had set up a shebeen, a drinking parlor. It was popular not only with the residents but also with the squatters living in a camp called Phola Park just beyond the large, barracklike hostel. As the event was reconstructed later by residents and the police, a man from the squatter camp went to the shebeen to drink, got into a fight, and was stabbed to death by a man from the hostel. Up until then, everybody seemed to say, people had co-existed in relative harmony, despite the underlying strains: the single men from Zululand living in the men-only hostel, had housed Zulu girlfriends in the squatter camp; the squatters used the water faucets at the hostel. But after the stabbing, the dead man's family gathered supporters and went to the hostel to demand retribution, and fighting started.

There had been earlier, smaller incidents, in Sebokeng, south of Johannesburg in the industrial area called the Vaal Triangle—where unrest first built in September 1984—and at Kagiso, west of Johannesburg. The fighting at Thokoza, however, ignited a much broader conflict. Initially, as at Kagiso, the Zulus chased the Xhosa men from the hostel. Then they set to work raiding the squatter camp, possibly to rescue their girlfriends, but even more motivated by the urge to strike back. The township residents, not directly involved in the first phase of the fighting, organized to some extent in the various affiliates of the ANC and COSATU—and forced again into unwelcome choices—seemed to side with the squatters.

On August 15, as the death toll rose beyond 140, the squatters tried to counterattack, using the same short spears, clubs, and knives as the hostel residents had done. They charged across the scrub on a cold winter's morning, planning to storm the hostel. Then the rules changed. From within the hostel came the distinctive crackle of AK-47 assault rifle fire. Some fell as they charged, thrown back by the impact of the bullets. Others slowed, confused and fearful. The lines faltered and broke.

Elsewhere, hostel residents in the adjacent settlement of Katlehong set fire to another squatter camp nicknamed "Crossroads" after the more famous slum in the Cape. There were people inside the shacks when the torches came, and when the flames subsided, "we just [kept] on finding bodies," a policeman said.

From then on, as the fighting spread to Vosloorus and back to Kagiso, igniting parts of Soweto on the way, the labels became tribal.

The Zulu and Xhosa languages both stem from the same Nguni root and share much common vocabulary. Zulu itself had become a lingua franca in places like Soweto. But a Zulu could detect the accent of a Xhosa person speaking the Zulu language. Life came to depend on gruesome and pathetic challenges. A group of men armed with spears would accost another person, point to the nose and say, in a muffled way: "What is that?" If the answer came in the wrong accent or language, it would mean death. People were burned, stabbed, shot. Commuters on the train from Soweto to Johannesburg were murdered and tossed onto the tracks. The role of the police and clandestine security force unit seemed increasingly ambiguous. On August 24, President de Klerk declared twenty-seven black townships "unrest areas," in effect resurrecting the state of emergency he had lifted three months earlier in three of South Africa's four provinces to demonstrate his good faith to Mandela.

By then, though, the township residents and the squatters spoke simply of "the Zulus," demanding that they be sent home. And the hostel dwellers, with their glistening spears and battle-axes and red headbands that identified them in battle, spoke derisively of "the Xhosas" who claimed that the Zulu chief—Mangosuthu Gatsha Buthelezi—would rule no more now that Mandela was free. As they advanced, so the frightened women told me in Kagiso, "the Zulus" had resurrected one of their nineteenth-century war cries—"Kill the wizards," the words once used by Dingane, Shaka Zulu's successor, to order the massacre of Afrikaners lured to his kraal during the Great Trek. Now, everything seemed upturned: the adversary was no longer a white intruder, but a black compatriot of a different tribe.

No one, either, would take the blame. In Vosloorus, a Zulu leader who identified himself only as George told me his side of the story as he crouched by a hostel wall, clutching a sharp spear and a battle-ax. "Since Mandela was released, they have been coming to us, saying:

'Your chief is finished. Buthelezi will not rule. Mandela will be king and you will be ruled by a Xhosa.' Then we heard they were going to attack us. So we attacked back." Across the way, a man of Xhosa descent who had made a living selling meat to the residents of the hostels and who had fled the fighting told it the other way round. "We had heard the Zulus might attack. Then they danced and sang their war songs. Then they attacked." Midway through this account, a man staggered from the hostel across the way, trying to run as he bled, pursued by young men with spears. On the road that separated the hostel from the police station a car squealed to a halt and a black plainclothes cop in baseball hat and slacks leapt out, leveled a pistol at the pursuers, and snapped off three quick shots. The chase was abandoned.

In Kagiso, to the west, Julia Khubeka, a supermarket employee, told one of those recurrent stories of helplessness that had echoed from Zaire to Zimbabwe to Mozambique and Angola. The nights were worst, she said, for that was when the hostel dwellers came marauding. "In the day it is quiet," she explained, "but when it comes to sunset, you start saying: What next? You start worrying." The fighting had caught her at a night-time prayer vigil for a neighbor, John Ntanga. "They came from the hostel, smashing windows, even at the church," she said. "They shouted: 'Kill the Wizard!'" And we could not even pray for Mr. Ntanga's soul."

But the mayhem did not happen in a vacuum. And, it seemed, it drew its fury from three principal elements: Chief Buthelezi's potent ambition and self-importance; white mischief; and the inability of the ANC either to implant its organization throughout the land (it had not had much time to do so) or to acknowledge the resultant limits of its influence.

Chief Buthelezi had always been an ambiguous figure, tall and imposing, yet given to diatribes—in print and vocally—that seemed to diminish his stature. Initially an associate of Mandela, and a member of the ANC Youth League, he had corresponded regularly with the ANC leader during his twenty-seven years in prison. They called one another friends. In his youth, Buthelezi had attended South Africa's Fort Hare University, then a veritable academy of black revolution; Robert Mugabe was an alumnus, as was Robert Sobukwe, the founder of the Pan Africanist Congress. But the breach with the ANC and the mainstream protest movement came in the 1970s, when the chief, who seemed to want one foot inside the system and the other outside of it, accepted the title of Chief Minister of the Zulu homeland, KwaZulu. According to the ANC, that meant he was working with the system and was thus a collaborator. According to the chief, it meant he had thwarted Pretoria's design to strip the 6 million Zulus of their citizenship because he refused to accept KwaZulu's independence. His protestations met with suspicion. In the 1976 Soweto riots, his followers turned against black protesters. In 1978, at Sobukwe's funeral, black anger against him was so great that the mourners jeered and spat upon him.

But he had a power base in the Inkatha movement, which claimed a membership of one million and had a very clear tribal identity. During the Botha era, both the Afrikaners and many white liberals came to see him as the potential black interlocutor they so badly craved as a bulwark against the radicalism of the ANC/SACP alliance. In some ways, Chief Buthelezi obliged: he opposed sanctions, disinvestment, the armed struggle. In some ways, he did not oblige: in 1983, he urged whites to oppose Mr. Botha's reforms because, he said, they would bring only bloodshed.

During the mid-1980s, he embarked with white businessmen from Natal on what was called the Indaba, a Zulu term for a gathering and discussion. The Indaba became a protracted, non-governmental negotiation that produced a formula for power sharing whose authors projected it as a model for the rest of the country. It foresaw a fusion of the KwaZulu homeland and Natal Province as a non-racial entity that would be governed by a black premier (Chief Buthelezi) held in check by a two-chamber legislature in which whites would be able to exercise vetoes. In a way, it was not far from what the British had sought to implant in Zimbabwe. Incensed by this impudent effort to upstage his own reform program, President Botha rejected it out of hand in 1986.

According to Gerhard Maré, a scholar at Durban University who has chronicled Inkatha closely with a critical eye, what the chief was trying to do was to position himself as a "federal leader" and to shake free the label of a homeland sell-out that the ANC so eagerly attached to him. The chief "wanted to do his best to escape from being only a

Bantustan leader," Mr. Mare said, and he saw Natal "as a stepping stone to national politics."

In that way, when the day came for a national negotiation, the chief would be able to lay claim to a large say in the country's future, and a place at the negotiating table in his own right, while mere homeland leaders would remain caught and emasculated by their reputation as stooges of the white regime.

President Botha's rejection stymied the plan, leaving the chief to contemplate the alarming inroads the ANC—and particularly its labor ally COSATU—was making in his traditional fiefdom. With clandestine government money, the chief set up his own labor movement; but when it came to squeezing higher wages out of the employers, it was COSATU that led the field and attracted his followers. The lifting of pass laws also worked against Inkatha. With the migration from the depleted, eroded hills of Zululand to Durban's ever-expanding fringes, many of his supporters found themselves outside the movement's rural dominance and drawn to the ANC. Thus, in early 1987, the chief set about securing his base, sending loyalists to demand and coerce membership in Inkatha and the purchase of a party card, frequently in the most brutish of ways.

As so often in South Africa's recent history, the recruitment drive forced choices on people who did not necessarily want to make them; and, as before in the history of the Zulu nation, the actions of an autocratic ruler split the tribe. Just as Shaka sent Mzilikazi fleeing northward in the nineteenth century until the Zambezi River drew a northern boundary to the diaspora, so too did the competition between Chief Buthelezi and the ANC set Zulu against Zulu in the hills and valleys and townships of Natal and KwaZulu. An impressive martial tradition that had inflicted what was then the worst ever defeat on British imperial forces by an indigenous army at Isandhlwana descended into a chaotic civil war that claimed 4,000 lives in three years. Neither side had the magnanimity, nor the influence, nor the will to halt it. As the struggle wore on, it seemed to lose all ideological underpinnings, its origins forgotten in the vengeance killings, the ambitions of small-time warlords and the bloodletting between clans whose mutual hostilities dated to Shaka's times.

Mired in this conflict, Chief Buthelezi approached Mandela's release with the ambivalence that had marked his career. Publicly, he welcomed it, implying that he had done much to bring it about. In his private counsels, though, he saw it as a challenge to be met, countered, and overcome. The photographs in the newspapers now showed Mandela and de Klerk side by side, supplanting the wary courtship he had conducted with Botha. Mandela had become the Afrikaners' interlocutor, robbing the Zulu chief of the very role he had foreseen for himself—and his tribe—in the country's future.

When negotiations were held, it was the ANC and its leaders, not Inkatha, that met with de Klerk and his ministers. In African political terms, Buthelezi risked being sidelined: "moderate" blacks had gone out of fashion, and he was being left behind. He confided to his intimates after Mandela's release that the time had come for a move into the Transvaal, the industrial heartland, to establish credentials beyond his narrow and bloodstained regional power base. He knew it would be difficult, because he had drawn only a low turnout at his last rally in Soweto and, in South African politics as much as anywhere else, the figures count as a measure of support and legitimacy. Neutral opinion surveys, moreover, gave him only marginal support in the Transvaal. Yet the alternative was political eclipse, which he considered far less than his due, either as a politician or as the leader of the nation's largest, proudest tribe. He retitled Inkatha the Inkatha Freedom Party, no longer a cultural movement, and sent his lieutenants forth to marshal the hostel dwellers as the vanguard of his latest campaign to achieve national standing.

In 1990, communism as a means of holding power and as an ideology had died almost everywhere else except China. But in South Africa, it was still the time of the comrades and, as in the mid-1980s, it was the comrades who took to the streets to challenge the new menace from Inkatha. It was an uneven fight, in part because the "hidden hand" bore suspicious resemblance to the hand that had so deftly manipulated black divisions from Angola and Mozambique to South Africa's townships in the mid-1980s.

When the ANC and its followers urged the police to evict the hostel dwellers, the police responded persistently by shielding them, citing tired myths of Afrikaner respect for the Zulus. But as so often before, the "hidden hand" found its work made easier by the same divisions it sought to exploit. The comrades wanted vengeance, not only for the dead of the Transvaal's townships, but also for the 4,000 dead in Natal. What they certainly did not want was to see their leader, Nelson Mandela, embrace the man who, by their lights, had brought this blight of violence upon them: Chief Gatsha Buthelezi.

And for his part, the Zulu leader seemed to imply his own complicity in the violence even as he denied any part in it, saying that the killings would only come to an end when Mandela shared a public platform with him. That seemed to mean that the chief felt he had the power to call off the violence, but was not prepared to use it until he had made political gains. His tactics caught the ANC at its weakest point of transition and inner uncertainty—it was no longer an exiled liberation movement, but it had not yet become organized as a political party; the autocratic bush rules of Angola and Zambia were not appropriate to its new status of sudden respectability, but it had devised no alternative as yet; and it was divided over issues of power, politics, and personality—a debate that drew in many. Its offices at 54 Sauer Street in downtown Johannesburg were a model of righteous fervor and revolutionary disorganization; no one seemed able even to answer the telephone or return calls, let alone respond decisively to the country's deepening crisis. Its very authority was in question.

Mandela had appealed to the combatants of Natal Province to throw their weapons into the Indian Ocean. But no one did, and so the whole issue of the ANC leader's status as the voice of the black majority was called into doubt. His followers in Natal were the most vociferous opponents of his decision to suspend the armed struggle: how could he undertake the move, they asked, when they faced daily and deadly hazard from the warlords of Inkatha? At the same time, the Pan Africanist Congress was seeking a revival, hoping to draw support from those who found the suddenly moderate ANC too accommodating to white designs. While Mandela spoke of negotiation and compromise, the PAC, with its history of black consciousness and political radicalism, offered an agenda more likely to appeal to those who had seen no benefit accruing from the talked-of "new" South Africa. "We hold the simple truth that what has not been won on the battlefield will never be won at the negotiating table," said the PAC's Barney Desai— a far simpler and attractive message to those bred on violence than the convolutions of negotiation. The PAC's motto was fairly gruesome, too: "One settler, one bullet." Even ANC stalwarts, including the maverick Afrikaner priest Beyers Naude, acknowledged the ANC's predicament. The young comrades of the townships, he said, "do not believe in the sincerity of the government. They believe that the only way forward is the continuation and increase of the armed struggle."

But that was not all: the leap into the harsh light of legality and public scrutiny seemed to leave the ANC dazzled, struggling to catch sight of its own identity, its vision splintered through the prisms of internal debate and dissent.

The former exiles, used to the self-defined rectitude of "the struggle" at a safe distance, and unfamiliar with the hard rules of the townships, seemed uneasy with realities that did not fit the theories they had advanced from Lusaka or London.

Among the factions that emerged, there were the former long-term political prisoners, jailed during the era three decades earlier that had propelled Mandela to prominence, regarded now by younger activists as little more than symbols, benchmarks in the ANC's history but not attuned to newer realities. And then there were those like Lucas in Cradock, who had supported the UDF and sacrificed friends and freedom for it during the height of protest in the mid-1980s, and who now found themselves caught between past and future, yearning for the clear lines of the struggle against apartheid, and receiving none. With political cross-purposes eddying through it, the organization spoke with many inconsistent voices. Nelson Mandela said the armed struggle had been suspended, but Joe Slovo said it could easily be revived and Winnie Mandela said the suspension was no more than a strategy—something Walter Sisulu, a long-term political prisoner along with Mandela, then had to deny. Negotiations were under way, it was true, said Joe Modise, the head of *Umkhonto we Sizwe*, but that did not mean the struggle was over.

Without funds or, apparently, sufficient personnel, and without the time to spread itself around the land, the ANC confronted another problem: it had no means of controlling or representing those who fought in its name, and it had no way of separating its loyalists from privateers interested solely in tribal violence under the ANC's banner. If there was one strand of unifying thought, however, it was that Chief Buthelezi simply did not deserve the exalted status implied by a shared platform with Mandela. He had stood in opposition to every strategy that had brought change—from armed struggle to sanctions—he was a homeland leader who had turned the homeland police against the comrades. And now he sought to challenge the ANC's supremacy.

The morass of competing ambitions and visions was unsettling. In the mid-1980s, some vague semblance of organization seemed to underlie many townships. Now in 1990 there was none, as political leaders soon discovered.

In Kagiso township, matchbox homes gave way to scrub and there was no road sign marking the turnoff on the black-top from the nearby white town of Krugersdorp; only a board inscribed with the word "Abattoir" indicated the route to the real and figurative slaughterhouses. Kagiso was divided into two areas—Kagiso 1 and Kagiso 2—and between them lay the police station and the post office, both surrounded by security fencing. In August 1990, Archbishop Desmond M. Tutu cut short a visit to Canada to return home and seek peace among his people. On the stunted ground by the post office, he gathered the township residents opposed to the hostel dwellers around him, enjoining them to peace and reconciliation. He led them in singing *Nkosi Sikelele Afrika*—God Bless Africa—the national anthem of several black-ruled African countries and the ANC's own hymn to liberation. In response, the hundreds around him lofted spears and battleaxes, ignored his words, and marched off toward an inconclusive encounter with the hostel dwellers. Around a corner a shack blazed, bright in the winter's sun, and the small group of chanting men who had set it alight moved on in search of more excitement. The fervor, moreover, had begun to be seen by right-wing whites as confirmation of their worst fears.

Vereeniging is a small, conservative white town forty miles south of Johannesburg in the Vaal Triangle. It was here, in April 1902, that the Boer commanders met to discuss the terms of their surrender to the British in Pretoria one month later. The principal black township serving it is Sharpeville, the scene of the 1960 and 1984 massacres. Some of the houses in the older, white parts still have maroon tin roofs in the style of the early twentieth century, and the streets are broad enough to turn a span of oxen. Along one of those streets, in August 1990, 15,000 black demonstrators, escorted by many police-men and soldiers on horseback, advanced toward the town hall to protest killings by "Zulus" in their segregated townships. Watching them, André Erasmus saw the future and hated it. "What do they get out of this?" he said, shortly before he went indoors to load hunting rifles in case the crowd caused trouble as it passed his door. "And what do we get out of this? Nothing. We are supposed to be trying to reach an accommodation with them, but this just causes the opposite. I never hated blacks before, but after this, I will."

What the ANC got out of its first legal protest in Vereeniging was fairly clear: it secured the right to break the icons of apartheid by injecting an organized, black political presence into the sanctum of white lives, from which the black majority had, for years, been barred. But such victories could not be scored without hostile reactions among those sensing defeat. The sentiments expressed by Erasmus, a store manager in his early fifties, were not unusual among a large white minority that was approaching President de Klerk's new order with a blend of trepidation, ill-feeling, hostility, and outright fear. Even some of the white liberals who had secretly championed the ANC during its exile—when it was more a notion than a reality—had begun to recoil as they realized that the worst-case scenarios of a violent tran-sition might be upon them. And it was the culture of the white right that offered the most obvious beacon because it shone with unequivocal racial hatred.

The one-star hotel in Ventersdorp, set among the great corn and wheat estates of the western Transvaal, offered visitors very little beyond cheap rooms, a bar, and the wisdom of a man called "Buks" van Deventer, an Afrikaner who made his living by traveling the farmlands with a team of men—"my Swazis," he called them, referring to their tribe— and purchasing the right to fell blue-gum trees, which he then sold to the paper mills near his home in the eastern Transvaal. Buks wore a dark mustache that slashed across a battered face reddened by sun, booze, wind, and years. His graying hair was neatly plastered down with some patent preparation. He dressed in a short-sleeved safari suit, with shorts and kneesocks.

Over neat, rough brandy, Buks spoke easily about racial relations, his disappointment with President F. W. de Klerk, and his ideas on how the game of races should be played. "Never show fear," he said, reminding me of George, my one-time guide in the townships of Natal, who had said the same when we met a Zulu impi. "You must never show fear," Buks intoned. That was rule number one, and he seemed to suggest that de Klerk's policies had broken the rule. Rule number two was a corollary: instill fear. Back home, in the eastern Transvaal, Buks said, he was an officer in the local "commando"—a kind of militia established by the South African Defense Force that took its name from the same Boer units that had harassed the British nine decades before. Sometimes, Buks said, he and his commando patrolled the black townships, and, unlike the police, they never encountered difficulties because the township residents knew that the commando carried only rifles with live ammunition and had no truck with tear gas, rubber bullets, or other non-lethal equipment. He explained his views in a companionable way, seeing no need to apologize or justify them in the presence of whites, whose company he found reassuring. Often, he said, he and his friends would take a weekend to hunt in the bushlands of the northern Transvaal. He found shooting animals distasteful, and went along for the pleasure of being with friends. "I couldn't kill a kudu," he said, referring to a species of buck. He thought for a minute, then went on to add with a rueful laugh, "I'd kill a kaffir, but I could never kill a kudu." That, it seemed, was the essence of rule three.

Such conversations were not unusual. Ventersdorp is a particularly conservative town; indeed, it is the home of Eugene Terre Blanche. But just about anywhere, in the small, stale bars of country hotels, the conversation would be the same, and sometimes the actions would follow: in the Orange Free State, on the same day that André Erasmus expounded his views in Vereeniging, a similar black protest march took place in the town of Welkom, and an AWB member in his sand-colored, paramilitary gear fired a crossbow into the crowd of marchers for no reason other than their skin color.

For President de Klerk, the right-wing whites meant a troubled constituency, and in the black townships, they meant a lot more. As the killings followed one another, the stories began to accumulate of white involvement in what had become nightly terror as hostel dwellers rampaged. The accounts, at first, seemed to overlap, as if they might have been no more than a retelling of received wisdom, rumor, gossip. But even on close and insistent questioning, people would say: yes, there were white men helping the "Zulus," they brought them in their police trucks, they took them away again, they asked them, in Afrikaans, if they were through with their looting. Whites wearing balaclava helmets were accused of opening fire on blacks from the roofs of hostels, from speeding mini-buses. That was the "hidden hand" de Klerk had acknowledged was at work.

The suggestion seemed all the more plausible in view of past practices that were coming to light at the same period. A single-judge government commission had sought to delve into the operations of the Civil Cooperation Bureau—the particularly euphemistic title of a clandestine military unit devoted to dirty tricks, including, its adversaries believed, political assassination. The Bureau, it seemed from the skimpy and patchy testimony of uncooperative witnesses—former employees who refused to remember anything about their work—had drawn together army and intelligence operatives along with freelancers, some of them leftover killers from the Selous Scouts in Rhodesia. Its critics held it responsible for a spate of political killings over several years. Griffiths Mxenge in Durban, David Webster from Johannesburg, and Anton Lubowski in Windhoek had all been murdered in mysterious and brutal circumstances. All three of them were prominent activists opposed to Pretoria's writ.

Significantly, the authorities refused to permit the inquiry to delve into dirty tricks committed beyond South Africa's frontiers—a restriction that inspired speculation about the Bureau's role in Mozambique, Angola, and Namibia. As the inquiry, conducted by Justice Harms, pressed for more detail, however, the Bureau took the expedient step in mid-1990 of dissolving itself, a move that left many civil rights activists pondering whether it had simply reconstituted itself under another, even more clandestine and euphemistic name.

The Harms inquiry was notoriously feeble. But the very existence of the Civil Cooperation Bureau showed that those who thought like Buks van Deventer and André Erasmus had the skill and the patronage to run a clandestine unit far from public scrutiny within an institution of state—the army. Its existence became known only when former operatives defected, or professed knowledge of it on Death Row to avoid execution for their crimes. The results of clandestine warfare techniques, of destabilization, were not hard to find.

ANC officials gave convincing accounts of phony pamphlets being distributed in the townships, urging people to tribal war in the name of Nelson Mandela. Another leaflet, on ANC letterhead and apparently signed by Walter Sisulu, announced that the "heroes of the struggle," returning from exile, would be quarantined for AIDS screening— disinformation easily believed considering that the ANC's headquarters-in-exile was in Lusaka, at the heart of Africa's AIDS belt, where specialists estimated that at least one fifth of the adult population was infected with the virus. Any doubt of a link between white subversives and Inkatha seemed dispelled when Chief Buthelezi's main lieutenant in the Transvaal, Temba Khoza, was stopped at an official police roadblock and found to be carrying four AK-47 assault rifles in the trunk of his car—weapons he would not have been able to locate without assistance in circumventing South Africa's gun laws and control of captured weaponry such as AK-47s.

President de Klerk himself had no apparent interest in the violence, for it undermined Nelson Mandela, whose credibility and authority were central to the idea of negotiating a way out of sanctions and decline. Ironically, it did not help Chief Buthelezi's cause, either, because the fighting proved that his support lay in the narrow social band of the hostels. But the bloodshed did benefit his white adversaries—both inside and outside the security forces—for it could be depicted as proof of two points: first, that it was impossible to negotiate with "these people"; and, second, that de Klerk was leading the land into chaos. And de Klerk, mysteriously, did nothing to stop it.

If conservative Afrikaner policemen sided with Inkatha, they were in part responding to years of tutoring by official propaganda that held Inkatha and the Zulus to be "good blacks" while the ANC, Nelson Mandela, and his cohorts represented all that was evil. And, if the police commanders reporting to President de Klerk could say with total honesty that they were unaware of the dirty tricks, that did not mean that their subordinates had such clear consciences. Eugene Terre Blanche had frequently bragged of a following among the often poorly educated white policemen, and the activities of the Civil Cooperation Bureau proved that devious minds were available, too, to direct the brute strength of destabilization in townships. In the end, though, surveying the burned shacks, the bodies as suddenly useless and deprived of purpose or vanity as they had been in Kolwezi, no one could avoid the question: What on earth had these small, sad skirmishes been for, and why had they been so easy to ignite?

Epilogue: Just Causes,
Hidden Agendas

"It is an ideal which I hope to live
for and to achieve. But if needs be
it is an ideal for which I am prepared
to die."

—NELSON MANDELA at his trial in 1963,
and again after his release in 1990

In the beginning was the Cause. And the Cause was just.

If there were a revolutionary catechism of the comrades' time in Africa, a primer of insurgent dogma, that is how it would begin. The Cause—freedom, justice, and democracy—was at once the justification for revolt, the rallying cry of those embroiled in it, and the agenda for the future.

Amorphous discontent might lead to grievances and possibly uprising. Guns could facilitate insurgency. But without a defined and clearly articulated "just Cause" to give direction and win support, there could be no lasting victory, as the Shaba warriors of 1977 and 1978 had discovered. The Cause was both motive and intention.

Africa's post-colonial wars and conflicts were about power and the ability to usurp it—or regain it—in the name of a revived and different national and political identity. Often, the result, in the most simple terms, was to replace one elite with another. But Africa's comrades could never have achieved the transformation from colonial to indigenous rule on the scale they did without the ability to harness raw numerical, racial, and sometimes tribal power behind an identifiable and visibly legitimate cause.

The Cause marshaled forces on two fronts: in the direct confrontation with the adversary on the ground; and in the theater of international politics and diplomacy, where the insurgents' prime weapon was moral and political pressure on those who provided their enemy's economic and diplomatic support.

Ultimately, the physical fight became almost subservient to the diplomacy it fed. In South Africa, for example, there was no hope of any kind of military victory over a continent's best-armed and most resolute forces. Pretoria's weakness lay elsewhere, in its international economic dependencies and in its abhorrence of isolation. The insurgents' most decisive battles were fought to produce sanctions and ever greater ostracism. And the justice of the Cause made it impossible for all but the most cynical outside constituencies to ignore its implicit demand for change.

The Cause, moreover, staked out the moral high ground and confronted the adversary with an impossible dilemma. When the French strategist Beaufre told Afrikaner generals that they needed to implement "thoroughgoing reforms" to undermine the malcontents, he was evoking one of the basic riddles of counterinsurgency: "thoroughgoing reforms" could only really undermine the Cause by fulfilling its requirements. But how was that possible without yielding victory to the insurgents? How was it possible to win the hearts and minds of the people when those same hearts and minds wanted a completely new order and new leaders?

The wars that patterned southern Africa reflected different histories, personalities, and phenomena in each theater of conflict. But in those great tracts of southern Africa where the "comrades" came to hold sway, their conflicts bore some striking broad similarities.

In every case, from the Portuguese Empire to South Africa, the majority of the people bore a profound and justified grievance against those who ruled them. And, in every case, those who led the majority had come to conclude, as Mandela said of his own struggle in 1963, that "our policy to achieve a non-racial state by non-violence had achieved nothing."

The insurgents had the numbers on their side, a demographic edge, but the regimes they faced invariably possessed vastly superior firepower. That automatically dictated recourse to guerrilla warfare. "If war were inevitable," Mandela said in the same seminal speech at his trial in 1963, "we wanted the fight to be conducted on terms most favorable to our people. The fight which held out prospects best for us and the least risk of life to both sides was guerrilla warfare." The principle and the rationale were the same throughout the region.

The insurgents sought, or were obliged to seek, guns and bullets, and it was communist countries that supplied weapons, training, and diplomatic support. "Although there is a universal condemnation of apartheid," Mandela was moved to observe, "the Communist bloc speaks out against it with a louder voice than most of the white world." A blend of ideology and warfare developed: the most promising graduates of the guerrillas' own training camps went on to the Eastern bloc for advanced tuition in the techniques of insurgency, and were exposed to an ideology that reflected their condition and embraced the notion of violence as a prerequisite for revolutionary change—even though they freely admitted that Eastern Europe seemed no utopia.

By contrast, the white regimes, the targets of insurgency, were virulently anti-Communist, drawing their support from important segments of Western society, including, usually, conservative politicians and the corporations that benefited from access to the region's twin economic assets—cheap labor and abundant natural resources.

And—throughout the region—those differences fed upon and nourished the easy distinctions of the Cold War. Only when the Cold War was over did the United States countenance the pro-democracy movements that stirred, in the early 1990s, in Kenya, Zaire, and Zambia. Until then, considerations of global competition assumed far greater importance than any honest examination of just causes. The United States sponsored South Africa's intervention in Angola in 1976 to prevent a Soviet advance, not to promote democracy; the Reagan administration formulated its policy of "constructive engagement" to shelter P. W. Botha from pressure in the 1980s because the alternative seemed threatening to a tradition of Western interests dating back to Cecil John Rhodes.

British multinationals held stakes in the mines of Rhodesia, Namibia, and South Africa. Americans drilled Angola's oil, and South Africa marketed its diamonds. Before divestment, the billboards in South Africa itself showed IBM and Ford locked into an economy and political system that provided blacks with jobs, but benefited primarily the white minority. Mercedes and BMW set up some of their biggest assembly plants outside Germany in South Africa, and their products, primarily, graced white driveways. (The seductive allure and status of a BMW was sought in Soweto, too.) Only when "the struggle" had become an irreversible and undeniable fact of life did corporations intimate readiness to switch sides. Lonrho might have made money in Rhodesia; but it also paid hotel bills run up by Joshua Nkomo's insurgents at various peace conferences before independence. When "the struggle" and its attendant controversies in the United States turned relatively small economic investments into large sources of political discomfiture and annoyance, American corporations active in South Africa shed their stakes.

Given the economic disparities between the combatants, and the lessons both sides learned from their foreign sponsors, many of the comrades saw clear parallels between their position and the fundamental premise of socialism that divided the world between oppressed and oppressor. Comrade was more than just an honorific, it was a statement of a condition.

The cause that permeated the oratory was freedom—with its acolytes of justice and democracy—ostensibly the same individual freedom that the French, the Americans, and the British had fought for and won for themselves over many centuries. In the wake of World War II, Africa's colonial and minority elites could no longer claim legitimacy in an era that feted self-determination as the basis of political management. India's freedom in 1947 set a precedent that would not be ignored. A decade later Africa's Gold Coast became independent Ghana, and three years after that, Harold Macmillan told the South Africans themselves to brace for the wind of change that brought independence to much of Africa in the 1960s.

The colonial regimes drew on discredited Victorian notions of control, paternalism, and expansionism. The insurgents, by contrast, avowed commitment to those values that were, notionally at least, the bedrock of Western civilization—freedom and democracy. How, then, was it possible to refuse them?

The diplomatic battle waged by liberation movements for the hearts and minds of Western public opinion was designed to maintain the exclusivity of their claim and to deny their enemy's access to sympathy. For every speech and statement aligning their guerrillas with the quest for freedom, Joshua Nkomo and Robert Mugabe in Zimbabwe insisted on the perfidy of Ian Smith's regime, seeking thereby to counter the instinctive sympathy many Britons felt for their kith and kin in Rhodesia: there could only be one bull in the kraal of international legitimacy and sympathy.

The Cause was inseparable from the ability to wield power in its name. Lenin's one-party state meshed comfortably with the belief of the bush warriors that, having won the war, they should secure the peace, too. Having killed the wizard of alien rule, they would cast their own spells to hold their nation in thrall and thus fulfill the hidden Agenda.

The independence struggle itself thus became the legitimator of the post-independence regime. Having won independence in the name of democracy and justice, the new regime cast itself as the embodiment of freedom, and the person who led the regime came to be depicted as the very essence of the new order; opposition became treason, an affront to liberty, a denial of freedom. Kenneth Kaunda in Zambia clung to that bizarre rationale for twenty-seven years after independence from Britain in 1964, permitting democratic elections only after events in Eastern Europe left his notions of one-party rule in tatters. The transformation of a democratic ideal to rule by clique and crony marked freedom's progress in Kenya, Zaire, Uganda, and many other African countries too. Ten years after the flag was furled in Harare's Rufaro Stadium, Robert Mugabe still hankered for legislation to turn his de facto one-party state into de jure rule by himself and his loyalists. To the victor, the spoils.

The call to liberty in parts of southern Africa was a call to freedom from alien rule that did not automatically imply Western notions of freedoms such as individual choice and the right to oppose. The definition of liberty was an evocation of consensus within a single political body that spoke for the nation and its leaders, just as a tradition in Africa rested on consensus around the chief. Multi-party rule, by contrast, was depicted as a source of division, often tribal. Yet ethnic distinctions could not simply be laid to rest under political monoliths.

In Zimbabwe's war from 1972 to 1979, the liberation movements led by Robert Mugabe and Joshua Nkomo were supposedly allied in the Patriotic Front, a notional body that withered with independence when the not-so-hidden tribal agenda took over: Mugabe's followers won the majority Shona vote, Nkomo's followers won the minority Ndebele vote, and the land knew no peace until the Ndebele interest was subjugated to the Shona interest. Moreover, every government and party leadership Mugabe announced after independence paid careful attention to a distribution of the spoils of power between the fractious subclans of the Shona—the Karanga, Manica, Ndau, and so forth. From the shared interest of a broad struggle against minority rule in the name of an amorphous majority, the competition had narrowed to smaller units pursuing principally self-interest. That was the hidden agenda that underlay the internal feudings of the Patriotic Front long before freedom came.

The ANC in South Africa sought to be different. It offered the broadest definition of shared interest. Even though many of the ANC's leaders hailed from the Xhosa tribe, anybody opposed to apartheid, irrespective of skin color, could join the fight. The PAC narrowed the definition: how could whites, who were the oppressors, free themselves from their own oppression, the argument ran; therefore only blacks, or at least non-whites, could join the ranks that fought for the just Cause. In practice, Chief Buthelezi's Inkatha narrowed the definition further still, to the Zulu nation. That limited Inkatha's appeal, but it built on the powerful sense of shared identity and responsibility that lies at the root of tribal politics. The tribe is the ultimate welfare state, a recognition system built on language, custom, geography, faith. It ties people to their land and possessions. The lore of the elders, the tales of the village, and the sense of shared history and shared future anchor values in a complicated world. The tribe is where the sense of belonging and security begins and ends. The nepotism and corruption often associated with tribal politics is no more than an expression of the intuitive belief that, beyond the tribe, there is only peril. If the tribe denotes belonging and safety, then the converse also holds true: those outside the tribe represent hostility that can only be met with suspicion or aggression.

Guerrilla warfare was about pressure, not frontal assault. Its tactics were psychological more than physical, the ambush, not the setpiece battle. Its aim was to produce the sense of emotional siege that sapped the enemy's will and enhanced its readiness for negotiation on unfavorable terms. The Portuguese officers' coup in Lisbon in 1974 was the most dramatic example of achieving the goal, and, in a more complicated way, the Lancaster House conference in 1979 in London was another. In both cases, insurgency and its allied pressures had eroded the ruling minority's preparedness to continue with the fray, even though, physically, the battle had not been lost.

From the mid-1970s to 1990, the theories of confrontation, struggle, and counterstruggle were honed to match the terrain as the region edged toward the last epic fight in South Africa. And in the process, the notions of guerrilla warfare, insurgency, and violence became woven into a new culture that challenged everything the just Cause stood for.

Ungovernability in South Africa's townships was relatively simple to unleash, but difficult to turn back as a state of mind among people who came to see violence as the final arbiter. After the winter of 1990, the bloodshed in the townships of the Transvaal endured into the following year and revived the very imagery that Africa wished to disavow—tribal warfare and political intolerance.

Despite the long decades of Africa's fight for freedom, the sad reality was that neither Chief Buthelezi's impis nor their adversaries aligned to the ANC were free in any sense of the word. The long exposure to violence had bred its own rules of intolerance, and so they fought rather than talked, and the fighting defied anyone to sit down and talk about it until the battles on the streets of the black townships were over.

Winnie Mandela, the controversial First Lady of South Africa's struggle, insisted that the Boers, the Afrikaners, had taught her and her people the capacity for implacable hatred (although Shaka Zulu seemed adept in the same syllabus). And once the lessons had been learned, they turned the struggle against itself, as the beating of a fourteen-year-old political activist, Stompie Mokhetsi, in Mrs. Mandela's own home at year's turning in 1988—and his subsequent murder by one of her aides—seemed to show. With our tires and our matches, Mrs. Mandela had said in the mid-1980s, we will liberate South Africa. The comment drew rebuttals from the ANC, which insisted that the "necklace" to which Mrs. Mandela was alluding was not approved policy.

Many in the struggle—although not her loyal husband—disowned

Winnie Mandela and were dismayed when she became the ANC's secretary for social welfare, even as she faced trial on criminal charges relating to the demise of the young Stompie. But her comment about the necklace nonetheless found a broad and resonant echo among the street warriors and raised the question: Could the just Cause ever create a just society if its attainment evoked so many practices and values that contradicted its most fundamental assumption of human decency? Apartheid had been a violent degradation of an entire people, but if the revolt against it ran on the same currents of violence and indifference to human suffering, where would the cycle of bloodletting break?

Africa produced its own answers, contradictory "models" that deny easy categorization.

In the 1970s and 1980s Angola and Mozambique descended into chaos, as outsiders and insiders alike seemed bent on ensuring. But in Zimbabwe, despite Mr. Mugabe's quest for political monopoly, a remarkable racial and ethnic tolerance descended on the land, even though economic decline and the unconnected pestilence of AIDS came to gnaw at the social fabric. Zimbabwe's war had killed 30,000 people, but Ian Smith was still free to rail against the new order. Once the wars had been fought—between black and white, between black and black—southern Africa displayed a capability for reconciliation. For South Africa's whites, there was something to learn, too, from Namibia: once white minorities relinquished political control, the new black elites registered no objection to their continued economic dominance; majority rule did not, after all, eclipse the life in the sun. And, by late 1991, the values that rose from the ending of the Cold War had pushed Angola, Kenya, Zaire, and Zambia toward a new political experiment in tolerance after the wasted years of rule by elite.

But of course, as people had often told me when I arrived there in 1983, South Africa was different, more complex, rich, and seething. The kraal was much bigger, and so too was the number and nature of the bulls.

South Africa was not a colony and, unlike the Belgians, the Portuguese, the French, and the British, its Afrikaner rulers had nowhere else to turn to when the pennants were furled. Its black majority had not fought a rural war conducted by trained guerrillas who could then be absorbed into a new army, as had happened to the fighters of Zimbabwe. Theirs had been an urban war, conducted by far more amorphous legions, which ended the campaigns unschooled and un-skilled, tutored only in the ways of street violence.

Once, I had assumed that South Africa possessed the riches to sustain change, with all its diamonds and gold, even if the will to reform was absent. But, as the gold mines went deeper, the ore body grew poorer, and the number of people and squatters swelled, that, too, became a questionable supposition: the will to change had arrived as the wealth was beginning to run out, too late to help the just Cause overcome reflexive violence and intolerance.

That, at least, is one conclusion from the still-unsettled competition between just Cause and hidden agenda. Keen to see the best where history had displayed the worst, I want the just Cause to win: if South Africa is doomed, there is little hope for the region. South Africa alone offers the economic sophistication and the expertise to redeem the setbacks and defeats elsewhere, some of its own creation, some of Africa's own. But if the intolerance continues, fanned by extremists on both sides, then a land as big and generous in its endowments as South Africa will finish up denying its own capacity to be big enough for everyone, whatever their color.

When I arrived in Africa, I sensed only vaguely the issues of place and identity that framed the outsiders' presence in Africa.

My job had trailed the time of the comrades from Maputo and Luanda and Lusaka to Cape Town. It had taken me from the horror of Kolwezi, Zaire, in 1978, to the corresponding horror of a bleak black township in Port Elizabeth, South Africa, in 1985, where a man kept the body of a son on the back seat of a car in a yard for several days, too fearful of the repercussions to tell the authorities that his boy had been shot dead in confrontation with the police and had thus been a malcontent.

When I left, I knew that the outsider would never completely find a real home in an adopted continent. And yet, I knew that somehow I would be drawn back, that the editors who sent me to Africa had inadvertently exposed me to a magic and wizardry that would never completely dissipate. The newsstand billboard I espied on the way to Jan Smuts Airport in Johannesburg proclaimed that I had been hostile. That was not true, but I could no longer claim innocence.

The forecasts of doom and decline had come true in many of the lands where I had tried to see hope. In the uplands of central Angola in 1977, even a Cuban medic tending lepers seemed optimistic, but there had been much bloodshed and decay before the stirrings of reconciliation in 1990. In Zaire, President Mobutu's personal wealth still equaled the national debt even as he was pressed toward change and took refuge from his own people aboard the Presidential yacht, moored on the Congo River. In many places, the hidden agenda had come to supplant the just Cause, so much so that no one even bothered to hide it any more, and I had seen its protagonists and pretenders strut uninvited across the stage in Chad and Uganda, Somalia and the Sudan.

I flew out of Johannesburg after a brief visit in mid-1990, looking down on the myriad swimming pools that bejeweled white homes and on the smog that cloaked black townships. It was just over fourteen years since I had flown into Africa, via Cairo and Nairobi to Lusaka. Far below, made insignificant by altitude, were all those places that had forced the immediacy and passions on me, a foreigner, an observer trying to be neutral. Somewhere down there was the Zambezi, the Centenary Club, the clearing that had once been called Assembly Point Lima. In the gloaming, 35,000 feet below, lay Guy Scott's croquet lawn near Lusaka, and the murderous villa in Kolwezi. I doubted I would ever be able to say—or want to say—it was all behind me.

GLOSSARY OF ACRONYMS

ANC. The African National Congress. Formed in 1912, it is the principal black liberation movement in South Africa supportive of multi-racial struggle against apartheid. Led by Nelson Mandela.

AZAPO. The Azanian People's Organization. The leading Black Consciousness internal group in South Africa.

COSATU. Congress of South African Trade Unions. South Africa's biggest black labor federation, formed 1985. Allied with the ANC and the SACP (q.v.).

FNLA. National Front for the Liberation of Angola. Led by Holden Roberto. Zaire-based liberation movement in Angola's pre-independence war. Now defunct.

FNLC. National Front for the Liberation of the Congo. Led by Colonel Nathaniel M'Bumba. Angola-based insurgent movement that invaded Zaire in 1977 and 1978. Now believed defunct.

Frelimo. Mozambique Liberation Front. Principal guerrilla organization during pre-independence war in Mozambique. Took power at independence in 1975 under the late Samora Machel.

Inkatha. Zulu cultural organization in South Africa founded in 1975 by Chief Mangosuthu Gatsha Buthelezi. Renamed the Inkatha Freedom Party in 1990. The name refers to a distinctive form of Zulu headgear.

MK. *Umkhonto we Sizwe* (the Spear of the Nation), Soviet-armed military wing of the ANC (q.v.). Founded by Nelson Mandela in 1960. Commanded by Chris Hani, also a member of the SACP (q.v.).

MPLA. Popular Movement for the Liberation of Angola. Soviet-backed liberation movement in Angola's pre-independence war and winner, with Cuban support, of post-independence civil war in 1975–76.

PAC. Pan Africanist Congress. Formed in South Africa by Robert Sobukwe as splinter from the ANC (q.v.) in 1959 to advance the belief that only blacks can win their own freedom.

PAIGC. Liberation movement that fought Portuguese in Cape Verde and Guinea-Bissau and took power at independence in 1975. Moscow-backed.

POQO. Chinese-armed military wing of PAC (q.v.). Based in Tanzania.

RENAMO.   Mozambique National Resistance. Created in 1976 by white intelligence operatives in Rhodesia to destabilize Mozambique. Transferred to South African bases in 1980.

SACP.   South African Communist Party. Moscow-backed movement formed in 1921 to support white miners. Allied with the ANC, MK, and COSATU (q.v.).

SWANU.   South West African National Union. Small, Chinese-backed liberation movement in Namibia, later sponsored by South Africa as an alternative to SWAPO (q.v.).

SWAPO.   South West African Peoples Organization. Led by Sam Nujoma. Principal liberation movement in Namibia before winning power at independence in 1989. Armed by the Soviet Union.

UDF.   United Democratic Front. Formed August 20, 1983, as umbrella organization grouping six hundred community, civic, and other anti-apartheid associations opposed to P. W. Botha's reform program. Allied with the ANC (q.v.).

UNITA.   National Union for the Total Independence of Angola. Led by Jonas Savimbi. Loser in Angola's civil war of 1975–76. Revived its campaign with help from South Africa, then the United States, from redoubts in southern Angola. Made peace with the MPLA (q.v.) in 1990.

ZANLA.   Military wing of Zanu (q.v.), based in Mozambique, prior to independence of Zimbabwe.

ZANU.   Zimbabwe African National Union. Chinese-backed liberation movement that fought the most sustained guerrilla war against white rule in Rhodesia. Won power at independence in 1980. Led by Robert Mugabe.

ZAPU.   Zimbabwe African People's Union. Oldest nationalist movement in Zimbabwe before independence in 1980. Led by Joshua Nkomo. Backed variously by the Soviet Union and some figures in British big business.

ZIPRA.   Military wing of ZAPU (q.v.), based in Zambia before Zimbabwe's independence. Soviet-armed.

CHRONOLOGY OF SOME AFRICAN EVENTS

1482. Portugese mariner Diogo Cão, becomes the first European to observe the mouth of the Congo River on the west coast of Africa.

1652. Dutch voyager Jan van Riebeck arrives at the Cape of Good Hope to establish a victualing station and thus begin Afrikaners settlement of South Africa.

1816. Shaka Zulu assumes leadership of the Zulu nation and embarks on the Mfecane—"the crushing"—of opponents.

1835–38. The Great Trek brings Afrikaners inland from Britain's Cape colony to found their own republics in the Orange Free State and the Transvaal.

1838. Zulus under Dingane, Shaka's successor, massacre Afrikaner pioneers led by Piet Retief. In subsequent reprisal at the Battle of Blood River, Afrikaners defeat Zulus after making a covenant with their God.

1884–85. Congress of Berlin divides Africa into spheres of interest among European states, principally Germany, France, Portugal, Belgium, and Britain.

1886. Gold is discovered on the Witwatersrand of South Africa.

1890. The Pioneer Column of British settlers, inspired by Cecil John Rhodes, presses north from the Transvaal to found Rhodesia.

1893–96. Settlers in Rhodesia put down revolts by both Shona and Matabele people.

1899–1902. Anglo-Boer War in South Africa ends with defeat of Afrikaner armies by the British and the end of independent Boer republics in the Transvaal and Orange Free State.

1910. Creation of the Union of South Africa entrenches white power and further disenfranchises blacks.

1912. Formation of the African National Congress as the South African Native National Congress.

1913. Land Acts in South Africa create native reserves on less than 10 percent of the country's surface area.

1914. Formation of the Afrikaners' National Party.

1921. Formation of the South African Communist Party to protect the rights of white miners.

271

1947. India's independence begins the unraveling of the British Empire following World War II.

1948. The National Party comes to power in South Africa and begins enacting apartheid legislation.

1950. South African Communist Party banned.

1958. At a conference in Khartoum, the Soviet Union decides to support six "authentic" liberation movements—the ANC, Frelimo, SWAPO, PAIGC, MPLA, and ZAPU.

1959. Pan Africanist Congress formed under Robert Sobukwe as radical splinter of the African National Congress.

1960. At Sharpeville township, South Africa, sixty-seven blacks protesting the pass laws are massacred by police. The ANC and PAC are banned. State of emergency declared. The ANC commits itself to "armed struggle." The ANC forms its military wing, *Umkhonto we Sizwe*, with Nelson Mandela as commander.

The Belgian Congo becomes independent, leading to widespread secession and chaos.

1963. Nelson Mandela is jailed for life on treason charges in South Africa.

1964. Independence of Zambia.

1965. Ian Smith makes Unilateral Declaration of Independence in Rhodesia.

In the Congo, Mobutu Sese Seko takes power in a coup supported by the CIA.

1972. Forces from the Zimbabwe African National Liberation Army begin a guerrilla war against white minority rule in Rhodesia.

1974. Officers' coup in Lisbon heralds the end of Portugal's empire in Africa.

1975. Independence of Angola, Mozambique, and Guinea-Bissau.

Civil war in Angola draws in Cuban, Zairean, and South African regulars, white mercenaries, Chinese arms suppliers, and the CIA.

1976. Blacks protesting the use of Afrikaans as a teaching language rise up in Soweto.

In Rhodesia, white intelligence operatives create the Mozambique National Resistance movement from disaffected Mozambicans.

In Angola, Jonas Savimbi's National Union for the Total Independence of Angola retreats to Cuando Cubango province after losing the civil war.

South African troops withdraw from Angola.

1977. First Shaba War in Zaire. Guerrillas based in Angola advance on Zaire's copper and cobalt plants but are repulsed by Moroccan forces at Mutshatsha.

Steve Biko, Black Consciousness leader, dies in police custody in South Africa.

1978. Second Shaba War. Guerrillas occupy Kolwezi, Zaire, leading to widespread massacres and mass exodus of European expatriates. French Foreign Legion and Belgian commandos fly to Zaire, supported logistically by the United States Air Force.

1979. The Wiehahn Commission in South Africa recommends the legalization of the black labor movement.

The Lancaster House conference in London agrees to terms for a ceasefire and majority rule in Rhodesia.

1980. Rhodesia becomes independent as Zimbabwe under Robert Mugabe. RENAMO is moved from bases in Rhodesia to South Africa.

1983. President P. W. Botha wins a referendum among whites on his proposals for racial and political reform.

1984. Elections for people of Indian and mixed-race descent, held under the Botha reform plan, are widely boycotted.

In September, violence in Sharpeville begins more than two years of protest in South Africa.

1985. Limited state of emergency of South Africa. American banks sever credit lines.

1986. Nationwide state of emergency in South Africa. U.S. government imposes sanctions.

1987. Civil war begins in Natal between ANC and Chief Mangosuthu Gatsha Buthelezi's Inkatha movement.

In Angola, Soviet-supported government forces and UNITA guerrillas backed by South Africa and the United States reach a stand-off at Cuito Cuanavale.

1989. South Africa withdraws from Namibia as part of American-brokered deal also supposed to get Cubans out of Angola. Namibia becomes independent under Sam Nujoma's SWAPO.

P. W. Botha is replaced as South Africa's state president by F. W. de Klerk.

1990. De Klerk orders the legalization of all opposition groups and the release of Mandela. Negotiations begin between the government and the ANC.

Fighting between the ANC and Inkatha in the Transvaal claims eight hundred lives.

1991. Township violence continues. The white-dominated South African parliament repeals major apartheid legislation. In Zambia Kenneth Kaunda is defeated in elections and steps down. Opposition legalized in Zaire.

1992. Negotiations between South African government and wide array of opposition groups, including the ANC, but not the PAC, Inkatha or white extremists.

INDEX

ABOUT THE AUTHOR

ALAN COWELL was born in England. As a correspondent for Reuters he was based in Germany, Turkey, Zambia, Lebanon, and Zimbabwe. Since 1981, he has reported for *The New York Times* from bureaus in Nairobi, Johannesburg, Athens, Cairo, and Rome, where he is now bureau chief.